HOWLING TESTIMONIALS

Praise for Wulf Moon's Super Secrets of Writing

FROM NOVELISTS

"Wulf Moon is a terrific writing teacher, and in How to Write a Howling Good Story, *he shares the tips and tricks that have made him one of today's hottest authors. His advice is spot-on; follow it and you can launch a major career. This book is pure gold."*

—Robert J. Sawyer, Hugo Award-winning author of *The Oppenheimer Alternative*

"When Wulf does public speaking, he really puts a lot into his effort. When I was starting out, I did the same thing. I asked, 'What can I give this audience that maybe no one else knows about or has thought about?' and then I tried to give my everything for it. People noticed. Wulf Moon is showing you exactly how it's done."

—David Farland/Wolverton, *New York Times* bestselling author, founder of Apex Writers.

"Wulf Moon's Super Secrets have helped me leap forward in my writing skills more than any other writing courses I've ever taken—and I have a B.A. in Creative Writing! I wish I'd come across his Super Secrets years earlier. They have shaved at least ten years off my learning curve for writing short stories. Moon's Super Secrets have proven more effective than my entire degree."

—Crystal Crawford, author, CCrawfordWriting

"Want to hear a secret? Wulf Moon WILL improve your fiction. He's helped me and he'll help you. Wulf Moon knows what readers want, and that's a story that evokes deep emotion. It's the secret behind his SUPER SECRETS, and the difference between delivering a story that's simply entertaining versus one that's utterly unforgettable. Do you have a story that could use help? Get in on this secret formula to success."

—Steve Pantazis, award-winning author of *The Light of Darkness* series

"I learned SO MUCH from the SUPER SECRETS and your workshop! I listened and studied the lessons intently, and I went back over my current novel and used the techniques to strengthen every page. It's the only book I've written that I've had full confidence in, so much so that I personally submitted it to a prestigious writing contest. In March of 2021, I was notified that I was a WINNER in the Canadian Book Awards! Thank you for guiding me to where I needed to go. Your Secrets have helped me take my writing to a whole new level."

—Tina Griffith, author of the Canadian Book Award Winner *Til Text Do Us Part*, one of her thirteen novels and thirty children's books

"The SUPER SECRETS helped me grow as an author. How to plot a story, set the stage and be descriptive, and pinpointing the protagonist's heart's desire to win readers over. I started writing a novel at thirteen but failed to get it published. Learning the Super Secrets helped me deepen the story and kill my darlings. I became a published author at sixteen, and now at eighteen, I've written twenty-two novels and have won five international awards. The Super Secrets helped me grow from writer to author, and I recommend them to anyone who dreams of writing a book and getting published."

—Hermione Lee, award-winning teen novelist

FROM A HOLLYWOOD SCREENWRITER AND TV PRODUCER

"I wanted actionable advice on writing short fiction and found the goods in Wulf Moon's Super Secrets. As a newcomer to this form—so different than the screenplays I've been writing for 20+ years—Moon's insights condensed my learning curve and spared me untold hours of revisions. If you're ready to put in the work, the Super Secrets are well worth your time."

—Terri Hughes Burton, Screenwriter, TV Producer (*Star Trek: Discovery, The 100, Warrior Nun, Eureka*)

FROM SHORT STORY WRITERS

"For years I'd been sending my stories to Clarkesworld, *a premiere speculative fiction magazine, only to get a very quick 'No, Thanks' from Neil. Then, Wulf Moon taught me the importance of putting the protagonist's 'Heart's Desire' up front, on the first page, and I made sure to include that in my latest story. What do you know, Neil bought the story! Thank you, Wulf! Your teachings have taken my career to a whole new level!"*

—Lou J. Berger, author

"I began writing speculative fiction in late 2019. But it wasn't until 2022 when I took two masterclasses from Wulf Moon that I found myself leveling up. I landed my first three pro and semipro sales, joined Moon's Wulf Pack Writers group of ambitious, hard-working fellow writers, and had fun along the way. The Super Secrets are like rocket fuel!"

—Jennifer Lesh Fleck, writer

"After years of rejection letters, I doubted I'd make it as a writer. Then I discovered Moon's Super Secrets of Writing and everything changed. They're easy to follow, fun to read, and guaranteed to improve your writing. I can't recommend the Super Secrets enough!"

—David Hankins, Winner, Writers of the Future Vol. 39

"Moon promised me that if I put in the work he gave me, I'd reduce my time to publication. The Super Secrets helped me move from not even sniffing a sale, to winning the Mike Resnick Memorial Award, and winning the Writers of the Future Contest. Moon is not just a keeper of secrets. He's a keeper of promises."

—Z.T. Bright, multiple award-winning author

"I have been a member of Wulf Moon's SUPER SECRETS Challenge and have completed all of his workshops. They've been absolutely invaluable and I attribute applying them to making my first professional sale in a #1 best-selling anthology. The SUPER SECRETS help you 'see' what works and what doesn't, and armed with that knowledge, you can consciously apply those skills to make an emotional—or even award-winning—story. You can bet I'll be first in line to buy his book when it comes out!"

—Brittany Rainsdon, author, *Writers of the Future Vol. 37 & Vol. 38*

"By learning and applying Wulf Moon's Super Secrets, I went from being an aspiring author to making my first pro-level sale within eleven months. As a matter of fact, my first sale started as an exercise I wrote during one of Moon's Masterclasses. These are the secrets of how to succeed at writing, presented in a way that no one else is teaching today."

—Catherine Weaver, author

FROM TEACHERS

"I did my PhD in English Lit at Oxford University, and for the last 12 years I've been teaching English in Switzerland. Last year I attended Wulf Moon's fundraiser Webinar for DreamForge Magazine and was so impressed I joined the Wulf Pack Writers group. I'm just awed by Wulf Moon's teaching abilities and his group's limitless supportive energy. I'm glad we can encourage each other in the Wulf Pack to overcome all the obstacles that stand between us and the stories of our dreams. Wulf Moon and his Super Secrets have made a huge difference in my writing, and after trying all these years, they led to my first sale and publication in a professional anthology!"

—Daniel M. Cojocaru, DPhil (PhD) Oxford University

"Wulf Moon knows what makes a story connect with the readers, and the Super Secrets present that knowledge in a fun, easy-to-understand manner. Yet there is a depth in them that very few books on writing manage to convey; they are timeless and true. I want to touch the hearts of readers, and the Super Secrets keep teaching me ways to make my writing better. After using the secrets and attending Moon's workshop, I still return to them for every project, and there is always more to learn from them. I have even found myself using their insights when I teach my high school literature class."
—Christoffer Miller Dahl, English literature teacher, Norway

"The Super Secrets have advanced my writing skills more in the past six months than in the last six years writing without them. From plot structure and effective dialog, to magic swords and the heart's desire, Moon's guidance helped me hone my craft and earn my first professional sale."
—Darren Lipman, teacher and author

FROM THOSE THAT KNOW

"This book won't sit on a shelf. It's gonna live on your writing desk or rest by your favorite comfy chair. And it'll have sticky notes on lots of pages, and dog-ears too. I run through Wulf's Super Secrets every time I write a piece and always end up going back and revising based on something he wrote. It's not just excellent advice. Wulf has a talent for relating writing craft and making it enjoyable. If you want to write good stuff, this is a must-have."
—Chuck Thompson, attorney & author

"A must-have for writers seeking to craft leaner, meaner stories that sell. I know Wulf Moon. I've seen his Wulf Pack writers take the stage at prestigious award events. I've heard them praise his Super Secrets as the secret to their success. Wulf Moon's Super Secrets work!"
—Dave Chesson, *The Kindlepreneur*

HOW TO WRITE A HOWLING GOOD STORY

THE SUPER SECRETS OF WRITING

WULF MOON

STARK PUBLISHING

Wulf Moon Enterprises
PO Box 249, Carlsborg, WA 98324 USA
www.thesupersecrets.com

Published by Stark Publishing
www.starkpublishing.ca

First Edition September 2023

eBook ISBN: 978-1-7390474-6-7
Trade Paperback ISBN: 978-1-7390474-5-0
Hardcover ISBN: 978-1-7390474-4-3

Portions of this book were first published in the following articles:

"Wulf Moon's SUPER SECRETS: Title is Your First Hook: A Rose by Any Other Name is Not Just as Sweet." Copyright © 2023 by Wulf Moon Enterprises. Published in *DreamForge Anvil* Issue 13, September 2023.

"Wulf Moon's SUPER SECRETS: Escalating Tension: Crank it Up!" Copyright © 2023 by Wulf Moon Enterprises. Published in *DreamForge Anvil* Issue 12, June 2023.

"Wulf Moon's SUPER SECRETS: Magic Sword." Copyright © 2023 by Wulf Moon Enterprises. Published in *DreamForge Anvil* Issue 11, March 2023.

"Wulf Moon's SUPER SECRETS: Heart's Desire." Copyright © 2022 by Wulf Moon Enterprises. Published in *DreamForge Anvil* Issue 10, December 2022.

"Wulf Moon's SUPER SECRETS: SET. YOUR. STAGE." Copyright © 2022 by Wulf Moon. Published in *DreamForge Anvil* Issue 8, June 2022.

"Wulf Moon's SUPER SECRETS: 'Write Smart Dialogue,' Moon exclaimed emphatically." Copyright © 2022 by Wulf Moon. Published in *DreamForge Anvil* Issue 7, March 2022.

"Never Let Go." Copyright © 2019 by Wulf Moon. Published in *How I Got Published and What I Learned Along the Way* by Camden Park Press.

Dedicated to my Wulf Pack Writers group
that have run beside me on this journey.

"For the strength of the Pack is the Wolf,
and the strength of the Wolf is the Pack."
—Rudyard Kipling

CONTENTS

Introduction   xvii

SECTION ONE: The Principals of Story Structure

1. YOU CAN'T SKI WHAT YOU CAN'T SEE   1

2. THE NINE ELEMENTS OF STORY STRUCTURE   4

Behold! The Secrets to be unleashed: 5

LIGHT. YOUR. FORGE!   5

1. Your Protagonist   7

2. In A Setting   7

3. With a Heart's Desire (That Creates the Reader / Hero Bond)   8

4. The Inciting Incident, AKA The Problem   9

5. Magic Sword   10

6. Try   11

7. Fail   12

8. Climax   13

9. Denouement   14

3. THE PROTAGONIST   16

The Reader / Hero Bond   17

Creating Real Characters to Create a Real Bond   20

Character Agency   21

4. SETTING: SET. YOUR. STAGE   23

SET. YOUR. STAGE.   24

When the Curtain Opens   26

The Need to Proceed   27

All the World's a Stage, But the Stage Can't Hold a World   30

Costuming Our Hero   31

Environment is a Character   32

Scene Changes: It's Not Over Until It's Over   33

Danger, Will Robinson!   34

5. HEART'S DESIRE   36

What is Heart's Desire?   37

Make a Statement of Heart's Desire   37

Ripping Away Heart's Desire   39
In light of this, ask yourself these questions before you
write your next story: 43

6. INCITING INCIDENT AND THE PROBLEM   45
   When To Introduce the Inciting Incident   46
   Big Problems Yield Big Stories, Tiny Problems Yield
   Wimpy Stories   48

7. MAGIC SWORD   51
   The Origins of Magic Sword   52
   What's the Modern Version of a Magic Sword?   53
   Beware the MacGuffin!   55
   The Prevalence of Magic Sword in Storytelling   56
   Deploying Your Magic Sword   58

8. ESCALATING TENSION: CRANK IT UP!   60
   Try/Fail Cycles   63
   Try/Succeed   66

9. THE CLIMAX   69
   The Purpose of the Climax   70
   Magic Sword   72
   The Sacrifice   73
   Heart's Desire   75
   Positive Result Climax, Negative Result Climax, Neutral
   Result Climax   76

10. THE DENOUEMENT   79
   The Denouement   80
   Paid in Full   81
   Character Growth and Full Circle Endings   83

11. SECTION ONE REVIEW   86
   1. The Protagonist   87
   2. Setting   87
   3. Heart's Desire   88
   4. Inciting Incident and The Problem   88
   5. Magic Sword   88
   6. Escalating Tension: The Try   89
   7. Escalating Tension: The Fail   89
   8. Climax   90
   9. Denouement   91

SECTION TWO: Writing Craft

12. FROM LUMPY CLAY TO POTTERY MASTERPIECES   94

13. "WHERE DO YOU GET YOUR IDEAS?"   98
    The Idea   99
    Collecting The Raw Material   99
    Go Big or Go Home   102
    Strike While the Iron is Hot!   106

14. POINT OF VIEW AND PAST OR PRESENT TENSE   108
    First Person POV   110
    Second Person POV   110
    Third Person POV   112
    Past Tense or Present Tense?   114

15. THE LOGLINE   117
    Elements of a Logline   118

16. TITLE IS YOUR FIRST HOOK: A ROSE BY ANY OTHER
NAME IS NOT JUST AS SWEET   121
    A Story About a Title's Importance   122
    The Importance of a Smart Title   125

17. CHARACTER NAMES: CHOOSE WISELY   128
    The Problem   129
    This Super Secret comes with an assignment: 133

18. GENRE CUE UP FRONT!   134

19. OPEN YOUR STORY WITH YOUR PROTAGONIST   137
    Why You Should Open With Your Protagonist   138
    Proactive Protagonists   139

20. START YOUR #$%@! QUEST, WE'RE ON THE CLOCK!   141

21. "WRITE SMART DIALOGUE!" MOON EXCLAIMED
EMPHATICALLY   144
    The Danger of Saidisms   145
    How to Write Smart Dialogue   146
    Action Beats   149
    Kill "As You Know, Bobs"   151
    Finalis   153

22. KYD: KILL YOUR DARLINGS   155
    Too Many Notes   156
    The Problem   157
    KYD: Kill Your Darlings!   158
    1 - Driving to the Story   158
    2 - Purple Prose   159
    3 - Infodumps   159

4 - Backstory / Flashbacks 160
5 - Character Movement Mechanics 161
Practice Makes Perfect 162

23. TRUST YOUR READER 165
Trust Your Reader 166
The Story Doesn't Happen on the Page 170

24. YOU HAVE FIVE SENSES—WHY AREN'T THEY ON THE PAGE? 174
Weaving With the Full Sensory Array 177

25. MAKE IT WORK! 181

26. SECTION TWO REVIEW 184

SECTION THREE: Belief Determines Reality

27. SHARING YOUR WORKS WITH THE WORLD 188
Quality Control 190
Sending Your Stories to Markets 193

28. BABY STEPS 195
Short Stories 196
Novels 198
Baby Steps 200

29. TO EDIT OR NOT TO EDIT, THAT IS THE QUESTION 202
Editing Your Manuscript 204
Moon's Hybrid Flow System 206

30. BETA READERS, WRITING GROUPS, FREELANCE EDITORS 214
Beta Readers 215
Writing Groups 216
Freelance Editors 218

31. PROPER MANUSCRIPT FORMAT FOR THE WIN! 222
Professional Manuscript Format 223
"Last Words" 224
Shunn's Guide 229

32. COVER LETTERS 233
Cover Letters: What's Their Purpose? 234
What Goes In a Cover Letter? 235
What Does a Proper Short Story Cover Letter Look Like? 236

33. NEVER LET GO 238
    The Larval Stage 239
    Writing Contests 240
    Broadway vs Off-Broadway 243
    My Breakout Moment 246
    Never Let Go 247
    Bullet Points for Emerging Writers ... 249

34. DEALING WITH CRITICISM, PART ONE: ... 251
    Constructive Criticism 253
    Clinical Destructive Criticism 256

35. DEALING WITH CRITICISM, PART TWO: ... 260
    Public Comments and Reviews 263
    Professional Commentaries 265

36. THE SECRET INGREDIENT 269
    Cook vs. Chef 270
    The Master Chef Mindset 272
    The Secret Ingredient 274

    Afterword 277
    Glossary 281
    100 Howling Good Writing Prompts ... 291
    Acknowledgments 295
    On-Demand Workshop Recordings ... 299
    WorkBook Companion 301
    About the Author 303
    Notes

INTRODUCTION

You've turned the page. Good. You've found me. And so our journey begins.

I'm Wulf Moon. I bet you're a writer, or want to be a writer, and like all of us on this path, you're trying to find your way. I've been writing stories since I was five years old. My Ojibwe grandmother raised me in those years in the woods of Spooner, Wisconsin. I begged for stories from her every night in front of the pot-bellied stove and if I was a good boy, I got my wish—fireside tales that fired my imagination. If I had a time machine, those are the days I would go back to. Since I don't have a time machine, I write.

Everything I learned about storytelling—from intriguing characters to challenging trials to surprising plot twists and endless "you'll find out tomorrow night" cliffhangers—well, it all came from Grandma and her wild imagination. No one was better at casting you under a story's spell and when she released you, it was never enough —you always begged for more.

That was her *Secret*. To leave you begging for more.

I've been winning writing contests using this secret ever since I was ten years old. And I've added quite a few of my own secrets over the years. My first claim to fame? First prize and a twenty-five-dollar credit from Scholastic Publications for a Scooby Doo poster I painted for our book fair with the slogan *Reading Books Should Not Be a Mystery*. For a little kid, I painted a darn good Scooby Doo. Loved that cartoon and that crazy snack-loving dog.

At fifteen, I wrote my first science fiction story. It won the national Scholastic Art & Writing Awards—the same contest that first discovered Stephen King, Joyce Carol Oates, John Updike, and a host of iconic names in the arts. *Science World*—a magazine with a circulation of 500,000 copies per issue in its heyday—bought and published my story that same year, making "The Last Ray of Light" my first professional sale. It helped that there was an energy crisis going on in the late seventies, and that my story centered on a hyperloop vactrain long before Elon Musk started talking about them.

I enjoy writing in a variety of genres, and in nonfiction. I've won over forty writing contests to date. One was grand prize in the largest international flash fiction contest I've heard of—around 30,000 entries over the course of one year. I also won a romance writers' contest where I had the privilege of writing the conclusion to Nora Roberts' contest novella, *Riley Slade's Return*.

In 1999, I won Paramount's *Star Trek: Strange New Worlds* Contest with my story "Seventh Heaven." A Borg love story—what could be sweeter? In 2019, my young adult story "Super-Duper Moongirl and the Amazing Moon Dawdler" won the Writers of the Future Contest —the largest talent search for speculative fiction writers in the world. Published in their international bestselling anthology, *Writers of the Future Vol. 35*, this story also won a Best of the Year award. I still receive fan mail and comments on the story from all ages, one of the latest from, surprisingly, a vocalist in a popular heavy metal band.

Thousands of readers from around the world vote each year in the Critters Readers' Choice Awards, and I've been awarded the Best Author award for the last four years at time of writing. My Super Secrets of Writing Workshop has won Best Writing Workshop for the last four years as well. In 2022, I published *The Illustrated Super Secrets of Writing*—a compilation from my writing series published at *Dream-Forge* magazine, which is also the workbook companion to this very book. It won Best Nonfiction Book of the year in these same Readers' Choice awards.

I am honored and frankly tickled so many readers love my work. And it's my heart's desire to help emerging writers level up their technical craft and storytelling skills so that they too can be published and read by appreciative fans. And if a writer is already published or independently published? There are always benefits from improving the stories we tell.

Great stories can change the world, one heart at a time.

Here's where you come in. There's nothing wrong with being a hobby writer, which is writing for one's pleasure as the mood moves us. But I assume you picked up this book because you long for something *more*.

Most of us that write want our words to be read. We are communicators and have a deep need to share our stories with others, to touch their hearts, to spark their dreams, to show them worlds of possibilities, maybe even to reveal to them their own untapped potential.

To do that, we long for readers. The best way to find them is by getting our work published, and by winning awards that will get our work *noticed*. Crafting excellent short stories and novels will make that happen.

Producing quality product is the principal way you build a writing career.

As a writing instructor, I've used my knowledge to help countless writers achieve their first professional sales, win prestigious writing contests, and launch their writing careers. In the last four years since I launched these methods, one dozen writers from my Super Secrets Workshop and my Wulf Pack Writers group have won the Writers of the Future Contest. Anyone in the know understands the enormity of this accomplishment. Thousands from around the world enter this contest *every quarter*. To my knowledge, no other writing group or writing program has turned out so many winners in such a short period of time.

Other alumni from my workshops have won Baen Book's Adventure Fantasy Award, the Mike Resnick Memorial Award, the Canadian Book Awards, and more. Many I've mentored and edited now have professional and even bestselling writing careers, all because they learned the fundamentals of storytelling by studying the *Super Secrets of Writing* (presently around 850,000 online views), and they did the work.

Knowledge is power ... but only if you figure out how to apply it. That's why I'm here. That's why I wrote this book.

Do you long to be published and win writing awards that will get your work noticed and read? My Wulf Pack Writers did. And I helped them find a way to make that happen in *record time*.

Whether you're a hopeful short story writer, a novelist, or a screenwriter, *what could these writing principles do for you?*

Nothing, if you don't read them. Nothing, if you don't apply them. Nothing, if you don't try.

But everything can happen ... if you *do*.

Would you like to learn how to write a howling good story?

Turn the page.

SECTION ONE

The Principles of Story Structure

"You must learn the rules before you break them."

Sir Edward German, composer
The Bookman, July 1921

1

YOU CAN'T SKI WHAT YOU CAN'T SEE

Downhill skiers have a saying: *You can't ski what you can't see*. Oh, you can try, but I don't recommend it. Skiing blind in a white-out? Not only can you barely move forward, you're likely to wipe out. You can't see the snow conditions in front of your skis, nor the turns in the course ahead. Worse, you could easily hit a tree. Game over.

And yet, years ago when I was a skier, I found myself on Mt. Bachelor in Oregon, attempting my first black diamond run. I'd been skiing beginner and intermediate runs for some years by this point. The time had come to challenge my abilities with a stretch goal.

The trail I chose had one of those typical black diamond names like *Devil's Backbone* or *Widowmaker* to give you that boost of encouragement just before you dropped off the edge of the cliff to face your doom. I mustered my courage, pushed off, and heard that rumble against my bases that gives every skier a thrill. I had never skied so fast before; the slightest dip in the snowpack sent me airborne.

Halfway down, I managed to pull off to the side of the run and stared at the remaining steep descent. My arms and legs jittered like a strung-out junkie's. My mind believed I was skiing beyond my abilities and told me if I continued, I'd wipe out at high speed. With that state of uncertainty and fear coursing through me, my logical side was indeed correct. Not a good state to ski in for a guy with a broken back that liked to pretend that he didn't have one. I had no idea how I'd make it the rest of the way.

Fortunately, I kept a flask of liquid courage in my breast pocket for just such occasions. As I took a big swig, I heard a strange call descending from uphill.

"Left ... Right ... Left ... Right."

A skier zoomed past, his bases growling against the snowpack like an angry bear. His speed taking that slope surprised me the least. What shocked me was the orange caution sign on his back: BLIND SKIER.

Another rumble followed. A second skier passed. He also bore a sign: BLIND SKIER GUIDE.

As they soared past the next bend in the trail, that call faded into the distance: *"Left ... Right ... Left ... Right ..."*

I pocketed my flask. Hell. What was I so afraid of? If that guy could take on *Widowmaker* completely blind, what could I accomplish being able to see? Seeing a blind man conquer what seemed impossible for me moments before gave me fresh courage. I believed in myself again, and not only finished the course with that ecstatic rush of victory, but I also realized some important life lessons that day:

1. *Belief determines reality.*
2. *What we think is the absolute limit of our ability is not even close.*
3. *Everything worth achieving is on the other side of fear.*

Am I telling you that if you've never skied before you should head up to your nearest mountain, rent a pair of skis, take the lift to the first black diamond run you see, and with a confident mindset you'll make it safely to the bottom like all the other pros?

Not if you enjoy life and limb.

Note that I said I had been working my way up for several years before taking on that black diamond. I had advanced my skills and honed my muscles during the summers on a ski machine. And I had taken lessons every year from experienced instructors that watched me go down runs and gave me personalized instruction on how to improve.

I'll bet you that blind skier did all of that and more. And the most important ingredient of all that he utilized to successfully navigate the mountain?

He hired a guide.

In writing, good writing, it is no different. We need belief. We need to advance our skills and hone our writing muscles. We need to take in instruction and do smart practice to improve our writing craft. But if we have the good fortune to gain help from an experienced guide, doesn't it make sense that we'll reach our goals faster? Isn't that smarter than blundering about in the fog for years? Wiping out in an unseen snowdrift? Or going off the course and hitting a tree?

You can't ski what you can't see. Not without a guide. This is what the Super Secrets are all about. Blazing the trail for you. Lighting up the path.

Let me show you the way.

This first section of the book begins with the elements of a working story. Grasping foundational principles that make stories work is the first step to being able to apply them in our own stories. We'll build on our skills from there.

Come on! The mountain awaits! Fresh powder!

We'll take *Widowmaker* another day.

THE NINE ELEMENTS OF STORY STRUCTURE

C ue the mysterious voice. Ready?

   The Secrets of a Howling Good Story.

What? More cowbell? Are you crazy? Maybe a touch of reverb to give it that back-of-the-deep-dark-cavern effect. Ready? Here we go. Take Two:

The Secrets of a Howling Good Story.

We good? Reverb at the right level? Great. Quiet on the set!

The Nine. You have heard these legends told, of nine Secrets from the days of old, when forges burned hot and hammers rang bold. They are the stories of mortals who sold their souls, to create from crude ore one tale of pure gold.

Yes, writer, you know of what I speak. For you can see it too, in your mind's eye. A story incomplete, seeking what is missing with all its might in the fog and confusion of lidless night. Gather your power. Come to the fiery mountain, where we shall dare to stare into its molten heart of doom. Cast your story into the fire and bring it forth in radiance anew. Howl as you seize the nine elements of every successful story and apply Moon's alchemy to bind them to your living creation.

You have heard of the Seven Point Plot. This one ... is The Nine. From these nine essential elements, every successful story is created. If you have wondered how to craft a story, if you have been confounded by your story not selling, this chapter will teach you how to turn lead into gold.

BEHOLD! THE SECRETS TO BE UNLEASHED:

1. *Discover the Nine Secrets of every working story. Analyze what makes them kick and scream and drag you down into the heart of darkness, only to lift you from the ashes into blazing glory.*
2. *Explore how authors use these Secrets in your favorite stories to bind you to their power and cast you under their spell. The scales shall fall from your eyes; you will be forever changed.*
3. *Learn how to bind the Nine to do your will. Using* How to Write a Howling Good Story, *we will take your idea and give it fur and fangs and a sporty bowler hat. Or a holocaust cloak. You decide.*
4. *Stand back! Farther, you fools!—you have a wraith on your hands! Learn how to safely unleash your beast into the world and prepare for world domination.*

LIGHT. YOUR. FORGE!

Okay, so I plagiarized this material from the description I wrote for one of my masterclasses. It's my version of the Seven-Point Plot you see many writers teaching today, but with a couple of important additions that these writers don't teach. They likely learned Seven-Point Plot from the same source I learned it from—the late Hugo Award winner Algis Budrys' book *Writing to the Point*. I learned Seven-Point Plot from A.J. himself, as he liked to be called. And A.J.? He learned it from a famous literary agent. If you want to go back further, we all learned how to plot our stories from the ancient Greeks and their three-act structure, which in the simplest terms is that every story has a beginning, a middle, and an end.

We stand on the backs of giants.

I've already discussed three-act structure in the workbook meant to complement this book: *The Illustrated Super Secrets of Writing, Vol. 1.* I won't belabor it by repeating it again here. Three-act structure is a simple system of storytelling that has stood the test of time. But it's missing elements we've come to expect in today's stories, and so the model needed to advance. I've utilized the Seven-Point Plot in my storytelling ever since I took AJ's "Sarah Jane" workshop where he drew stick figures of his protagonist Sarah Jane on a chalk board and told us a story about her, using his Seven-Point Plot format.

It's a solid system. There are other systems—this isn't the only way to tell a story—but it's solid. It's why so many have copied it and taught it to other writers. A.J.'s premise was that if you included his seven essential points in every story you wrote, you'd start selling. And indeed, writers have.

But over the years, I discovered additional essential elements that are necessary to enhance the system. I believe you need them if you not only wish to write stories that sell, but wish to write stories that are howling good—stories that not only engage the mind, but more importantly, reach the heart.

Stories that touch readers' hearts create a deep emotional experience they won't soon forget. They'll talk about your story to others for years to come, and they'll seek you out to find more. If you enter those stories in contests, they'll rise to the top, touch the judges' hearts, and win awards. Major awards can launch your writing career.

But first, let's study the fundamentals of my *Nine Elements of Story Structure*. You can't ski what you can't see. So let me show you all nine. If you're trying to get your stories published in Western markets, you will benefit from learning these. In fact, like A.J. with his system, I believe you'll start selling if you do, even win awards in time as you gain experience in wielding them. And if you have been published but a story or novel isn't selling, reviewing it against this plot structure can reveal areas that might be weak or missing in the tale that's causing it to have lackluster performance.

We want our stories to shine! Fire up the forge!

1. YOUR PROTAGONIST

Stories are first and foremost about people. That's because we're people, human beings, and we like knowing about the other person's life and what makes them tick. We learn from others in real life, both the good and the bad, and it's no different in stories. Even if the main character of the story (known as the protagonist) is an alien from another galaxy, a talking horse, or a sentient rock, they are funhouse mirrors of *people*.

A story *has to be about somebody*. I will also argue that the person it's about should be *interesting*. And even if they're troubled and flawed, they should exhibit some actions that make us identify with them and draw us toward them. More on the reasons for that in another chapter. For now, let's stay on target. We're just establishing the foundation stones of a working story. Here's our next:

2. IN A SETTING

Now you have to put that person somewhere. This is called a setting. Think of a play. Unless it's avant-garde—or *gasp*, a play populated by mimes—there's going to be stuff on that stage. Maybe even a nicely painted backdrop to give some depth and dimension to the scene. The director will want to establish what location these actors are at, what time period they're in, the time of day, and more. The stuff around the stage cues in the audience to the big picture that isn't really there, just hinted at.

This is important to note. All the world's a stage, but you can't fit the world *on* a stage. The director must be discerning and selective, choosing props that establish setting clearly without overdoing it. If the curtains open on the interior of a stable, there might be a few bales of hay stacked up, a pitchfork leaning against a wall, and a backdrop painted with some stalls and horses. The director of a play doesn't ask her set designer to build out an entire stable. They hint at the larger

7

environment of a stable by carefully adding symbolic items that key up a vision of a stable, mostly in the viewer's mind.

The same is true in a story. Scenes have to take place somewhere. Describing the setting at the opening of each scene establishes where this story is taking place, and the description makes sure that all the characters and items important to the scene are in it.

~

3. WITH A HEART'S DESIRE (THAT CREATES THE READER/HERO BOND)

This is the one no one tells you about. Instructors will walk you through their plot model and say, "A story is about a character in a setting with a problem." Ever heard that? I have, in plenty of workshops I've attended. And you do need a problem or something for the protagonist to push against, or your story will have no tension, no drama, and no character growth. But drama alone does not make a meaningful story. The problem or power opposing your hero is meaningless if it isn't attacking something near and dear to your protagonist's heart.

Heart's Desire is the most important element of a story, and it's crazy to leave it out of the equation. Without Heart's Desire, you can have one of Hollywood's "roller coaster thrill ride" plots, you can put your character through the wringer with multiple problem cycles, but your reader will have little to no emotional attachment to your character and the journey they're on.

It's been said that stories are about people that want something, and someone else is trying to keep it from them. But you must go deeper. Much deeper. Heart's Desire is revealing on the page what the protagonist cares about most dearly. Once you have established what truly motivates them, what they care about more than anything else (at least in the confines of the story), THEN you rip it away from them, creating the soul-crushing problem. Now the problem is going to matter because your hero cares, so we care.

When readers know what the hero desires above all else, when it's threatened, readers will sense the stakes are high. And if you've done your job right with early characterization, readers will already identify with your protagonist, and they too will begin caring about what your hero holds most dear in their heart. When you crush or rip away your protagonist's hope of keeping or obtaining what is most dear to them, it's not just your hero that will be cut to the heart. Your reader will be, too. They'll bond with your protagonist, and they'll go through hell and high water with your hero to find out if they get their Heart's Desire or not.

Heart's Desire is what makes readers care.

4. THE INCITING INCIDENT, AKA THE PROBLEM

So, you've introduced your interesting character, you've placed them in a setting so we know what their normal world is like, and you've shown us the thing deep down inside of them that they cherish most. They may already have it in their possession and pray they never lose it, or they don't have it in their possession and hope they'll find the way to obtain it.

Your next job? Dash their chances of getting that cherished thing all to hell, or if they already have it, you rip it from them. For the story to have dramatic tension, there must be an opposing force, and it must have the power to drop its ugly size sixteen combat boot down on the protagonist's Heart's Desire and squash that sucker flat. The rest of the story will answer the question: *Will they succeed in getting back the thing taken?* Or, if it's something they hope to obtain or achieve: *Will they get their Heart's Desire in the end?*

Without a strong desire met by a strong opposing force, there's no tension. And if nothing is put in jeopardy for your protagonist that they care deeply about, why would they ever leave the comfort and safety of their home to go out into the dark and dangerous world to go get it?

The paramount rule of any story is to hold the reader's attention. This is how you do it. A powerful Heart's Desire *placed in jeopardy* by the inciting incident motivates your protagonist to stand up and fight against the soul-crushing force.

5. MAGIC SWORD

Here's another one I've never heard discussed in writing classes, and I'm betting you haven't either. Magic Sword. This fundamental story element is in virtually every story or novel you read, every play or movie you watch. Yet no one teaches you to put it in your stories! You have to figure it out on your own, or come across a brief blip about the concept in a book, as if it's too inconsequential to mention. Let's fix that right now. You're a writer that wants to succeed. You need to know this.

What is Magic Sword?

Magic Sword is the thing of power that can defeat the opposing force *if* the protagonist can just get their needy hands on it. Or perhaps they already have it in their possession, but they have no idea how to wield it effectively. Whatever the case, when a protagonist is faced with a force that they can't beat, they seek something beyond their reach that might have the power to turn the tables. It's most visible in fantasy quest stories: the hero loses what they hold dear to a powerful villain, someone tells them about a sword / talisman / chalice / wizard in a distant land that could help them, and the hero sets out to gain this weapon or ally that can lend them the power to defeat their enemy.

What about stories and novels that aren't fantasy? Like detective stories or romances or thrillers. Surely they don't have a magic sword in them, how ridiculous! *Wrong*. It's there, its simply got different wrappings, different trappings. And once I show you what it is and what it does, you'll be looking for it in everything you read, everything you watch. And you'll be making a conscious effort to put one in your stories. But for now, trust me on this. There's a whole chapter coming up where I'll make my case.

6. TRY

Stories need escalating tension. Your protagonist wants something. Someone else—the antagonist—is keeping it from them. So, after the inciting incident occurs—often called the problem—the protagonist comes up with a rudimentary plan to defeat their enemy, and then they act on it. They *Try* to get the thing desired.

The attempt to solve the problem is important. Many beginning writers have their hero swept along by circumstance. They create reactive characters instead of proactive ones. But a character that's swept along by the opposing force isn't pushing against it, they're being controlled by it. There's no character growth if the protagonist isn't at least trying to solve the problem. In real life, we respect people that try to change unfortunate circumstances. Even if they fail, we respect that they *tried*.

And since stories are about us as humans in one way or another, we expect the same of the characters in stories. We need to see them actively engaged in attempts to try to right the wrong, to turn the tables on bad circumstances, to better their lives or the lives of others. The Try is a fundamental plot point because it's a fundamental principle of humanity.

It is vital to remember that tension in your story comes from your protagonist pushing against an opposing force. The more powerful the force, the more the push required to move against it. This is what creates plot tension. No tension, boring story, readers quit reading. Editors quit reading. Judges quit reading. And that means no happy sale, no shiny award.

Make sure your protagonist is trying, even fighting, to get the thing you told your readers they desire.

7. FAIL

If obtaining Heart's Desire came easily to our character, we'd have no story. It's not fun reading stories like that because in the real world, life isn't easy, it's a struggle. Things of value are normally hard won and hard to hold on to. Normally, before we achieve a great thing, we have to fall flat on our face a few times and pick ourselves up and try again to get it. There's even a saying on this we teach our children: *If at first you don't succeed, try, try again.* Failure is just the lesson that teaches us how to succeed the next time. Or the time after that. As the saying goes, try, *try* again.

Failure is implied before success. We learn from our mistakes. They force us to strive to do better the next time. When the stakes are high, multiple tries and fails go with the territory.

A Try/Fail Cycle is when your protagonist comes up with a plan to try to get the thing desired. They initiate the plan. And fall flat on their face. To increase the story's tension, the failure must make things get worse, putting your hero even farther from their goal.

They have that heroic streak, meaning they don't give up when the chips are down. They try again, with a better plan this time because they learned from the fall, and realize they're going to have to do better if they hope to win. But even with their best plan yet, they fail. And things get even worse. The dark night approaches, all hope is lost.

Or so it appears.

Before we move on, there is another way to play this. There is such a thing as Try/Succeed cycles. A character can succeed in an attempt, and things still get worse. That's why I prefer the term Escalating Tension—it works for both. More on that in another chapter. For now, your story has had two tries, two fails. The most important Try is yet to come.

8. CLIMAX

In a short story, the final try / fail or try / succeed cycle is called your Climax. This is where the stakes are highest. Your hero has gathered their power for one last Hail Mary, and because they've gained knowledge through their previous attempts and have built up their muscles, they can actually throw the Hail Mary and make it into the end zone. What seemed impossible before is now possible because they grew in strength and knowledge and at last have a real chance at winning.

Of course, their antagonist has probably grown into even more power during this time, especially if they've been facing off before this. The antagonist may even have beaten the protagonist to the Magic Sword, the thing of power, and know how to wield it against them. To achieve the highest stakes in a story—and thus ultimate tension—the final try should be a desperate do-or-die battle. No, this doesn't mean there must be clashing swords and one must behead the other like in all the *Highlander* stories. But it should be clear everything is on the line for the hero—they're all in. Everything to gain, and everything to lose. Everything in the story funnels into the outcome of a final face-off with their opponent.

Your hero may not win. This would be a Tragedy. Just as in real life, not all stories have positive outcomes. So, the Climax could actually become a Fail, and there are lessons learned even in these tales. Sometimes our heroes were actually chasing the wrong desire, and learn too late the price for doing so.

But it's good to remember the reader has been hoping for your protagonist to find a way to beat the impossible odds, and they get a happy release of hormones when tension and defeat change to triumph. Therefore, many climaxes are a Try / Succeed cycle. The protagonist went on a journey, they proactively did their best to defeat their dragon, and after getting scorched a couple of times, they figured out how to vanquish him. Hurrah! Victory at last!

But wait! The story is not over ....

9. DENOUEMENT

Your hero just vanquished their enemy after a steady rise of escalating tension. Your reader has been sitting on the edge of their seat, racing through the pages to find out who will win this battle. Now you need to bring them back down from the heights to enjoy that warm fuzzy feeling, knowing this person they bonded with will now be okay. The hero got what they desired. They saved their world in the nick of time … and perhaps saved the world for everyone else as well. Except the bad guy. He can go wallow in the gutter in shame and disgrace. Or maybe he's in a shallow grave.

Denouement comes from the French word for unknotting or unwinding, and it's a fitting term for the scene that follows the climax in short stories, or often a series of scenes after the climax in novels. All those mysteries in the story are unraveled in the end.

Anyone that's watched a Scooby Doo cartoon knows this scene. The "ghost" in the haunted mansion is finally captured in the climax. Next, it's unmasked. Everyone gasps as you find out the friendly neighbor was scaring everyone off to steal the hidden treasure in the walls. Fred and Velma explain all the tricks used to make the ghost appear real. That which was knotted up is now untied, made plain for the reader to see. Questions are answered. Wrongs are made right. Scooby gets his Scooby snack for a job well done. Life goes on as the team drives into the sunset in The Mystery Machine.

Denouement is also known by another term: the Validation Scene. True, any unsolved mysteries in a story must be unraveled by the end. But even more important is the validation of the story itself, and the hero that took the journey. You opened your story making a statement of the protagonist's Heart's Desire. It's also a contract with the reader, promising them what the story will be about. You end the story by stating through your characters whether or not the hero achieved their Heart's Desire, and it's also to validate the hero for a job well done.

Every *Lone Ranger* movie did this. After the bad guys were defeated, town folk would look on admiringly as the Lone Ranger rode off into the sunset. Someone would say, "Who was that masked man?" Their awe and admiration mirrored our own awe and admiration. Our hero beat impossible odds and saved the day.

So, there you have it. Moon's Nine Elements of Story Structure. Now you are fully armed with weapons pulled hot from the forge. Let's assemble the elements and do target practice with each.

Hi-ho, Silver! Away!

3

THE PROTAGONIST

Name some of your favorite main characters from the stories you love. I've got a few. Charlie Bucket. Bilbo Baggins. Paul Atreides. Mickey Haller. Jean-Luc Picard. What makes them memorable?

Charlie loved chocolate, but he could only get a candy bar once a year because his family was dirt poor.

Bilbo Baggins loved hearth and home and would never think of going on an adventure. Nasty disturbing uncomfortable things. Make you late for dinner!

Paul Atreides was plucked from his lush world and life of privilege, stripped of all he held dear except his mother, and had to use his wits to survive the deadliest planet in the known universe.

Mickey Haller was an attorney that did business in the back of a Lincoln Town Car, hoping to upscale his practice by finding high-society clientele.

Jean-Luc Picard served as the highly skilled captain of the Federation starship USS *Enterprise*. But because of these skills he was constantly sent in to solve problems where angels feared to tread.

What's the common denominator?

Fascinating characters behind the eight-ball from the very start of the story facing extraordinary circumstances. You can see it in my list. I bet you can see it in yours, too. The main character of a story—known as the protagonist—must be *interesting*. They need to be someone we'd like to spend some time with, or at least some time studying, because we're curious about who they are and what makes them tick. They have puzzles within their personalities that would be interesting to see unraveled. Perhaps some of those puzzles are in our own character or in the lives of people we know. Perhaps we'd like to see how someone else deals with the knots. Whatever the case, if we're going to read a story about someone, we need to see something interesting in them that stirs our curiosity.

A character, an interesting character, is the first element of a story. Stories are about someone. And that person has to pique our interest so that we are willing to invest our precious time to figure them out. Most of us enjoy puzzles. People and what makes them do the things they do are the most interesting puzzles of all.

THE READER/HERO BOND

Once we've named our character and given them some simple but unique definition, our next job is to show the reader the protagonist's normal world so they can interact in it and reveal the type of person they are. Note I said reveal, not tell. It's a lot more fun to watch a character interact with others and then draw our own conclusions than to have the writer narrate those conclusions for us.

Part of the fun of reading is discovery, and that includes discovering who the protagonist is and most importantly, whether we like them or not. Unless it's an antihero story where you're giving us a bad person and are redeeming them in some way by the end (or giving them their just desserts), readers normally want a hero they like. Someone they discern has some good moral character within them, even if it's buried deep. For your protagonist to become a hero, we should see glimmers of the undeveloped hero within. I'll also argue that even in an antihero, there better be some shiny bits revealed early on in them somewhere, or most readers aren't going to want to spend time with them.

We spend time with people we like. As in the real world, so too in stories.

You reveal your protagonist with their unique quirks or flaws—this makes them human—but you also reveal through thoughtful or kind actions that your protagonist is good, someone your reader might even become friends with or at least respect if they met them in the real world. Is the mother worn out coming home from a hard day's work and snaps at her child, but quickly apologizes? We respect that. We're not always playing our A game each day, and neither should our characters. But when we see kindness and consideration rise up in spite of life's stresses, we value this in real life, and we value it in our fictional characters as well. Remember, stories are a funhouse mirror, distorted perhaps, but still reflecting realities within our humanity and world.

Some call this technique *Save the Cat*, but this is something deeper. I call it the Reader/Hero Bond. It's not a formulaic act at the beginning of your story, i.e., saving a cat out of a tree like Mr. Incredible did at the opening of *The Incredibles* movie. Winning stories MAKE. US. CARE. Winning stories MAKE. US. LOVE. the hero. From beginning to end.

Combinations of thoughtful acts and small sacrifices from the very beginning of the story tell us this child is golden, this college student is authentic, this jaded detective deep down inside has a good heart. We need to know this person you're presenting to us to hang our hats on for the rest of the story is the REAL DEAL. Yes, you can twist all of this, but first learn the principle like a pro. Then learn it some more. One day when you're really skilled through smart practice and you've proven yourself with respectable sales, you can twist most anything and get away with it, even surprise the reader. Until then, learn the ropes. Creating a real character we can empathize with from beginning to end is a master skill. To sell stories to respected markets and win awards, you must become the master.

What is the Reader/Hero Bond? It's a series of *kind acts and noble thoughts* that start in the very beginning of the tale and build throughout the rest of the story. Each small act of kindness adds up to the bigger revelation: that your protagonist is a decent human being (or alien, robot, sentient rock, etc.), and although flawed, they have strength of character, often higher principles, admirable qualities that will lead your reader to like, care about, maybe even fall in love with them.

Fall in love with them? Isn't that a stretch? Ask skilled romance writers. Talk to rabid fans of a series. Better yet, look up *fictofilia*.

Let's assume you've been on a first date, and it led to more. What made you like the person? Were they courteous and thanked the wait-staff? Or did they talk about killing and rape? Did they talk about their love of hiking, how they'd like to travel more, maybe shared a favorite hobby that was the same as yours? Or did they diss all the people they work with, calling them foul names and ranting that they will get even with them one day? Or instead, did they talk about good friends and good times shared? What did favorite books, TV shows, movies, and songs reveal?

It doesn't take long to form a picture about someone. If their likes and values are similar to ours, we start to identify with them. If we find more commonalities or characteristics we respect, we start to like them. And as we spend more time with them and discover these things are genuine, feelings can and often do go deeper.

As a writer, that's your job. Whether it's a short story or a screen-play or a novel, you are sending your protagonists out on a date, even several dates, hoping the reader will spend some time with them and fall in love. If you can accomplish such magic—getting a live reader to bond tight with a fictional character—you aren't doing sleight of hand. This is not some quickie parlor trick. This is the deep magic that can only be pulled off by a skilled magician. This is the Reader/Hero Bond.

That's your objective. To bond a reader so tight to your protago-nist, they are no longer fictional, they become a real person to them. Through carefully orchestrated actions, you bring the reader under your spell and bind them emotionally to your hero.

It won't happen immediately. At first it will be simple parlor tricks. All magicians begin this way. And then they practice, and they grow.

They study the masters. They join elite magic clubs. And one day, they can snap their fingers and make you fall in love with a total stranger. Because they know all the tricks to bring you under their spell.

I always hear Mr. Burns from *The Simpsons* cartoons at this point. *"Then we get to crush the hopes and dreams of this little person they've come to know and love, and we get to watch them cry. Exxxcellent!"*

It's a sadistic business we writers have. We must torture our protagonists. And you'll love every minute of it when you effectively pull it off, whether you made readers bawl like babies at the end, made them laugh out loud, or made them cry out *"Yes!"* in triumph.

Because you bonded the reader to your hero. They became your hero's close friend and walked right beside them on their journey. They might have gone even deeper, melting into your hero, experiencing the journey vicariously as if *they* were your hero. It's a good thing.

CREATING REAL CHARACTERS TO CREATE A REAL BOND

There are as many ways to create an interesting character as there are people that have ever walked this earth. Be a student of humanity by watching and interacting with the people around you. Get out from your writer she shack or writer man cave and engage in social activity. You'll develop realism in your characters from this. Study historical figures, read biographies. Watch for mannerisms in people that make them unique. Plagiarize their lives—the good, the bad, and the ugly—and season your characters with realistic traits that reveal:

1. They're quirky.
2. They have vulnerabilities.
3. They have a fatal flaw.
4. They exhibit noble strengths.
5. They might be a hopeless dreamer.
6. They could be a survivor of tragedy.

7. They have wounded souls.

8. They love animals, they love their kids.

9. They make sacrifices for others.

10. They are troubled by injustice.

11. They have a highly spiritual nature.

12. They see light where others see darkness.

13. They pick themselves up no matter how many times they fall.

These are just a few among the infinite possibilities of characteristics in your hero that readers will likely identify with. If you're skilled enough to create a character that resonates with many, you can write about them again and again. You might even have an award-winning story on your hands, or a blockbuster novel. Because you did the deep magic of making an imaginary character feel *real*.

CHARACTER AGENCY

What makes a hero? A dictionary would say it's a person who is admired or idealized for courage, outstanding achievements, or noble qualities. But it's more complicated than that. That's because what is considered outstanding in one group might be considered mediocre in another. What might have been considered heroic in one time period or culture might appear barbaric in another age. Heroes and what makes the stuff of heroes is relative.

For the purpose of heroes in stories—the protagonist—these are people who are not passive. They don't run from their problems, or if they do, they find the courage to turn around and go back and face them. They don't allow themselves to be swept along by the opposing force, or if they do at first, they find their courage and turn around and swim upstream to find the source. Heroes are not passive. They are proactive. They grab the bull by the horns, even if they might get gored if it means saving others. This is called *Character Agency*.

I won't delve deeper into this topic here. I wrote an entire chapter on character agency in the companion to this book, *The Illustrated Super Secrets of Writing, Volume 1*. It's a workbook. I recommend you read it. But since we're here now, I'll throw you a bone from the workbook. You need to know this.

Character agency is an essential story element in Western culture. Readers expect protagonists to actively engage the problem, the opposing force, and do their best to push back and figure out how to overcome it. Most beginning writers' stories fail miserably in this regard. Their heroes are passive observers, watching all the action, avoiding all the tough problems, and in the end may even be rescued by someone else. These stories are not fun to read because there are no stakes for the protagonist, no real threat, no tension to hold attention. There is no character growth because they never *tried* to grow.

Thor said it best in the movie *Thor Ragnarok*: "But me, I choose to run toward my problems, and not away from them, because that's what heroes do."

Your hero may start in a weak state, she may have been swept along by circumstance in the past, but in your story, your hero is going to stand up and do her best to change her fate. She's going to rise up against all odds to determine her own destiny. She won't allow anyone else to choose it for her. Not this time. Not ever again.

That's a hero your readers will cheer for. That's a hero they'll respect … maybe even fall in love with.

Now go create your fascinating protagonist facing extraordinary circumstances. Use the points in the list in this chapter as a sounding board. Make readers believe in your hero by mastering the deep magic of characterization.

4

SETTING: SET. YOUR. STAGE

You're tired of watching *The Big Bang Theory* reruns and decide you need to broaden your mind with a little culture. So, you head to the theater district, go to that booth with the half-price tickets, and the seller says she's got great seats for *Marshmallows Getting Roasted*, truly avant-garde. Avant-garde? You don't speak French, but it sounds like advancing guards getting roasted, just the kind of cultural piece you've been craving! You plop down fifty bucks, head into the empty theater, and the curtain opens on the glorious stage where the magic that transports you to another time and place happens.

Only this stage is white. The background is white. There's not a prop in sight. You squint, and there might be two players standing in the center, but they're in puffy white marshmallow costumes so they're really hard to make out. Oh good, they talk. You were worried they might be *mimes*.

"Hello Marsh Mallow."

"Hello White Mallow. You're certainly looking puffy today."

"Why thank you. Did you hear about Cousin Minnie Mallow? She got roasted."

"No!"

"Yes!"

"No!"

"Yes!"

"I did not. I spilled out of the bag and rolled in the dirt, and they tossed me."

You squint. Was that a third marshmallow on the stage? Where did she come from?

"Oh, my bad, Minnie. So glad they didn't shove you on a pointed stick and roast you over the flames."

Oh good, some drama. They must be at a campsite, about to be eaten. But then—

"We're all glad!"

You squint. Was that a bag's worth of marshmallow actors standing on the stage? Where did they come from?

"Someone's coming!" they say in unison. "Let's hide in the cupboard!"

Oooh-kay. Why didn't they say they were in a kitchen in the first place? And as the play rolls on with not a prop in sight, with marshmallows spilling onto the stage out of nowhere, with nothing to identify them with but identical puffball costumes, you quietly slip from your chair and escape. Those reruns at home are sounding pretty good again. So does a cup of blistering hot chocolate, and you know just what you're going to top it with.

SET. YOUR. STAGE.

I can't tell you how many times I've written SET. YOUR. STAGE., in all caps, on a manuscript I'm editing. The story opens with characters talking, but I have no idea who they are, what they look like, where they're at, what they're doing. The scene is like white marshmallows acting on a white stage. I keep waiting for setting clues to appear as to where we're at, hopefully some indication as to what these people look like, but it rarely comes. The writer is so busy telling their story, they forgot that the reader can't see what's in their head. They forgot that, as the director of their story, the writer needs to *set their stage*.

True, the intrepid reader might forge ahead, but they're forced to stare at a blank stage where they're left to guess at what the environment and characters look like. In order to read on, they fill in the gaps by setting the stage themselves. They'll make assumptions as to locations and time periods, character gender and age, even whether the scene is happening indoors or outdoors. In effect, the writer is asking the reader to be their own production designer ... without furnishing them any set designs. Chaos ensues. Why?

As the story progresses, the reader discovers their assumptions were wrong. They come to find out the Ashley character that they gave a slender build and dressed up as a dandy Southern gentleman is actually a homeless woman in Detroit who is nine months pregnant! Or that posh room they pictured in a Georgia mansion turns out to be the gilded captain's quarters on an interstellar spaceship. Or they discover many pages later the newspaper the heroine put over her head isn't repelling a Kansas rainstorm, it's protecting her coiffure from water pistols fired over the crowd in a sticky, rice-covered theater.

Lack of set direction from the writer causes mental whiplash for readers. They are forced to slam on the brakes, back up, and restart the opening with new information revealed far too late in the scene. Setting whiplash is also responsible for unhappy editors ... only they don't have the time nor the interest to back up and build out a new set in their minds. They'll send the story back with a form that says, *"Not right for us but good luck sending it elsewhere."*

Let's not make that mistake. Making readers fill with anticipation at the opening of our story is a critical part of our job; confounding them is not. We know we must provide clear and efficient coding that sets the stage and channels the reader down our own Yellow Brick Road, with the promise of the Emerald City gleaming on a backdrop in the distance. If we clearly define who our protagonist is, if we set our stage properly from the moment the curtain opens, our audience won't scratch their heads in confusion as scenery, people, and props pop out of nowhere later on. When they see a properly developed opening, they'll ease back into their seats, settle in for the ride, and let the magic happen … because we set our stage like the professionals we are.

So how do we make that kind of theater magic happen? What are the necessary setting elements readers need at the start? How do we help them visualize our characters? How much detail is needed? And once we've described our world in the opening scene, do we dust off our hands and say our work here is done?

Like all good directors, let's take a moment and analyze our *stagecraft*.

~

WHEN THE CURTAIN OPENS

Every story begins like a play. You might have a clue what a play is going to be about because of its title, but until the curtain opens, a mysterious void hides behind it. But rest assured, unless it's an improv or a no-set production, the director and her design team will have put tremendous effort into turning that void into a setting that will enhance and illuminate what the story is all about.

A properly set stage is an art form. Smart, creative set design can enchant an audience before an actor utters a single word. Long before opening night, the director will have had many meetings with the production designer and her team to select the colors, scenery, backdrops, costumes, lighting, sound, and props that will create an evocative setting for each scene in the production.

Stagecraft has many elements, and careful attention is given to each department to create place, period, and mood. Does the play open in a park? Then the set will need a bench and a few trees on stands. Edwardian era? Get the props department to find a period streetlamp. Takes place in London, and there's going to be a chimney sweep scene? Tell the art department to research period buildings and create sketches for the set pieces and backdrop. What about costuming? The script says the protagonist is a governess, but she can also fly.

We'll need apparel that must look prim and proper, and yet allow her to, I don't know, fly casual ....

A writer, too, must give careful thought to their stagecraft if they want their production to be a hit. There are many elements to stage-craft, just as there are many elements to a smart opening of a story. But it all boils down to this: What does my reader need to proceed?

THE NEED TO PROCEED

Unlike a play, the setting of a story is not already created on a stage, imme-diately absorbed by the audience as the curtain opens. A writer has to establish their setting in the reader's mind, providing them in the opening scene with all the textual prompts necessary to enter their world, attach to their hero, and go on the journey they've created. The reader needs to quickly visualize who the story is about, and they need setting context to provide the necessary details in order to see a vision in their mind and move forward. The more potent, evocative, and accurate the word choices are crafted for an opening scene, the faster the reader will settle into the world, identify with the protagonist, and kick back to enjoy the ride.

Think about the questions a reader immediately wants answered at the beginning of a story. These are the same questions you have undoubtedly asked as a reader, so this test shouldn't be hard.

- Who is this story about, and are they interesting in some way?
- What's the name of the protagonist, their gender, do they have any features or clothing to visualize them by, and is there a clue as to their age?
- Where is this story taking place, and what does the immediate area look like?
- When is this story taking place?
- Are there crucial elements in this scene I'll need to remember later?

- Why should I care about the protagonist? What do they desire?
- Is their problem big enough to hold my interest?
- What genre is this?

There are plenty of other questions you might ask, but these are critical ones. The faster we answer these questions, the quicker we build our set and its players, the easier it is for the reader to step over the threshold and enter the story trance—in effect, to enjoy our wondrous play.

If we provide proper coding from the very beginning of our story, giving the reader the essentials they need to create the proper vision, they won't have to tear down the set in their minds several pages in because we failed to reveal key details until later. It will build out accurately and beautifully from the start, with us enhancing our stage and props as we need to through the progression of our plot.

Now, note the question at the top of the list. Why do readers need to know who the story is about ASAP? Because of the basic definition of what makes a story. A story is about 1. a character, 2. in a setting, 3. with a problem. Readers need to know who they're supposed to be rooting for, and then whether or not they're interesting enough to spend time figuring them out. It's basic storytelling.

Want proof? Note how the *Epic of Gilgamesh*, considered the earliest surviving work of literature, opens:

I WILL proclaim to the world the deeds of Gilgamesh. This was the man to whom all things were known; this was the king who knew the countries of the world. He was wise, he saw mysteries and knew secret things, he brought us a tale of the days before the flood. He went on a long journey, was weary, worn-out with labour, returning he rested, he engraved on a stone the whole story.

See that? The ancient Sumerians knew how to tell a story! The writer opened by *naming* the hero of the tale—Gilgamesh—and then told the reader why they should be interested in him. Was he worth reading about? You bet! This man was a king, worldly-wise, had accomplished deeds and had been to places no one else had. In fact, there's a narrative hook by the third sentence: *he saw mysteries and knew secret things.* Gilgamesh was an international man of mystery!

I'll give you a modern example. It's one of mine, the opening to "Super-Duper Moongirl and the Amazing Moon Dawdler" in *Writers of the Future, Vol. 35:*

I'm Dixie. I'm twelve. Well, almost. My birthday is coming up, so close enough. I wear red. God gave me red hair, but I picked the rest, from my red space Keds—Mom hates them—to my matching silk cape—Dad loves it—because capes are cool, and when you drape them right, they hide the tubes.

I have a dog. He's a MedGen robodog, looks like a chrome Doberman pinscher. He breathes for both of us, and he juices up my air with higher oxy. I named him Moon Dawdler, because, duh, we're on the Moon, and because, double duh, he dawdles, doing his blinkies and sniffies with everything, making sure I'm safe before we enter an airlock, or head to Moonshine's for burgers, or go to the arboretum for a run, or take the tunnels back to Norden Moonbase Resort. Mom and Dad run it for some rich dude that's about to head the first mission to Mars.

Mars. I'm the first girl on the Moon, and I can't breathe on my own, so who would have believed that? But Mars? That's a whole 'nuther world. But they'll make a base there too, and I'd love to see it. One step at a time, my physical therapist used to say, and look where that got me so far!

Note how quickly I provide the story's heroine, her name, her age, identifying physical traits, narrative hook, unique character cues to make you identify with her, costuming, secondary characters, location, genre cue, and more ... all in three paragraphs. As the director of this production, I've set the stage in the opening. You even know where future scenes in this production will be held, because I've given you a glimpse into the grand vista of Dixie's world. There'll be no surprises when I take you to some of these locations later. It's all there, listed in your program at the very start. You've got a lay of the land.

∽

ALL THE WORLD'S A STAGE, BUT THE STAGE CAN'T HOLD A WORLD

Another question in that list is *Where is this story taking place?* We've established that a professional director sets the stage they place their players upon. They put a great deal of thought into it. They don't clutter the stage, they create a thoughtful backdrop and place just the right number of props to give the *impression* of the world, location, and environment their players live within.

This Super Secret is called *Hint at the Grand Vista of Your World.* You can't cram your entire world into the opening scene, anymore than you can cram an oak tree into the space of a bonsai. Many beginners try, creating an endless laundry list of setting and world details, often dumping in the intricate milieu of their world. Wonderful, we're glad they know all that stuff, it adds depth to the tale they're telling. But guess what? The story doesn't need it. Just the facts, ma'am. Trust me. Better yet, trust the reader. A little dab will do ya. *Especially* in the opening.

J.R.R. Tolkien was the king of detailed backstory. You can see it all in *The Silmarillion.* But when he started to write *The Hobbit*, did he stuff all that history into the opening? Fortunately for us, he did not. He opened with his main character, in a setting, with one of the most memorable openings of all time:

In a hole in the ground there lived a hobbit. Not a nasty, dirty, wet hole, filled with the ends of worms and an oozy smell, nor yet a dry, bare, sandy hole with nothing in it to sit down on or eat: it was a hobbit-hole, and that means comfort.

Had Tolkien opened with a chunk of backstory from the First Age of Middle Earth, it's unlikely we'd have the same feelings about this tale. Fortunately, Tolkien knew his business. In spite of the grand vista of his world and history and all his mighty heroes, he started his story with what appeared to be the simplest of all his races: the hobbits. And then he gave the opening another twist. Of all the marvelous places he had created in his world, he decided his opening setting would be a hole in the ground. Then, he twisted it again. This hole was the *opposite* of what every reader knows a hole to be; this one was a place of comfort. How can that be? We don't know, and Tolkien hooks us with the contrast. Curiosity piqued, we'll read on.

COSTUMING OUR HERO

Unless we're actually writing a story about marshmallows (plagiarist!), it's good practice when we introduce characters to give a brief description of their features. This is important. Readers need to know who the protagonist is, and to visualize that person, they need a little definition. Emphasis on *little*, at least for short stories. You have more leeway in novels because you have more space. Still, the features you choose should be specific, short, and should evoke a reflection of the hero's character within. Is the heroine shy and unassertive? You could give her mousy brown hair. Is the hero an insomniac? Bloodshot eyes could foreshadow his troubled sleep. Some idea of build and height can be helpful. But do we need the cut of his chiseled chin, the tiny mole at the right corner of her mouth? Unless it's relevant to the plot, casting aside such detailed descriptions is a smart idea. Not only do they bog down pacing, the reader supplies these details from their own memories and experience. The writer inserts just enough descriptive code into their prose to spark the vision.

We also should select costuming for our characters. As Mark Twain said, "Clothes make the man. Naked people have little or no influence in society." In fact, what they wear often makes a statement as to their position in society. A smart costume can tell you whether a player is an elite socialite or an angry rebel even before they open their mouths. And yet, some aspiring writers neglect to give even one item of clothing to their poor characters, and readers are forced to read about naked, nebulous marshmallows prancing about the tale with not even a graham cracker to cover them.

ENVIRONMENT IS A CHARACTER

Setting is the surroundings in the location where your scene takes place. Bland descriptions do a poor job of evoking emotions and lack sensory texture that aids the reader in not only visualizing the story, but *feeling* the story as well. Saying Christopher sat on a park bench works, but it's not enough to provide specificity, nor will it evoke much of an emotional response. Powerful settings include rich sensory details.

Is Christopher in London, and is he an aristocrat? Put him in Hyde Park at noon on a crisp autumn afternoon, his bowler hat doing little to warm his head. Is he worried the socialite Isabelle he plans to propose to won't show? Make the oak trees moan as a cold breeze blows, dropping brown leaves as dry as the skins of mummies. The bench could be wrought iron, and the longer Christopher waits, the more the cold seeps through his cape and creeps under his skin. A rider passes, the horse's hooves clopping in hollow thuds against the cobbles. The horse lifts its tail and steaming manure drops, permeating the sweet scent from the roses he purchased for this hopeful day with a pungent barnyard stench. Church bells toll, and as the hour of their meeting time passes, Christopher's heart sinks. Isabelle did not come.

Setting can do multiple duties. Not only does it reveal surroundings, but it can also create tension, even foreshadow events to come. If we think of environment as a character in our stories, we can do so much more than use it as a backdrop. We can use it to set mood in each scene, even have it bear down on our protagonist, heightening tension.

Here's a quick example of this from author Steve Pantazis in his nine-novel series, *The Light of Darkness*:

If not for the clouds and bleak shades of gray in the mountains, Petrah might have missed the brewing darkness, the shadow that blocked the light and the promise of a peaceful day.

Just like in a play, environment is a moody character.

SCENE CHANGES: IT'S NOT OVER UNTIL IT'S OVER

Even when aspiring writers recognize they need to craft a brief but evocative setting for their opening, often when they start a new scene, it's as if they forgot everything they learned. Apparently, they figure they did all that work for the opening scene, and now that the story launched, they don't need to do anything more for subsequent ones. Not so! The first stage rocket got the story off the ground, but if that spacecraft is going to achieve orbital velocity, the next stages in the story will also need to be fired. Ignite the opening of each scene, and the story will stay on target for its final destination.

What might help writers with this issue is to think of each scene as a mini short story. A story has a beginning, a middle, and an end. Scenes do, too. They need to open with a setting, so we know where we are. They need an indication of how much time has passed since the last scene, so we know where we're at in the time stream. And even though we know our protagonist by this point, we still need to drop them into the setting, along with any other characters that are with them.

Too often will I edit a scene for a writer with the setting established, but they fail to indicate who else is with the main character. Suddenly, Juan hands the protagonist a rusty machete, and I have to ask, "Where did Juan come from? Was he just beamed down from the starship *Enterprise*?"

Set Your Stage includes setting up your players. If they were with your hero at the opening of a scene, you need to show it at the start, not surprise the reader an hour later in the timeline after we assumed your hero was alone in the jungle. New characters and necessary props must be introduced. While they can be shown *entering* the scene later, they can't materialize out of thin air. Well, unless you have a transporter and a replicator.

~

DANGER, WILL ROBINSON!

A word of warning. You might look at all you need to accomplish at the opening of a story or novel and think that to apply all of this, you'll need many pages, perhaps the entire opening scene, and a long one at that. But gone are the days when readers would greedily eat up a forty-eight-page introductory about Salem's Custom House, as they did in Nathaniel Hawthorne's *The Scarlet Letter*. Today's reader has little patience and expects you to set your stage quickly and get on with the show. So much so, many writers advise throwing any stage setting to the wind, and instead advocate starting the story in the middle of an action sequence. Here's a Latin phrase you've heard of: *in medias res*.

Dropping into an action sequence—*in medias res*—can be very exciting. But just like Hollywood movies that open with a car chase, you'll need to be a trained professional to pull this off. Why? All the introductory elements we've discussed will still be demanded by your reader. They *need* this information to follow your story, to form an attachment to your protagonist, to invest in the thing desired, and to care about whether your hero gets their prize or not. But in a true *in medias res* opening, the writer gives the reader none of these things as the curtain opens. It all has to be tossed in as the story progresses, often as backstory and flashbacks.

Here's the danger: Until the flashback or necessary information is dropped in about why this action scene is happening (and more importantly, *why I should care*), I, the reader, have to suspend my needs, trusting that the author will deliver the goods later in the story in a satisfactory way. Because of inexperience in works by newer writers, I often find this doesn't happen. Some even drop into a flashback on the first page to get these details in. Nowhere is it more important than in the opening to move the story forward—the writer has to push the beast forward with zero established momentum—and then they wipe out momentum gained by going back in time.

What's a writer to do? Too much detail drops the opening into a slog, too little (or none at all with *in medias res*) leaves the reader irritated because they don't have a clue as to what this story is about.

Truth is, we need to be like Goldilocks with her porridge. Not too hot, not too cold. Not too much, not too little. Proper balance makes it *jusssst right*.

I enjoy well-chosen details, and a picture of the protagonist's normal world that reveals who they are before they get slammed with a problem. But it's good for writers to realize they can start their story rolling with a lot less than they think. They don't have to put the whole forest on the stage. A smattering of cardboard props and a painted backdrop will give the idea, and that's all readers need for their imaginations to fill in the rest.

SET. YOUR. STAGE. Hook your reader as the curtain opens with a vivid description of your character and the environment they exist in. Show us their heart from the start. Make us fall in love with them, or at least identify with them and the problem they will face. Help us not only see the world they live in, but to *feel* that world with choice sensory details. Grounding your reader with interesting settings and unique characters in the opening lines will make your story come to life. Nebulous marshmallows and talking heads will not.

If you make your audience *oooh* and *ahhh* as the curtain opens, and deliver each time it opens on subsequent scenes, no one's going to walk out. By paying smart attention to your stagecraft and story, those readers will give you a standing ovation at the end.

Bravo!

5

HEART'S DESIRE

I n one of my Super Secrets of Writing workshops, I open with a
basic statement about storytelling: "Your job is to swiftly establish
a setting, place your hero in it, tell us what their heart's desire is, and
then rip it from them." The attendees' eyes go wide, and I do believe if
I turned out the lights, I'd see lightbulbs popping on all over the room.
By the end of the workshop, everyone is aglow—they realize they've
just discovered gold, and they're going to be mining it in their stories
for the rest of their lives.

Heart's Desire. Over the decades, I've taken countless workshops,
seminars, and writing courses from college professors to *New York
Times* bestselling authors. Many of those teaching were experts in their
field, yet none of them talked about the concept of Heart's Desire. Oh,
they spoke plenty about the Problem, the Catalyst, the Inciting Incident. And it's true: stories normally open with a character, in a setting,
with a problem. But without establishing Heart's Desire, a story might
have a world-shattering problem that creates a screaming fast-paced
plot, but it won't have the emotional elements necessary to stir readers' emotions.

Good stories, great stories, *moving* stories must engage, not just the
mind, but above all else, *the heart.*

~

WHAT IS HEART'S DESIRE?

Heart's Desire is a person, thing, or state of being that the protagonist values and desires. It can be something precious to them that they hope to gain, or something precious that they have and don't want to lose. Or, as in the movie *Taken*, it can be a combination of both. In the opening, the protagonist played by Liam Neeson desires to rebuild his relationship with his estranged daughter—something precious he hopes to gain—and then she gets kidnapped by sex slavers in Paris—something precious he does not want to lose. By the end of the tale, there's a payout on both.

Heart's Desire can take many forms. It could be anything that is of deep importance to your protagonist: a young man's need for that rite of passage by owning his first car (think Sam Witwicky and the rusty '77 Camaro in *Transformers*); a sorority girl seeking acceptance to an Ivy League college to win back her boyfriend (think Elle Woods and her need to get into Harvard in *Legally Blonde*); or a lawyer, tired of defending deadbeats, that craves a higher level of clientele (think Mickey Haller in *The Lincoln Lawyer*). Anything is game as long as it matters dearly to your hero. It's also a binding emotional hook if your readers can not only identify with that desire, but also crave that desire for themselves.

You've got a winner when your hero becomes the reader's avatar to explore their own feelings, desires, and emotional needs as they go along on the journey you've created in your story.

~

MAKE A STATEMENT OF HEART'S DESIRE

Think of J.R.R. Tolkien's *The Hobbit*. After establishing one of the most memorable opening statements of setting and character ever—*In a hole in the ground there lived a hobbit*—Tolkien tells us how cozy the lifestyle is for one homebody named Bilbo Baggins. If we haven't discerned

Bilbo desires nothing better than an uneventful life of comfort and his seven squares a day, Tolkien makes sure we understand this when the wizard Gandalf appears at his doorstep.

Gandalf: "I am looking for someone to share in an adventure that I am arranging, and it's very difficult to find anyone."

Bilbo: "I should think so—in these parts! We are plain quiet folk and have no use for adventures. Nasty disturbing uncomfortable things. Make you late for dinner! I can't think what anybody sees in them .... Sorry! I don't want any adventures, thank you."

Does Tolkien leave us with any question as to what Bilbo desires most of all? Peace and quiet in his family's warm home of comfort. Can we identify with that feeling? Certainly! We ourselves have probably said, "There's no place like home." Having a bit of life experience under our belt, we know unexpected adventures can indeed be nasty disturbing uncomfortable things. And unexpected guests that clean out fridge and pantry in one night? *No thank you!* We can identify with poor Bilbo's world being turned upside down. We'd likely feel the same in his circumstances. In fact, knowing how to engage his audience, Tolkien counted on it.

Tolkien is not subtle in that opening about Bilbo's desire to stay at home. He has Bilbo repeat it, over and over, just so we don't miss it. It's a statement of Heart's Desire. And, after showing us how dear this heart's desire is to Bilbo, like any good writer, Tolkien proceeds to rip it from him. The very next day in fact. Just to kick a hobbit where it really counts—in their larder—Tolkien sends into Bilbo's home thirteen hungry dwarves with terrible table manners and a quest to take back their ancestral home from a vicious dragon named Smaug.

A writer cannot be too blunt about Heart's Desire. Let me restate that. *A writer cannot be too blunt about Heart's Desire.* It's what the story is truly all about for the protagonist, and it answers two important questions every reader asks at the beginning of a story: WHAT'S THIS STORY ABOUT? and WHY SHOULD I CARE? We're only human, after all. We want to know we've got a good reason to invest our time and emotions in this character and their tale. So get to the *heart* of the matter, and get there quickly. A statement of Heart's Desire does just that. It's the author laying it on the line, spelling out in the opening scene exactly what the protagonist holds most dear. It's a sign lit up on the story's marquee saying *THIS IS WHAT IT'S ALL ABOUT*. Don't be bashful about this. Be bold. Hit it with a spotlight. Inquiring minds want to know.

Inquiring minds *need* to know.

~

RIPPING AWAY HEART'S DESIRE

When the Problem is first introduced into the story (this is called the Inciting Incident), the Problem's ugly size sixteen combat boot usually drops directly onto the path of the hero's Heart's Desire. Now, everything about obtaining or protecting that desire is put in jeopardy. And if our hero hopes to secure her heart's desire, she must go on a quest to get rid of that giant obstacle that's keeping her from obtaining it. You desire more than anything to return home, Dorothy? No problem. You just have to figure out how to kill the Wicked Witch of the West. You'd love to have more than one small chocolate bar a year, starving Charlie? No problem. You just have to survive a crazy chocolate factory tour.

Does this mean the Heart's Desire in the opening is chiseled in stone, immutable? No. Quite often, a protagonist's Heart's Desire at the opening will change by the end of the story. Not always, but often. This is because one of the requirements for meaningful stories is that the protagonist must *change* by the end of the story. They need to learn some valuable personal lesson by the end, otherwise, their quest appears meaningless even though they might have saved the world.

Sometimes, the hero learns the thing they most desired was not the best thing to have desired. Sometimes, they find something more important to claim for their Heart's Desire. Sometimes they get their desire, but it's not at all what they thought it would be. Sometimes, they sacrifice their deepest desire in order to save others. Sometimes—and romance stories revolve around this one—they get exactly what they desired and live happily ever after.

There are many ways to play this, but strong stories open with your protagonist's Heart's Desire, and if you can sneak it into the first couple of pages, you're going to have a more potent story. We will know what your protagonist cares about, what they hope and long for, and we'll expect a payout in some way on this desire by the end of the story. And if you can make us care about your hero and his desire, we're going to feel troubled when you step in and dash that hero's chance at happiness all to hell.

Think about *Star Wars: A New Hope*. Young Luke cares about one thing—getting off that sand trap of a planet. He'll do anything to escape Tatooine, even join the Imperial Academy if it helps him get away! It's a naïve young man's dream—in seeking a way off Tatooine, he'd be trading Uncle Owen's tough farming yoke for the Empire's galaxy-crushing chokehold. But Luke only sees the Academy as his chance to get off the family farm and see the galaxy. In his mind, it's a path to freedom. Still young-person thinking, but we can identify with it because we were young once. We know that feeling of wanting to be out on our own.

Then the Empire kills his aunt and uncle while Luke's out searching for his 'droid. Luke immediately recognizes his desire to join the Academy was misplaced. The battles going on in the galaxy are not so far away after all. A deeper fire now burns within this young man's heart. He is consumed with the need to fight back. His Heart's Desire *changes*.

Luke expresses this new Heart's Desire to Obi-Wan. "I want to learn the ways of the Force and become a Jedi like my father." See? His Heart's Desire changed to one vastly more important, because he grew up in a hurry. Facing death does that. And for the rest of the tale, which spans three episodes (*A New Hope, The Empire Strikes Back, Return of the Jedi*), it is ever uncertain whether Luke will obtain his Heart's Desire. Even in the last episode, *Return of the Jedi*, when Luke has *become* a Jedi! Why?

Because Luke's Heart's Desire has deepened again. Now, there's something more important to him—saving his father. This quest is so dear to him, Luke is willing to sacrifice all if it means saving his father, now Darth Vader, from the dark side. He puts everything on the line— his friends' lives, the rebellion and all it stands for, even his own life and his work to become a Jedi—if it means he might find a path to his father's redemption. He comes within a hairbreadth of losing it all, but we discover that's what it often takes when the stakes to obtain your Heart's Desire are so high.

Here's another one: a classic romance adventure tale, *Romancing the Stone*. Repeatedly in the opening scenes we are told our protagonist—romance writer Joan Wilder—is lonely and would love to have a man like her daring novel hero Jesse in her life. Alas, she's clearly not the kind of person that would attract a character like Jesse, so she writes about her Heart's Desire instead.

But by the end of the crisis that was thrust upon her, Joan Wilder has made the tough choices that create growth. She has now become <spoiler alert!> a woman that can face off with criminals and killers, throw a switchblade, even roll the evil colonel off her and watch him tumble into a crocodile pit. Jack Colton, the man that's helped her through her trials, stares at her admiringly. "You're gonna be all right, Joan Wilder." She has earned his respect because she's now a different woman from the helpless one he first met—she has grown through her trials. And because of this, in the end, she obtains her Heart's Desire. Jack Colton returns, fulfilling her desire for a companion that was stated repeatedly at the story's start.

Joan Wilder gets her real-life version of Jesse.

You can find plenty of other examples. Go look for them in your favorite short stories, your favorite books, your favorite movies. Heart's Desire might be to reclaim one's honor, to find love, to live a quiet life inside your hobbit hole, but it's going to be there, and in great stories, you'll see it glowing in the heart of the protagonist early on. It won't be a mystery. There will be a strong indication or statement of Heart's Desire.

So, there you have it. A story should open with 1. A *Character*. 2. In a *Setting*. 3. With a *Heart's Desire*. 4. And then, the *Inciting Incident* (the *Problem*). 5. The hero recognizes they need more power to beat this problem, a *Magic Sword*. 6. They must *Try* to solve their problem. 7. They must *Fail* (or *Succeed*, but success creates more problems). 8. The tries escalate into a final *Climax*. 9. Win or lose, the story is concluded by *Denouement/Resolution*, which is really the validation that the protagonist achieved their Heart's Desire (or lost it if the story is a tragedy).

This is why we read many stories that don't grab our hearts. The story is technically correct—it's got most of these essentials, and it may have a hellishly difficult problem that challenges the hero in solving it. But without Heart's Desire, it has no heart. It's missing the emotional element wrapped up inside the protagonist because the writer never reveals it on the page. The writer must show us the desire burning deep inside their protagonist that motivates them to take on the risks involved in the quest.

The writer must give us a reason to believe and to care.

Make sense? Good. *This is the single most important lesson I teach.* I'm betting you'll see stories and movies in a new light from now on. And if you truly understand a thing, you have the knowledge to help you create that thing. Knowledge is power. This knowledge will transform your stories. How do I know?

I've seen it do so for *many* emerging writers that took my workshops on the subject. Many won major awards and launched professional careers after utilizing this knowledge in their stories. Focusing short stories, screenplays, and novels on Heart's Desire *works*.

I'll share just one example. Here's what happened to writer Lou J. Berger after he took my recorded Heart's Desire masterclass on the subject and applied it to his stories:

"For years I'd been sending my stories to Clarkesworld, a premiere speculative fiction magazine, only to get a very quick "No, Thanks" from Neil. Then, Wulf Moon taught me the importance of putting the protagonist's "Heart's Desire" up front, on the first page, and I made sure to include that in my latest story. What do you know, Neil bought the story!

"It didn't end there. A few months later I thought, 'What if I try Moon's technique with 'Kintsugi.' I had trunked this story because I had sent it to ALL the big venues, and EVERYBODY said 'No!' But there was a new editor at F&SF [The Magazine of Fantasy and Science Fiction], so I opened the file and inserted a Heart's Desire, right in the beginning, to explain why the main character was working so hard to help maimed battle droids. IMAGINE MY SURPRISE! SALE!!!

"Thank you, Wulf! Your teachings have taken my career to a whole new level!"

Do you hear me now? *Wonderful!* Then ask yourself: Do I state in the opening scene of my story what the protagonist's Heart's Desire is? It may transform as the story unfolds, but do I reveal a deep desire in the heart of my protagonist, something that they care so deeply about, they're willing to take great risks to achieve, or go to great lengths to get back?

If we fail to clearly reveal the protagonist's emotional motivation, our stories will fail to reach their fullest potential. Because we are missing a crucial element of successful stories ... Heart's Desire.

IN LIGHT OF THIS, ASK YOURSELF THESE QUESTIONS BEFORE YOU WRITE YOUR NEXT STORY:

1. *Do my first two pages reveal what my protagonist's Heart's Desire is? (You can take longer in novels but get it toward the opening.)*
2. *Does everything that follows in the story stay **completely focused** on the protagonist's attempts to obtain their Heart's Desire*
3. *Does my protagonist get the thing desired by the end?*
4. *For a character growth twist: Do they come to realize the thing originally desired may not have been the true or proper desire?*
5. *For a tragic twist: Do they get the thing desired, but it destroys them? (Think Paul Atreides in* Dune Messiah.*)*

Embedding Heart's Desire within our heroes makes for very real, and very human, stories. It's the engine that provides the motivation for our characters and gives them the ability to make great sacrifices to achieve the thing desired. More than that, Heart's Desire makes us reflect on our own motivations and choices we've made to gain our own important desires in life. They create the strongest stories because they're packed with emotional punch.

So put *Heart's Desire* into the primary equation for writing a story.

Don't make it a secondary or nonexistent thing. It is THE most important aspect of any plot because it's what motivates your hero and moves them to act. It's what makes a story moving. Memorable. Strong.

And strong stories that touch the heart win.

Do I see lightbulbs popping on? Good. I can turn out the lights. You can see your way out.

6

INCITING INCIDENT AND THE PROBLEM

"Your job is to swiftly establish a setting, place your hero in it, tell us what their Heart's Desire is, and then rip it from them." I stated this in the last chapter. We're now at the *rip it from them* part. Ouch. This is gonna hurt.

You've opened your story with a setting, you've created a unique protagonist we care about, you've shown us what *they* care about, we've had our introduction into your character's everyday life, and we've now made some assessments as to the kind of person your protagonist is. Good. We need this. This is our story baseline, whether it's a story about a housebound disabled youth, a woman working in a male-dominated corporation, or a handler in a K-9 unit stationed in Afghanistan. But unless it's a slice of life story, something significant needs to happen, and happen quickly. Why?

A story is about someone that wants something, and someone or something is standing in their way of getting it.

To hold our attention, a story requires the second part of that equation. Someone or something needs to stand in your protagonist's way of their getting the thing desired. This creates tension, and tension is what makes exciting stories that keep readers turning pages. When you create a character the reader becomes attached to, the reader won't like a bully stomping on that character. They'll get emotionally invested, and they'll read on to find out if your hero will figure out a way to beat their opponent and finally get what they desire.

This fundamental element of Story is known as the *Inciting Incident*. Most story models refer to this plot element as *The Problem*. I prefer the term Inciting Incident because it indicates an initial event that will incite the protagonist to take action against The Problem, the latter a more fitting term for the totality of the opposing force and the obstacles it creates throughout the story.

Inciting Incident is the size-sixteen combat boot that drops down on your protagonist's normal world and what they hold most dear (or hope to hold) and shatters it. Think of it like this: Inciting Incident is the combat boot that first stomps down on your character's life, and The Problem is the Nazi soldier that continues stomping throughout the rest of the story. Inciting Incident is pulling the trigger on the gun, the catalyst that will set off a chain of events that become the totality of The Problem that will challenge your protagonist.

Without some powerful incident that steps into your hero's normal life, they won't have the motivation necessary to leave the comfort and protection of their known world. They'll never have a reason to push back against the opposing force and prove what kind of stuff they're made of. Your job is to boot them out of that world. It's time to leave the nest. Face some challenges.

The Inciting Incident provides the catalyst that makes that happen.

∼

WHEN TO INTRODUCE THE INCITING INCIDENT

It's important to remember that readers don't come to stories to get another rundown of how mundane life can be. They're already doing the drill in their own world. They picked up your story to be transported somewhere else and expect you to take them on an adventure.

Sure, there's curiosity about how other people live, what makes them tick. Stories, after all, are about people. Many like delving deep into human relationships and complex emotional issues. They may even enjoy the workings of imaginary political systems through which they can evaluate their own, or exploring complex scientific theories in a space-traveling world. And there's much beauty in the lovely tapestry of prose.

But in fiction, just like at the circus, readers want to be entertained. That means Exciting. Stuff. Must. Occur. As the writer, that's your job. You're the ringmaster standing center stage that's supposed to make the magic happen.

The majority of your audience comes to your tale with one hopeful expectation: *Tell me a howling good story.*

They care nothing for your detailed wakeup scene, unless it's quite different from the way they wake up every morning. They care nothing for pages of genealogical line of descent in the opening, who begat who, because that kind of reading is as dry as uncooked oatmeal. They don't want an infodump on your cold-blooded alien race and how their physiology and digestive tract works. You can drop those twenty-three pages of backstory while you're at it as well.

Can you hear it? Readers begging you to get to the story? It's like the director calling out, *"Action!"*

"But, Moon," you might say, "they have to know my boy hero is from a famous fiefdom on a world under the thumb of a ruthless galactic emperor. And he's got skills—I've got him tutored by the best assassin in the empire, best fighter, too, and I need to list every discipline he knows because I'm skilled in the martial arts myself, you know. And we can't forget that his father is a duke in a long lineage of heroic leaders. In fact, I've carefully opened my story with an outline of the centuries each duke ruled so readers understand how important this family is! And readers need to know every one of their noble house's enemies, and a detailed history of all the clan battles. Oh, and I came up with this neat family history that his grandpa was a famous bullfighter and died from being gored by a bull. This is essential information! If the reader doesn't know this stuff, they won't understand my story!"

Really? I thought we were past this. You read my chapter on "How Driving to the Story Creates Accidents" in *The Illustrated Super Secrets of Writing* workbook, did you not? No? Well, there's the problem! You are forgiven. Let me sum up. Give us a tasty sip of your world so we can savor the flavor, but don't dump the whole barrel over our heads. Then send in the witch with her box of pain and a gom jabbar needle at his neck to test the boy. Let's get this party started! That's how Frank Herbert did it in *Dune,* and that's how you and I need to do it. Get to the story.

There's your rule of thumb. *Get to the story.* How? By starting your story as close to the Inciting Incident as you can. Sure, you need to give us a taste of character and world details. We need a little information to know who, what, where, when, maybe even why, but until you get to the Inciting Incident, there is no true action. The story is static. Another word for static? Inaction. And lack of action is *boring.*

Readers come to your story to *go on an adventure.* Until your protagonist has a good reason to leave their cozy hobbit hole with their tasty seven squares a day, why would they pick up and go into the wild on an adventure? Nasty disturbing uncomfortable things! Make you late for dinner!

You have to give your protagonist a reason to leave, and it's got to be a good one. It must be powerful enough to move them to abandon the comfort and security of home (the Ordinary World) in exchange for the risks that come with going into the unknown (I call it the Quest World). Give them the boot. Kick them out that door.

If they won't go, get a bigger boot.

BIG PROBLEMS YIELD BIG STORIES, TINY PROBLEMS YIELD WIMPY STORIES

Want to write a story that will hook your reader's heart and send them on an emotional roller coaster that will keep them clutching the safety bar with white knuckles all the way to the end? Then your problem needs to be soul-crushing.

What do I mean by soul-crushing? You established Heart's Desire in your opening, right? And if you're writing a deep story, it was something so precious and dear to your protagonist, they'd be willing to risk their life to obtain it, or willing to sacrifice their life to save it.

Good. Because when you introduce an Inciting Incident and subsequent Problem that's powerful enough to rip what's most precious away from your hero, they're going to be shaken to their core. They cannot exist without that which is being held from them. They cannot bear to live in a world where that precious thing is gone or placed in jeopardy. *That* is a soul-crushing problem. It can challenge their very identity and ability to exist, stripping them of what they hold most dear. It's the most powerful motivating force there is in Story because the hero can't live their life without it.

Want to know the problem with many stories? It's The Problem. It's a big nothingburger. There's nothing there to truly challenge the hero. It becomes much ado about nothing, and if a story feels like it's about nothing, it's difficult to hold the reader's attention because the stakes aren't high enough to get the reader to care. Where's the risk? Where are the challenges? Where's the danger? There is none.

Here's an example. Take a story about an executive a couple of weeks late on his mortgage because he forgot to make the payment and now must pay a late fee. Sure, that's a problem, but it's a wimpy one because that's a tiny sting, the stakes aren't high. Readers will take a bite, lift up the bun and demand, "Where's the beef?"

But how about the story of a homemaker mom with three young children that gets abandoned by her husband. She's six months late on the mortgage, the sheriff just stapled an eviction notice to her door with all the neighbors watching, and she has no job, no friends, and nowhere to turn. That's a soul-crushing problem. Her ability to exist and to care for her children is put in absolute peril.

High stakes. Stronger story. Plenty to chew on under this burger's bun.

I know you want to protect your protagonist. You care about them, or you wouldn't have spent all that time thinking about them, building a world with its milieu around them, transcribing it to the page so you can share their story with others. Chances are, there's a part of you in them, and nobody that's sane wants to hurt themselves.

However, your job is to tell a story. Hopefully a howling good one. So remember what a story is. *A story is about someone that wants something, and someone or something is standing in their way of getting it.* Get to the action fast by starting near the Inciting Incident, whether you're writing a short story, a novel, or a screenplay. Kick your hero out of their cozy world or they won't learn anything. You've got to put your hero through the wringer, you've got to give them hell. And if your goal is to write award-winning stories, make that problem they're forced to deal with a big one. It needs to be soul-crushing, world-shattering, challenging your hero to their core.

No pain, no gain. Bring it on. *Let's crush this!*

7

MAGIC SWORD

So your hero just got a butt whoopin' and is sitting stunned amidst the rubble. They had been sitting by the fireplace all hunky dory in their nice cozy home, and someone showed up and blew their hopes and dreams all to hell. Their Heart's Desire is long gone. They were too puny to stop the big bad wolf from blowing their house down and taking whatever he wanted.

They could wallow in all the detritus and cry out, "Woe is me!" But if they're a proactive hero, they aren't going to take this sitting down. They're going to stand up, chase that wolf down, and take back what that mangy monster stole from …. Oh. They'd just get their butt kicked all over again. And maybe that wolf would eat them this time —he just proved how tough he is. No, your hero isn't stupid. They realize if they're going to beat him, they're going to need a plan, and that plan will involve figuring out how to get the power necessary to put that wolf down.

So here's the next story element, an integral part of my Nine Elements of Story Structure. Once again, I've never heard this principle taught in any writing courses or seminars I've taken, and I've taken many over the years, from college professors, famous literary agents, and *New York Times* bestselling authors. And yet, as I analyze stories on both the written page and the movie screen, I see this fundamental item show up in virtually every successful story I read or watch (I'll cover an exception). What is it?

The *Magic Sword*.

～

THE ORIGINS OF MAGIC SWORD

The concept of a weapon of power wielded by the hero of a tale to defeat the antagonist or opposing force in story or myth is not new. It's an integral element of our earliest stories, whether it's the Norse mythology of Odin thrusting Gramr into a tree, the Shinto storm god Susanoo's sword Ame-no-Habakiri used to defeat an eight-headed serpent, or ancient India's tales of Lord Brahma that created the sword Asi to destroy malevolent Asuras.

In Western culture, we have Homer's *The Odyssey*, written almost three thousand years ago. Magic Sword took the form of Odysseus' bow where his wife Penelope challenged freeloading suitors to prove their worthiness by stringing her lost husband's bow and firing an arrow through twelve axes. All fail miserably in their attempts and the long-lost Odysseus, disguised as a beggar, proves the only one with the power to string it. He easily meets the challenge, thus proving his identity as both husband and king, and with his powerful bow in hand, quickly vanquishes his foes.

Fast forward almost two thousand years and we have the tale of The Sword in the Stone, melded into Arthurian legend by French poet Robert de Boron. In that tale, the mage Merlin set a sword into an anvil atop a stone, stating only the rightful heir of Uther Pendragon would have the power to withdraw it, proving their birthright as king of Britain. Many view that sword today as Excalibur, but the true magic sword by that name appeared later in the tale, a gleaming sword of power forged in an unworldly realm, given to Arthur Pendragon by the Lady of the Lake to vanquish his foes (although Merlin pointed out the scabbard was the true prize, as its enchantment prevented the wearer from ever bleeding to death in battle).

As the legend took its twists and turns over the centuries, and especially in the hands of Hollywood, Excalibur became indelibly etched as the ideal of the Magic Sword—a weapon of gleaming magical might that could only be wielded by the virtuous and worthy to vanquish their foes in battle.

~

WHAT'S THE MODERN VERSION OF A MAGIC SWORD?

I hear some of you saying, "Hold up there, Moon. I've read plenty of stories and watched plenty of movies with nary a sword in sight, magic or otherwise. How can you say Magic Sword is an integral part of storytelling?"

Magic Sword is an archetype—a recurrent symbol or motif in literature, art, or mythology that represents a thing of power wielded by the protagonist to defeat their enemy. As an archetype, it can take many forms, but the basic premise is always the same. The protagonist at the beginning of the story does not have it or does not know how to wield it, otherwise they would vanquish their foe immediately and the story would end at the beginning. That won't do, won't do at all! Our heroes need to prove themselves! They need to pass through some trials by fire to show what they're made of before we'll view them as worthy of vanquishing their enemy.

Remember, most stories revolve around this premise: From a weak state, made powerful. At the start of the tale, our heroes are weak, unable to defend themselves against a superior antagonist or force. But they are strong of spirit, and choose to go forth and find a way to conquer their adversary. Through the course of the tale, the hero gains allies, knowledge, and power, until they're finally able to utilize lessons learned to face down their opponent and vanquish them, or at least make them back off so the hero can go home and live a life of peace.

But how does a person confronted by a superior force that keeps them from their Heart's Desire figure out how to conquer their enemy? When faced with the Inciting Incident at the start of the story

—that soul-crushing problem that steals away their ability to get that which is most desired—most protagonists realize they aren't powerful enough to defeat the enemy on their own. Chances are, they just got clobbered, and maybe not just them, but their family, their friends, perhaps even their race or their world.

A proactive hero with some intelligence realizes they can't beat this enemy in their current state, they're going to need help. So they develop a plan to go find a person, place, or thing that can help them gain the power necessary to defeat their enemy. That person, place, or thing of power? It doesn't have to be magic, it doesn't have to be a sword, but it must have *the potential to provide the elements, power, or knowledge necessary to defeat the enemy.* That's a Magic Sword.

There are many ways to play this concept. A protagonist in a state of poverty could realize a prized scholarship would get them the education they need to change their future. An immunologist might seek a vaccine or treatment that could prevent a deadly pandemic from spreading. A young lady might be sick of being harassed by a stalker and take up defense training to protect herself. In each of these instances, the hero realizes they don't have the solution to their problem, but they have an idea of where they could go to gather more knowledge or power to themselves. After being crushed by the Inciting Incident, the hero often develops a rudimentary plan that will set them upon a journey to obtain the power to defeat their enemy. They go after the Magic Sword.

Sometimes they possess the thing of power but have no idea how to unlock it. Sometimes they know where the thing of power is and go on a quest to obtain it. Sometimes they don't have a clue what they could use to defeat their enemy, but they're told of someone who does. Whatever the case, the hero realizes they can't beat this enemy on their own or with their current skill set, so they go on a quest to obtain the power, skills, or knowledge necessary to win.

Even in detective stories and thrillers, the problem is *whodunnit,* and the detective goes on a quest to find that one slip up or decisive clue that will reveal the murderer's identity. When they find it, they have the power to put the murderer away, fulfilling our sense of justice. Without it, they could not. Magic Sword.

~

BEWARE THE MACGUFFIN!

Someone from film or acting school might say, "Isn't this just another word for a MacGuffin?" Sorry, my thespian friend. A rose by any other name in this case does not smell as sweet. The Magic Sword archetype has *real power* in stories. A MacGuffin does not—its power is illusory.

What is a MacGuffin?

A MacGuffin is a plot device that I describe as "much ado about nothing." It's a term credited to English screenwriter Angus McPhail, but Alfred Hitchcock popularized it, using the technique in many of his motion pictures. Hitchcock described the MacGuffin as an item in a story that the characters want, but it really doesn't matter at all. In a 1962 interview with French film director François Truffaut, Hitchcock said, "The main thing I've learned over the years is that the MacGuffin is nothing."

An early example of a MacGuffin is the Holy Grail in the Arthurian legends. The search for the Holy Grail drives the plot for Arthur's knights, but the Grail has no real significance by the end of the tale. It merely serves as a foil to send Arthur's knights into the world to be tested by trials. Or Arthur himself if you're watching Monty Python's version. And if you hope to pass the questions at the Bridge of Death, it's a good idea to know the airspeed velocity of an unladen swallow.

Another example is in the movie *The Maltese Falcon*. Detective Sam Spade discovers an unsavory cast of characters that seek to get their hands on what they believe to be a priceless falcon statuette, even killing for it. But after many lies and twists in the plot, the statuette is revealed in the end to be a worthless fake. Again, much ado about nothing.

A MacGuffin drives plot because the characters believe the item is important and they struggle to obtain it. In reality, it's a fool's errand, the item is worthless. It's the carrot on a stick that makes the horse trot forward, but it's a carrot made of plastic.

Make no mistake. Magic Sword is an archetype that holds great power, power to defeat the antagonist or opposing force. A MacGuffin's only power is that the characters in the story *believe* it has power.

Still skeptical that a Magic Sword exists in most stories? Let's analyze the use of Magic Sword in some popular novels and movies. When I show you, the scales will fall from your eyes. It's in everything. Oh, yes, my Precious. You'll see ....

～

THE PREVALENCE OF MAGIC SWORD IN STORYTELLING

Here's an obvious Magic Sword that everyone knows, and it was worn not on a belt, but on the feet of a young girl from Kansas. In L. Frank Baum's tale *The Wonderful Wizard of Oz*, Dorothy's house lands on the Wicked Witch of the East, killing her. What does the good Witch of the North give Dorothy? The Wicked Witch's silver shoes. These are no ordinary shoes. "The Witch of the East was proud of those silver shoes," said one of the Munchkins, "and there is some charm connected with them; but what it is we never knew."

Okay, I see your wheels turning. "Whoa, there, buddy. Those were ruby slippers!" Just for you, I'll switch to the cinematic version. When the ruby slippers appear on Dorothy's feet, the Wicked Witch says, "Give me back my slippers. I'm the only one that knows how to use them. They're no use to you. Give them back to me. Give them back!" And Good Witch Glinda says to Dorothy, "Keep tight inside of them. Their magic must be very powerful, or she wouldn't want them so badly."

Dorothy receives a Magic Sword early in the story. We know they have power because the Wicked Witch wants them so badly, and Glinda states they must be "very powerful." But Dorothy doesn't have a clue how to use them to return home. She's going to have to go on an adventure to prove herself worthy to use their power. And only through many trials, including almost losing her life as she tries to save others, does she earn the right to the incantation that will unlock her Magic Sword.

At the end of the movie, Glinda tells her to click her heels together three times and say ... say it with me now: "There's no place like home; there's no place like home; there's no place like home." And the Magic Sword—those ruby slippers—takes her to her Heart's Desire. Home.

Here's one for you lovers of legal thrillers: John Grisham's novel *The Firm*. Mitch McDeere, fresh out of Harvard law, gets an offer he can't refuse, and goes to work for a firm that has a curious rate of deadly accidents among its lawyers. *Spoiler alert.* By the time Mitch figures out he's working for a company whose biggest client is a Chicago mafia family, he's in too deep to get out alive. What's more, the feds pressure him to forgo attorney-client privilege to give them the goods on the Firm, which would cause Mitch to be disbarred. Damned if you do, damned if you don't. Mitch is in a no-win situation involving two powerful entities, and both will ruin him no matter what he decides to do.

Mitch desperately seeks a way out of the clutches of both the feds and the mob family. To protect what he has worked so hard for, he needs a way to keep his license to practice law on the one hand, and a way to save his life on the other. To beat both of these powerful entities, Mitch must come up with not one but *two* Magic Swords.

To satisfy the feds, he discovers a way to stick the firm with mail fraud for sending padded bills to clients through the U.S. Postal Service, a federal offense that will shut their practice down and put their attorneys behind bars. To keep the mob bosses from killing him, Mitch sends his brother out on a live-aboard sailboat carrying files exposing all their operations and holdings that could put the mob leaders away. If Mitch gets knocked off and fails to check in with his brother, those damning files go to the authorities. The mob bosses get the point: Mitch now has the thing of power to destroy them, and killing him would unleash it. In both cases, Mitch vanquished enemies that would have destroyed him, and he did so by using knowledge gained to forge his own Magic Swords.

One of my favorite Magic Swords is in the classic movie, *Casablanca*. Set in 1941 in Casablanca, Morocco, expatriate American Rick Blaine owns a nightclub, and desperate refugees gather there from across Europe to make deals for exit visas to America in order to escape Nazi control. The sleazy swindler Ugarte is under hot pursuit and calls upon Rick for a favor—that he hold an envelope for him until a deal can be finalized.

What's in the envelope? "Something that not even you have ever seen," Ugarte says. "Letters of Transit signed by General de Gaulle. They cannot be rescinded, not even questioned." Rick accepts them, and when Ugarte is captured and dies in custody, the Letters of Transit become Rick's by default. This document is a mighty Magic Sword, and by wielding it at the end of the story, Rick defeats the Nazis bent on keeping the leader of a resistance movement and Rick's former lover from leaving the country.

Can you see how Magic Sword is deployed in most successful stories? Go read or watch some of your favorites and pinpoint the moment the hero realizes they need it, their journey to obtain it, and whether they learn enough through their trials to become worthy to wield it. It's there, whether you're reading about Paul Atreides trying to get a handle on his destiny in *Dune,* or watching 17-year-old Daniel LaRusso facing his nemesis in *The Karate Kid.* It's the Time-Turner that Hermione Granger uses to save the day in *Harry Potter and the Prisoner of Azkaban.* It's the magic ring in *The Hobbit* which gave Bilbo invisibility, and without it Thorin and Company would have failed in their quest.

Now that you know what to look for, you'll be able to spot it. And when you see it showing up again and again, I think you'll agree that the Magic Sword archetype is a major plot element in virtually every successful story. Even in tragedies, which often occur because the hero failed to obtain the Magic Sword, or failed to grow and prove themselves worthy of wielding it.

~

DEPLOYING YOUR MAGIC SWORD

When you understand a tool, you can put that tool to work. And if you master that tool, you can have a distinct advantage over others that aren't even aware the tool exists. As you look at your own stories, ask yourself: Have I worked in my version of a Magic Sword? Does my protagonist have it at the beginning of the tale, or does she go on a quest to find it? Have I created adequate tests to prove she is worthy of wielding the Magic Sword at the climax?

Here's a Super Secret trick I like to do with Magic Sword. Introduce it in plain sight in the opening of the story so the reader understands it's available to the protagonist, but make it appear so innocuous, they don't realize how important the device could be. This can often be done by close point of view, where the protagonist herself doesn't realize its value, but through the course of the story discerns how it could be used at the very end.

An epiphany in what's known as the Dark Night of the Soul can be a powerful catalyst as the hero discerns there might be a way to use the item to their advantage. This is especially true if the Magic Sword was introduced in the opening, and the surprise wielding of it to defeat the opponent is sensible and logical. It takes skill to hide a magic sword in plain sight in a story, but the surprise critical deployment of an item that seemed impotent can be very satisfying, getting you high marks with readers, editors, and judges. We all enjoy a good surprise. P.T. Barnum made a great living by delivering the unexpected to his audiences. You can, too.

Do you see it there, glowing in the stone? That otherworldly light shining from a metal forged in the spectral fires of another dimension? Then grab the hilt, retrieve the Magic Sword, and claim your destiny by wielding this mighty talisman of power.

You are worthy.

8

ESCALATING TENSION: CRANK IT UP!

There's a legend about the 14th century king of Scotland, Robert Bruce, that is told to every child in Scotland to this day. In his first year as king, Bruce's army suffered a terrible defeat against the British at the Battle of Methven. The remnants of his fleeing army were scattered, and King Bruce, barely escaping with his life, hid alone in a cave. His soul sank under the weight of failure, snuffing his dream of freeing his countrymen from their English overlords.

And then, as some versions go, at the mouth of the cave the Bruce spotted a little spider attempting to build a web. The spider swung on a thread from its perch, only to miss its mark and drop to the floor. Up it climbed and swung again, only to miss and drop. Up it climbed, down it dropped, over and over again. But the spider never gave up. At last, it secured a line and strung its web, turning defeat into triumph. And in the hollow of that cave, that little spider's resolute determination inspired Robert Bruce, moving him to say, "If at first you don't succeed, try, try, try again." He sent word to his followers that he would rise once again against the English. They regrouped and routed the superior forces of the English at the Battle of Bannockburn in 1314.

The battle was real—I've been to the visitor center at Bannockburn and studied artifacts from that engagement. As for the various spider legends, it makes for a good story about their national hero, teaching Scottish children to keep trying and never give up. In fact, the principle of the legend is so strong, it spread beyond Scotland to the rest of the world. Who of us has not been told at some point in our lives, *"If at first you don't succeed, try, try again."*

The struggle against adversity even in the face of defeat is hard-wired into our humanity. If we didn't have this strength burning within us, we would not be alive today. Our ancestors would have dropped to their knees before the saber-toothed tigers and said, "Eat me. You are obviously stronger than I am. I know I don't stand a chance."

Instead of running in fear, some crafted weapons and stood their ground. They gathered in clans to defend themselves. And when those weapons turned man upon man, they designed ring forts and stockades and castles and fortresses. Defeat only made survivors more determined to rise again, to build it better, to secure a brighter future for themselves, their families, their people, their nations.

We value those that try again after they've fallen because to overcome defeat with success can mean our very survival. Our ancestors lived or died by this principle. And when they succeeded, they passed lessons learned on to their children. Nothing ventured, nothing gained. Speak softly but carry a big stick. You get knocked down, you get back up. Horse throws you off, get back in the saddle. Good things come to those that wait, but only the things left behind by those that hustle. You see? We respect the struggle, the Try, because the try means *survival*.

Does this mean every story must be a tale of do-or-die, a battle to the death where only the virtuous triumph? No, because life doesn't always work that way, and fiction is a reflection of the real world and our human experience. Maybe a funhouse mirror reflection, but a reflection nevertheless. Also, there are multitudes of things desired that might appear quite frivolous to others, yet are important to an individual. But it's good to remember what drives us deep in our core, and why determined struggle against all odds underpins mankind's cultures and therefore should underpin our stories.

Most of us don't believe things of precious value should be handed to just anyone, and especially on their first try. We know the more precious a thing is, the harder a person will have to work for it. Because that's how the world works. Unless we were born with a silver spoon in our mouths or won the lottery, if we want something precious, we're going to have to work for it and *earn* it. And when people know we've worked hard to earn something precious, even rising up through disadvantage or adversity to do so, we gain their respect. They know it didn't come easy. We've all heard someone say, "Well-deserved. She worked hard for that." Things of value require *struggle*.

This quote from a speech by Theodore Roosevelt to the Iowa State Teacher's Association in 1910 sums it up: "Nothing in the world is worth having or worth doing unless it means effort, pain, difficulty .... I have never in my life envied a human being who led an easy life. I have envied a great many people who led difficult lives and led them well."

If that's how it works in real life, shouldn't it work like that in fiction if we're to write believable characters reflecting life's struggles? Indeed. If our hero can walk through every obstacle in her path like it's a rice-paper wall in a Japanese *minka*, how does she earn the right to obtain her precious Heart's Desire? She did nothing to prove she deserved it. And if there's no struggle, if our hero comes prepackaged with every ability to defeat her adversary in the blink of an eye, it grinds against reader sensibilities. Because readers know the struggle, and while it may be fiction, for readers to buy into your story, it must *feel* real.

In fact, this is a well-known trope. The moniker for it comes from Star Trek fan fiction. It's called a *Mary Sue* story. Mary Sue represents a character that is charming, powerful, intelligent, and comes up with an instant solution to any trial she faces. Such stories can be funny, but unless we're intentionally writing comedy, do we really want people laughing at the naivete of our story? How will the protagonist learn anything from their journey if they already know it all? How can we have a story if our protagonist is superior in every way to the force opposing them? Without the struggle, there is no story.

What methods exist to create Escalating Tension in our stories?

TRY/FAIL CYCLES

When the protagonist leaves their Normal World and enters the Quest World, it's to make an attempt to solve their problem, to push back at the opposing force so they can bring normalcy back to their world and get what they desire that's being kept from them. They usually leave with a plan, but it's a rushed plan because they haven't learned anything yet, they start out with the same weaknesses that allowed their opponent to beat them or hold them back in the first place. But heroes give it their best shot. They may have shrunk back at first, but they're going to try and do something about this problem now.

Why must they try?

Because we long to read about heroes, not wimps that give up without a fight. We admire people that are willing to take on the struggle and fight the good fight. Never give up! Never surrender! I've said it before, but it bears repeating. The perfect answer was given by the character Thor in the movie *Thor Ragnarok*. "But me, I choose to run toward my problems, and not away from them. Because that's what heroes do."

Give your readers a hero, but with flaws and weaknesses just like us. Make them proactive, not reactive, so that they *choose* to run toward the problem. If they're forced to run toward it or are just swept along by circumstance, there's not much to respect. But to choose to put themselves at risk to save the day, to get back the one they love, to fight for their people's freedom and way of life against all odds? That's something we respect. That's a hero we can follow on their adventure … as long as it's from the comfort of our armchair.

And now the bad news. This attempt to confront the first obstacle must fail if you're using a Try/Fail cycle—an attempt by the protagonist to push back against the opposing force that fails. Let's face it. If your hero beat their opponent on their first try, there wouldn't be much of a story. Nor would the challenge have been great enough to make your reader feel the hero was worthy of any reward—they didn't try very hard, why do they deserve the princess? Again, for your story to be believable and for the hero to obtain their heart's desire, the reader must see them struggle to get it. They need to face obstacles, and they need to *try* to overcome them.

There's another reason for the Fail. Tension drives plot. When someone the reader cares about fails, they feel sorry for them. They themselves know the sting of failure, and it hurts to see someone you care about stumble and fall. Even a fictional character. If the writer did a good job of making you care about the hero, you want the hero to succeed, you hope they get their heart's desire. To increase the tension, the Fail should put them even farther from their goal. It should make the reader question whether this hope of the hero's will be possible to achieve. Uncertainty builds tension, and tension drives plot.

Here's another aspect of the Fail. It should make THINGS. GET. WORSE. I used to have those words in all caps taped below my monitor. My friends Dean Wesley Smith and Kris Rusch often spoke them when we lived in Eugene, Oregon, and they're an excellent reminder to keep ratcheting up the struggle. Every attempt to confront the opposing force or try to fix the problem should make matters worse.

For example. You decide you'll fix the leaking faucet that's driving you crazy with its *drip, drip, drip* by replacing the washer. You're not a plumber, but how hard can it be? So you unscrew the faucet and water sprays everywhere. Duh! You go under the sink and turn the water valve off, but it's old and rusty and breaks off in your hand. Now water is gushing from under your sink and across the kitchen floor. There's a main water valve on this house, right? Do you remember where? Did anyone show you when you bought it? Oh, no! The water is flowing across your new oak floor in the living room. You just paid a fortune to have that put in!

And on it goes, just like in every *Laurel and Hardy* movie. Things. Get. Worse. With every try there is a fail. Each failure makes matters worse, increasing the stakes, setting the protagonist farther from their goal. The worse it gets, the harder it is to see light at the end of the tunnel, the more your reader will wonder if your hero is ever going to make it.

When they finally do succeed against all the raised stakes that seemed impossible to beat, the reader is going to breathe a sigh of relief at the end and feel satisfied. Not because the hero got what they wanted, but because the hero had to *work* for it, even had to make sacrifices to get it. That's what makes achieving the thing they desired satisfying. They *earned* it.

How many times do you play these Try/Fail cycles? We've already discussed once is too easy. There's not enough challenge. But you can overdo it as well. If you tease a cat with a toy on a string and never let them catch the toy, the cat will get frustrated and give up. The same is true for your reader. So how many Try/Fails are necessary before the reader will view the attempts as worthy of the hero receiving the reward?

In short stories, the rule is three. There's an innate psychological reason for this. It's called the Rule of Three. The human mind likes thinking in patterns, and actively watches for them and seeks to create them in our everyday lives. The minimum number to form a pattern is three. This is because when we first see something occur, it's singular and can be attributed to chance. The second time we see something occur is notable, but we recognize it could still be a coincidence. But the third time? Our minds will see this as a pattern.

When we apply this to a short story, one try is considered hardly a try at all when it's a thing of value being sought. "What, you only tried once? Get back in there and try again!" Two tries, better, but it still seems half-hearted. "If you really wanted it, why didn't you try harder?" But three tries? Ah, there's the pattern of attempts that showed initiative. We even have a saying for that. "Third time's a charm." In baseball, we give the batter three attempts to hit the ball before they're out. If they couldn't do it in three tries, we let the next batter have their turn.

Is this an absolute rule? No, all rules can be broken or twisted, but it's good to know how the mind assesses the pattern of events in a story. The underlying principle is there. We expect to see multiple attempts before a result is achieved or something precious is gained. Deep down inside, we weigh whether or not the recipient of a special thing is worthy. Especially if we're deciding whether to consider your character a role model or hero.

Give your protagonist enough Try/Fail cycles so that if and when they finally succeed, your reader can analyze enough trials to make a good estimation of worthiness. If you hope they'll believe in your hero at the end and feel emotionally satisfied with their accomplishment, they'll need a pattern of events to weigh how well they overcame adversity.

Of course, novels require many more conflicts and trials as the protagonist pursues their goal over larger story terrain. But the results are the same. The hero must be tested to prove worthy of obtaining their Heart's Desire. Hopefully, they learn a few things about themselves and others as they face their trials in the crucible of fire. When they make it through the fire in the end, in a positive ending story we expect the fire of trials to have refined them. In a tragedy, we do not.

But for short stories, let's review the attempts to beat the opposing force. Once is too easy—your problem was not challenging enough; your protagonist did not prove worthy. Twice falls short of satisfying. You leave the reader wondering, *Did they really give it their all?* Four is overkill. **Third** time is the charm. They gave it the old college try. RESPECT.

You have to send your hero to hell before giving her a little slice of heaven.

TRY/SUCCEED

Here's a lesson I've never seen other instructors teach. Try/Succeed is another way to increase tension and drive the plot of your story. Stakes can go up and things can get worse *without* a failure after a Try. Consider Jake, an insurance salesman in a company whose Heart's Desire is to become an executive. No more traveling on the road! Each time he hits top sales figures for the month, the manager commends Jake in their sales meeting. Try/Succeed. Jake has a straight flush of six months in a row as top producer. Try/Succeed. And then the boss announces an all-expense paid trip to the Bahamas including a suite at The Royal at Atlantis. Jake works like a circus monkey for his boss for the rest of the year and wins the prize! Try/Succeed.

But what Jake is oblivious to is that all those smiling faces of his fellow sales associates at the sales meetings are not sincere. In fact, Bruce has been working for the company longer than Jake, and he resents this young upstart getting all the glory. Each time Jake gets his name on the sales board as top producer, Bruce moves from jealousy, to envy, to hatred. When Jake wins the trip to the Bahamas, Bruce's hatred seethes within him. If Jake had not been around, Bruce would have earned that award—he was in second place! Instead, he got the hundred-dollar gift card to Applebee's, and no number of boneless buffalo wings in that tangy sauce will sate his need for *revenge*.

You can see Try/Succeed work effectively in crime stories, especially bank robbery stories. Each time the bank robbers effectively pull off a heist, it's seen as a success from their point of view. What they may not realize is that as they move up from smaller banks to bigger ones, they're calling down more federal resources to catch them. Tension escalates because the reader knows this can't go on indefinitely, and they'll anticipate a major showdown at the end. If the robbers have sympathetic qualities, they may even worry for them, wondering if there's any way out, or if it's possible to redeem themselves. Try/Succeed can have plenty of tension with the right environment, plot, and proper characters.

This is why I prefer the term Escalating Tension. Whether your protagonist tries and fails or tries and succeeds, the result must be the same. Tension must escalate. The stakes in the story must ratchet up. Without escalating tension—the ever-increasing risk to the hero obtaining their Heart's Desire—the story will be as flat as an open soda left overnight on the counter.

Embrace the struggle. Make it hard on your characters. Put them into the crucible of trial and expose their flaws. Refine their noble qualities and bring forth the gold! Reveal who they are and guide who they will become by the tough choices they have to make. Let them fall flat on their face a few times. This is how we learn; this is how they should learn. When a reader cares about your hero and sees them facing a tough test, they're going to be engaged, wondering how they'll get through it, hoping they will triumph. When they fall, the reader will cry out, *Get up! Get up!* Every. Single. Time.

That struggle against the opposing force is how we create tension, and tension is what makes readers stay up all night turning pages. Put your protagonist at increasing risk, whether they succeed in a trial or fail.

As they say, *The struggle is real.* Escalating Tension is a fundamental story principle. For heart-pounding fiction, make sure you progressively ratchet it up in your stories. The plot shouldn't be loosey-goosey. It should twang when plucked like a taut bowstring. And if yours doesn't?

Try, try again.

9

THE CLIMAX

My favorite Westerns are the ones in the *Man with No Name* trilogy. There's no better gunslinger than the protagonist played by Clint Eastwood. He's gritty, he's tough, and he never gives up no matter how bad the situation looks. He's a guy you shouldn't like—he's a dangerous killer—but you like him anyway because he's written so well and shows he has a heart at just the right parts.

In *A Fistful of Dollars*, an unnamed stranger comes to the Mexican village of San Miguel and learns of a power struggle between two families: the Rojos and the Baxters. After seeing it for himself, the stranger (who does get called Joe) realizes he can pit the two families against one another and says, "That crazy bellringer was right. There's money to be made in a place like this." That's the statement of Heart's Desire.

Joe sets off a series of situations where each side thinks the other did a crime against them, and profits from each encounter. Each time Joe frames the other family, he succeeds (Try/Succeed cycle), and Joe makes more money from the killings. Tension escalates because we know Joe's got too much of a good thing going on, and we know it's just a matter of time before he gets caught. When he does, there will be hell to pay.

He gets caught as we feared, and Joe suffers—he gets beaten to within a hairbreadth of his life. But Joe is tough and crawls away and survives in a cave and finds a way to shoot a six shooter again. He also fashions himself a Magic Sword. No, it's not a literal sword, but it is made of iron. Joe cuts it from a boiler, he mounts it like a breastplate over his chest, and he conceals it under his poncho.

We come to the climax of the story. You know it well. You've seen it in almost every Western. The escalating trials have brought two forces out into the street for a showdown: the hero of the story, and the man who stands against him. Maybe some sagebrush rolls by, maybe it doesn't. I'm not sayin'. And as the sweat rolls down their brows and the camera pans back and forth on each opponent with eyes set with murderous intent, one thing's for sure.

Someone is going to die.

~

THE PURPOSE OF THE CLIMAX

If you're applying the principles I've outlined in the preceding chapters, you made a statement of Heart's Desire in the opening of your story. That statement was a promise by you to the reader on what this story would be about. Consider it a contract with the reader, and the Climax is where you pay up. You promised that your hooker on the streets of Hollywood would find true love by the end of the story? Make sure she doesn't sell out for less by the end, even if the choice will cost her dearly. You promised that the duke's son would turn the tables on their House's enemies, even becoming a messiah to the oppressed desert people? Then we better see him vanquish his enemies at the end and give back the planet to the indigenous people.

The Climax is the point at the end of the story where we find out if the protagonist gets what they wanted or not. This is the final attempt to overcome the opposing force, be that the man that kidnapped your daughter, surviving a killer storm on the sea, killing a whale hell-bent on destroying your ship, or turning back an alien invasion. The

Climax is the payoff for the reader, and it better not be chump change. They expect you to deliver the goods.

In novellas and novels, you build the tension up through multiple confrontations and twists and turns in the plot until the mighty head of steam is ready to blow the lid off the pot. In short stories, you don't have the luxuries of the "slow boil." The very definition of this story term is "short," or another way of saying it is: "Get to the point!"

Readers still want a good story, but in short stories, they expect them to be tight. They've cut out a half hour before leaving for work or after putting the kids to bed to have someone tell them a story they can finish in one sitting. This is why I recommend for short stories, the Climax is the **third** attempt to overcome the opposing force, or as some like to say, the third Try/Fail cycle (or Try/Succeed). There's a reason for this, and it's in addition to the Rule of Three.

Every one of these Tries take up space. You have to write the confrontation and the result for each of them. If a novel is like a meandering country estate, a short story is like a tidy beach bungalow. If you drag your story on with try upon try, the short story reader gets weary. They're on the clock! They chose to read a short story and came with short story expectations. That means short and tight and don't take your sweet time in getting to the point.

Have you ever heard someone circling all the details about an incident that happened to them and someone interrupts them and says, "Yes, yes, can you get to the point?" As Jar Jar Binks would say, "How rude!" But what they're actually saying is, "You're taking too long to get to the climax of this story. I've listened long enough. Give me the payoff. It's what I've been waiting for."

In short stories, with three confrontations against the opposing force—the third being the grand finale of the confrontations—you can not only satisfy that innate Rule of Three, you can tell your reader a *tight* story. Your reader won't be sighing and muttering, "When will this writer get to the point? They've had plenty of time to do so." Instead, they'll be like Goldilocks with her porridge. "Not too long, not too short. That story was *jussssst* right."

∽

MAGIC SWORD

The Climax is where the Magic Sword gets wielded with all its might to smite the opposing force in order to win the prize—the Heart's Desire. Remember, at the beginning of the story, the hero was too weak to push the opposing force back. Most likely, the hero got clobbered, and maybe the bad guy ran off with his girl. The hero sits amidst the rubble that was his normal life and cries out like Popeye, "That's all I can stands, I can't stands no more!"

But Brutus, Popeye's nemesis, well he's a tank, probably twice the muscle mass of Popeye. Popeye could ask his freeloading friend Wimpy for help, but he knows he'll just try to bum another hamburger off him. Popeye figures his anger will carry him, and he bares his arms and clenches his fists and rushes after Brutus before he can escape on his boat.

And Popeye gets clobbered again. Maybe with an anvil Brutus had hidden up his sleeve—hey, it's a cartoon! And as Popeye sits up with tweety birds spinning around his noggin, he sees his beloved Olive Oyl under Brutus' arm all wrapped in rope and crying out, "Help! Help!" Brutus laughs—*hah!-hah!-hah!*—as he tosses Olive Oyl to the deck and casts off the mooring lines. Popeye failed twice and now Brutus has made it to the boat and is about to get away! How could he have let down his beloved Olive Oyl like this? Because he's been outgunned and outsmarted by a monster, Popeye thinks, and he wonders if he's the lesser man.

And then, in Popeye's darkest hour, a thought bubble appears over his head. *Blip!* Inside is a vision of a Magic Sword. Only it's shaped like a can, sheathed in a green label, and upon its surface is etched one rune of power: SPINACH. Popeye reaches in his pocket and pulls out a can—who doesn't carry canned spinach for just such emergencies— and he tilts his head back and squeezes so hard the can bursts and dumps the nutrient-rich wad into his mouth.

Popeye's tattooed arms triple in size, and his fists become sledgehammers. He leaps across the pier, onto Brutus' ship, and with one mighty spinach-enhanced slug sends that hairy brute soaring across the sea. Then he spins Olive Oyl loose from the rope, gives a couple of toots from the pipe at his mouth, and off they sail into the sunset.

Now that's a Climax, complete with a Magic Sword to defeat the bad guy and obtain that which is most desired. It works. At least for kids in grade school, and adults with a bit of nostalgia. But to ratchet up the tension even inside a climax, there's a power tool in your box of tricks you'd do well to pull out now and then. And if you desire to write tales that grip the heart, you'll want to remember this tool and use it often. Because stories with this element rise to the top and win awards and make careers.

∼

THE SACRIFICE

We've established in the last chapter that the more precious the thing desired is, the higher the price the protagonist must pay to get it. The price not only proves its worth, it also proves the worthiness of the protagonist if they're able to achieve it. It should not be easy. In fact, it should be the hardest thing they've ever attempted in their life, likely at the extreme edge of their abilities or beyond. There's no turning back now. It's sink or swim, do or die. They fought like hell to get here, and now it's showtime.

In the final match for the Olympic gold, a skater must pull out all the stops. That perfect triple Axel in the short program might have gotten them high marks as they entered the long program. But this is the final round against the best in the world, and if they hope to pull off the win, they must do something amazing, perhaps a feat they've never achieved before, like their first quadruple Axel. (At time of writing, only one skater has ever successfully landed a quadruple Axel in an official competition—American figure skater Ilia Malinin.)

High stakes? Certainly. If you're a solo figure skater at the Olympics, you're after the gold. And if your score is tied at the start with a rival that secretly paid someone to break your legs—okay, that's too unbelievable, let me take it back a notch. If your score is tied with your rival that has one-upped you at every national competition, you'll be motivated to push your limit and try a move you're not sure you can do. If you succeed, your lifelong dream will come true. If you lose, years of sacrifice getting up at four a.m. to train and all those hard slams against the ice will have been for naught. And you'll have to stand on the stage next to your rival that's been mocking you event after event as she proudly displays her gold medal. For an Olympian, these are high stakes.

But they could be higher. Perhaps your protagonist is a skater from Russia. Let's call her Amaliya. A mob boss that's been giving her family trouble is an oligarch, and his daughter is Amaliya's rival. He delivers proof they've got Amaliya's brother, and if she doesn't throw the final round, he promises she'll never see him again.

Amaliya has worked her whole life to get to this moment, ever since she put on her first skates and stepped onto the rink and the sound of the blades singing against the ice became the music of her heart. As her skills grew and her parents recognized her talent, they sacrificed all to pay for trainers until she started winning competitions and worked her way onto a team. She had failed in other tryouts but at last, this was her year, she had done all her meets right to make the cut, to get on the team sent to the Olympics. And now, at the very end of her journey when she's about to triumph, she learns if she doesn't sacrifice her Heart's Desire, her brother will be sacrificed.

You could take it even higher. There's the potential of ultimate sacrifice—where the protagonist risks her own life to save her brother's. Maybe this Russian oligarch is with his cronies at the Olympics, and Amaliya knows where he is staying in the Beijing compound. She doesn't have a weapon, but she realizes she has her skates, and the edges of those blades are *deadly sharp* ....

You can see where this might go.

War stories play this one well, but you can play it in many others. The science fiction movie *Oblivion* with Tom Cruise's character Jack Harper has a satisfying twist on this one. Paul Atreides in *Dune Messiah* appears to make the ultimate sacrifice to adhere to Fremen law. And after we assume he died in that story, he shows up in *Children of Dune* under another guise, only to set himself upon a path that will surely end his life this time.

When we've created characters the reader cares deeply about, seeing them pay the ultimate price to save others can grip the reader's heart, even make them shed tears. I believe this to be the most remarkable magic in storytelling, to create a character from the stuff of dreams that's so real, our readers will actually be heartbroken when they watch our dear character make the ultimate sacrifice. That hero isn't real. They're imaginary. But for the span of the story and perhaps even beyond, they became real to the reader, even a friend or loved one of theirs. Real enough that when your hero gives their life for others and dies, the reader breaks down and cries.

That's the deep magic. Shakespeare certainly knew how to play this one. Hat's off to any writer that can pull this off.

HEART'S DESIRE

It's important in the climax not to forget the point of the whole story. You established what your protagonist desired. You took it from them or kept it from them. You sent them out on a quest to obtain it. They likely failed in their attempts a few times, and things got worse every time they tried. But unless their Heart's Desire is revenge, the climax is not complete without delivering on that opening question: Would the protagonist get their Heart's Desire or not? That's the point of the story. Sure, we can talk about internal plot arcs and external plot arcs, but if your opening holds a statement of Heart's Desire, it all boils down to this: Did they get what they wanted or not?

Defeating the antagonist is not enough. Pushing back the opposing force is not enough. We still have to show the reader the result of the entire chain of events that led to this do-or-die event. We have to answer that question. *Did they get what they wanted or not?* Why?

The reader expects payment on our original promise. We made a contract with them.

Does the contract have to pay out the exact terms stated at the opening? Do you have to deliver to the protagonist *exactly* what they desired in the opening? No. But you better have a good reason if you don't, because the reader expects to be compensated for the invest-ment they made in reading your story. If your climax delivers the goods, well and good. That's what you promised, and the hero got it. Contract fulfilled, the reader will trust you and if you told a good story, they'll come back for more.

But the reader also understands that the protagonist at the begin-ning of the story will likely change by the end. After all, they weren't strong enough, smart enough, wise enough, equipped enough in the beginning of the story, and needed to go on the journey and gather knowledge and power in order to defeat their adversary at the end. By that time, they may no longer be the same person anymore. What sent them on the quest in the beginning may no longer be a motivating force by the end.

A simple example of this is a trope in romance stories. Girl wants the beefcake guy because she's physically attracted to the type, and the plot revolves around getting him. But at the climax it's revealed that he's totally obsessed with himself and would never make a good companion. She takes a fresh look at that nerdy guy at the office that covered for her every time she came in late, and maybe he's not looking so bad anymore. Her values have changed because of the jour-ney, and therefore her Heart's Desire has changed. You're still deliv-ering on your protagonist's need for companionship. Contract fulfilled. In fact, your reader will likely consider this an upgrade to your original offer.

~

POSITIVE RESULT CLIMAX, NEGATIVE RESULT CLIMAX, NEUTRAL RESULT CLIMAX

When the hero got what they wanted at the climax, the Greeks called it a Comedy. If they failed, they called it a Tragedy. We still use the terms today. However, because we also use the term *comedy* to catego-rize stories that make us laugh, this title can be a misnomer. So let's designate the types of story endings for our times. It's going to make it easier for you, and a whole lot easier if you're talking to someone that doesn't understand story lingo.

A Positive Result Climax is the apex of the story's plot arc. Hero wants something, pushing against what's holding him back, stumbles a few times, has the dramatic final showdown, and gets what they wanted. Positive result. They worked hard, it may have seemed like they'd never get it, but they did!

A Negative Result Climax yields the opposite. Hero wants something, pushes against what's holding them back, stumbles a few times, has the final dramatic showdown, but loses the battle, does not achieve their Heart's Desire. Maybe even loses their life. From that baseline we established at the opening, this is a negative result. There can still be lessons learned from losing even a climactic battle, so it may not be so negative as it seems. But it's not what the protagonist wanted. Let's face it. Some people never learn, and so they don't deserve their reward at the end. As in life, so in fiction. Unless you're writing a redemptive antihero story—a character with bad traits that overcomes some of them to redeem themselves—their tale's climax will likely end with a negative result. Lessons can be learned from such stories, but they're usually a warning to the reader. Pursue a life of crime, you're likely not going to get rich, you're going to end up in jail.

Finally, there can be a Neutral Result Climax. It's not as dramatic as the others, but it can work. Both parties could face off in a final battle, and perhaps both realize the vacuous princess is not really worth the fight and they walk away. I chuckle at Princess Buttercup in *The Princess Bride*. She's Westley's heart's desire. He's cheated death— well, he was only *mostly* dead, but close enough—to fight against all the odds including Prince Humperdinck and his castle guards. Was she really worth the price? She treated him badly when he worked for her, she gave up on him to marry the prince, and she barely lifted a finger when *he* could barely lift a finger, let alone his sword to protect them. I think both men should have stopped and said, "Why on earth are we fighting for *her*?" But love is a fickle thing.

We come to the end. The Climax. Let me explain. No. There is too much. Let me sum up. After your protagonist has taken their journey and climbed the mountain's obstacles, they will get to the top. There, they will face a final showdown with their enemy in order to get the thing they set out to get. If they get it, great, they accomplished what they set out to do. Contract fulfilled. If they don't get it, there better be a good reason why not, because readers expected a payoff. Or, in rare cases, both parties might yield in the end, realizing opening Pandora's box may not be good for anyone, even though it appeared shiny to both of them at the start.

However you choose to play your Climax, the story is over, the players have had their day. One man is dead in the street, a bullet in his chest. To the victor go the spoils. The End.

But wait! This isn't the end! Just like in every good infomercial, there's *more* ....

10

THE DENOUEMENT

Did I mention there's no better gunslinger in Westerns than The Man with No Name? Did I also mention that *A Fistful of Dollars* has one of the best climax scenes in a Western? There were even subsequent Westerns that copied that scene. *Back to the Future II* gave a nod to it. But wait! It's also got one of the best *denouement* scenes in a Western, too! More on that in a moment.

This pretty bow at the end of your story package happens to be an essential story principle. Miss it and it's like building a house but forgetting to put the roof on it. The house might look respectable to the buyer on the street, but when he goes inside, he's going to say, "There's something not right with this place. Great entry, smart living room and kitchen, nice master bedroom and bath, but something is off, and I can't put my finger on it ...."

And then he looks up.

❧

THE DENOUEMENT

What is a denouement? And how do you pronounce it? As mentioned previously, "denouement" comes from the French language and is derived from a word that means to untie or unknot, as in all those knotted up plot twists. An easy way to remember how it's pronounced is to say *they knew ma,* only say it with a little dialect, *dey knew ma.* Denouement follows the Climax and finishes off your story.

It's also called the Resolution. And writing instructor Algis Budrys called it the Validation. Dictionaries define it as the final part of a story where the strands of the plot are drawn together and matters are explained or resolved. That definition works for the complexities of a novel with many plot twists and sneaky red herrings meant to mislead the reader. In a novel, the Denouement can be multiple chapters because a novel can have many characters with their own storylines. Some of the knotted-up plot twists may need to be unraveled to satisfy the reader, especially if a red herring was played and the reader was tricked into believing the poor butler had done it, when in fact he had not!

But short stories are supposed to be, well, *short,* so the wrap-up needs to be shorter. Ever read the last line of a fable to a young child? *And they all lived happily ever after.* That's a denouement, albeit a very short one. For short stories, the Denouement is usually a short final scene in the story that takes care of any unanswered plot questions, confirms that the protagonist defeated their adversary and got their reward, that they grew from the trials of the quest, and are now ready to return home and use what they gained to restore harmony to their normal world. Are we done?

Not so fast, *kemosabe.* Or as my Ojibwe ancestors would say: Not so fast, *gimoozaabi.* There are more components to this story element.

PAID IN FULL

We've established in the last chapter that the Climax is where you provide the payoff to the reader for your promise in the opening of your story. You told the reader your protagonist's Heart's Desire; you had the antagonist keep it from them. They've gone on a quest and overcame obstacles to get a thing of power to help them beat their antagonist. They've dueled it out and your hero won (if it's a Positive Ending story). He lifts his bloody fist over his fallen foe; she posts a snapshot of an engagement ring on her finger to social media. *Victory at last.*

Many beginning writers end their stories at this point. They lived to write that complex sword fight with all those laborious thrusts and parries, and at last they got to play their surprise twist at the end when they had their hero cry out, "I am not left-handed!" because *that's* never been done before. And after another set of thrusts and parries where the writer shows off his extensive knowledge of sword-play—*you are using Bonetti's Defense against me, huh?*—they have their hero vanquish their foe, lift their bloody sword, and cry out, "Take *that* for all those locker room wedgies you gave me!" THE END.

But that's not the end. It may be the end of the Climax scene, but it's not the end of the story. The story is not complete without delivering on the question established in the opening: Would the protagonist get their Heart's Desire or not? That's the driving force behind the story. So, did they get what they wanted? Pushing back the opposing force definitively, vanquishing the enemy, holding the ship together through the height of the storm, getting that guy to ask for her hand—these are all victories. But the reader still needs bona fide proof that the hero got what they came for. They are a suspicious lot.

They need validation that the promise was *paid*.

When we pay off a car loan, we expect to receive a receipt. Until we get that, we won't be completely satisfied. Yes, we know the contract has been paid off. We fought hard for that money and there were times when we didn't know if we would make it, but we stayed the course, fought the good fight, and came off victorious. The final payment left our bank account. The lender must surrender the title.

But until we receive written confirmation stamped by an authority figure that says PAID IN FULL along with the title, we're not going to sleep easy. It's not really over without proof it's over. Validation.

The late Algis Budrys used to say it's like a common trope done in the original *Star Trek* series. Suppose we see a pitched battle in the climax and though the enemy is defeated, one manages to lift his phaser and make one last shot at Kirk and a Red Shirt jumps in front of the blast and drops to the ground. Captain Kirk and Doctor McCoy stand over the young man. We know he's dead, he's a Red Shirt for crying out loud, we've seen this happen a million times. But no, that's not enough. We still need validation. And until McCoy bends down and runs that tricorder over his body, we don't have our proof until the authority figure says, "He's dead, Jim."

Algis Budrys, or A.J. as he liked to be called, said this was why every *Lone Ranger* episode didn't end with the victorious final shootout scene. No, the story wasn't over. One more scene was needed. Wrongs were righted, the cattle rustlers were driven off, the widow and her son had their ranch back. But you still needed to see the Lone Ranger ride that white horse out of town as the owner of the mercantile stepped out his door and said, "Who was that masked man?"

Someone outside the conflict had to verify that the Lone Ranger had fulfilled the unwritten contract—he came to save the day, he kicked butt and saved the day, and now he would ride off to the next adventure. We knew life would go on for the Lone Ranger. That mercantile owner just told us so. He even validated the quality of the job done. "Who was that masked man?" was always spoken with admiration. Attaboy, Lone Ranger. You earned that praise. You are worthy.

Let's go back to Clint Eastwood's character Joe in the climax of *A Fistful of Dollars*. I'm not going to say spoiler alert because the movie was made in 1967—I'm betting you've had plenty of time to see it. Did I mention it's my favorite Western? In that final high-noon showdown between gunslinger Joe and the ruthless Rojo family, Eastwood's character comes back from near death, risking all to save his innkeeper friend who is being tortured to death. He puts the Rojos down, even proving that a man with a pistol can beat a man with a rifle against the rival that almost killed him.

But the story isn't over yet, even with Joe victorious. For one thing, that was a helluva tense showdown, and as the camera panned back and forth from one eye-twitching gunslinger to another, you held your breath. They had Joe five to one, and he wasn't at his best, but he found a way to save the day. Now that Joe is safe—*whew!*—you need a few moments to catch your breath.

The director knew that, too, and had Joe walk over to his friend, changing the dynamics of the scene, entering the Denouement. The casket maker ran out and stretched his measuring line over the bodies, validating that they were dead. Joe was as good with that .45 as we had hoped, and he saved his friend and ridded the world of one heartless band of men.

Now is it over? Nope. We're only in the beginning of the validation scene and all that it's supposed to do. Just wait. There's more ....

CHARACTER GROWTH AND FULL CIRCLE ENDINGS

One expectation in Positive Ending stories is that the protagonist must change. They began the story not only with their good points, but with flaws like any other person. Chances are, they've got a big character flaw, and it might have been the very thing that got them into trouble in the first place. Maybe it's even the reason they lost their Heart's Desire, and now have to fight to get it back. Whatever the case, readers expect the hero to learn something during the course of the journey. It's called the internal character arc, but let's keep it simple. Readers hope to see the hero grow a little by the end of the story. Just like in real life, we expect the protagonist to learn from their mistakes.

A solid Denouement provides the proof the hero's character has grown.

Back to the Man with No Name, who had a name. Joe. When he first rode into San Miguel, both the bellringer and the innkeeper told Joe about the power struggle between the two rival families that ran the town. Joe stood on a balcony overlooking the place and said to the innkeeper, "Two bosses." He looked to one end of the town, then to the other. "Baxters over there, Rojos there, me right in the middle?" He paused. "Crazy bellringer was right. Money to be made in a place like this."

We knew what Joe desired. Money. You could sense his mind spinning with plans to get it. By the end of the story, that desire almost gets Joe killed. But we've seen him grow in the course of the story, even set a captive woman free so she can return to her family. He gives her his hard-won money to help her family escape and start a new life far away from that god-forsaken town. By the end of the story, we've watched Joe face a terrible ordeal and come out the victor. But we still wonder if Joe has learned his lesson.

Has Joe grown?

As he and the innkeeper stand on the porch overlooking the aftermath of the Climax, the innkeeper reminds Joe that the Mexican army will come looking for their gold. Joe's response?

Joe mirrors the words he spoke to the innkeeper at the beginning, reminding us of the original promise, but this time with a twist. "You mean the Mexican government on one side, maybe the Americans on the other side, me right smack in the middle? Unh-unh. Too dangerous." He tips his hat. "So long."

As a writer with expectations, I cheer inside every time I watch the movie and hear him say those lines. For one thing, I see his character arc fulfilled—Joe has learned his lesson and he's not going to let greed make him throw his common sense to the wind again. He almost lost his life playing his dangerous game, and he recognizes the price he paid is too high. He's able to walk away, even with all that gold sitting unprotected at the Baxter's. The Joe that first entered the town could never have done that. This Joe can.

But this Denouement features another powerful ending tool, and you should know it. It's known as the Full-Circle Ending. You don't have to play your ending like this, but it's my favorite tool in a Denouement. It's tricky to pull off, but done right, I believe it's the most satisfying ending you can write. Let me show you.

The plot of the story really began when Joe made his statement about two opposing sides, and him right in the middle. That statement began the entire chain of events that led us to the inevitable conclusion. By repeating his opening words in the Denouement, it brings the story all the way around to the beginning, reminding the viewer this is where we began. But now, those words have new meaning based on the journey Joe has taken. He's been through trials. He's wiser now, learned his lesson. True, he doesn't have all that money he desired. But he saved a tormented woman and her family with the money, and he used his superpower to rid the world of some very bad men.

Note that in this story, the Heart's Desire contract in the opening didn't pay out what was promised. Instead, because of the journey, it delivered something better. And as we watch Joe ride out of town on the same mule he rode in on, we can live with that, even cheer for that. The Man with No Name (his name is Joe!) is worthy of our admiration as he rides off to the next adventure. Life goes on.

Who was that gunslinging man?

When you write your stories, remember the story doesn't end at the Climax. There's one more scene to write—the Denouement. The reader needs those unanswered plot twists untied, they need to know your hero learned important life lessons, and they need validation you paid out on your original promise, or gave them an upgrade. And if you can do it with a full-circle ending like they did in *A Fistful of Dollars*, more power to you.

Did I mention it's my favorite Western?

11

SECTION ONE REVIEW

A s Emperor Joseph II in the movie *Amadeus* would say, "Well. There it is."

You now know the fundamental principles that underlie stories that *work*. With automobiles, drivers may not know all the things that make a car run, but they know what a car looks like, that it should start up as soon as they turn the key, and when they put it into drive and apply pressure to the gas pedal, it should move forward. Likewise with readers: They may not consciously know story principles, but they know a story should start right away, grab their attention, get up to speed quickly, and take them on an exciting journey toward a specified destination.

It's true that practice makes perfect, but smart practice in sound story principles will help you create good stories *faster*. That's because you now know the general pattern of what a story is supposed to look like. You've looked under the hood, and the mechanic has explained why the engine must have fuel, spark, pistons, crankshaft, and a power train so that the wheels can convert all that energy into motion by moving the car *forward*.

Let's review these nine story fundamentals so that we may commit them to memory. The next time our story stalls, we can lift up the hood and use these story mechanics to troubleshoot the issues. Better yet, if we know them well enough, we can build an engine that won't stall on the road, but will reliably carry our reader to the exact destination we wish to take them, and they'll have a helluva good time riding there.

Ready? *Writers, start your engines!*

~

1. THE PROTAGONIST

Stories are about people, and people with unique character traits are *remembered*. They have their flaws just like us, but if you want readers to care about your protagonists, you must give them admirable qualities as well: shiny bits that attract the reader and bind them emotionally to your hero.

~

2. SETTING

Stories need to take place somewhere, and a writer has the responsibility to clearly define that place and time for the reader to get a good mental picture from the start. SET. YOUR. STAGE. Be the good director of a play and practice smart stagecraft with an economy of props that say more with less. When you start new scenes or chapters in your story, be sure to SET. YOUR. STAGE. all over again. Don't assume the reader knows what the locale is supposed to look like if you fail to give them the necessary details. But don't overdo it, either. Like Goldilocks' porridge, not too cold, not too hot, not too little, not too much. Perfection is in the balance, and the balance should be *jussssst right*.

~

3. HEART'S DESIRE

Heart's Desire is the person, thing, or state of being that the protagonist values and desires above all else—at least in relation to your story.
It's something precious that they don't want to lose, or something
precious that they hope to gain. You can't be too blunt about this, and
it should be obvious for the reader to spot—this is what your story is
about! I recommend making a statement of Heart's Desire early in the
opening of your story so that you clearly define to the reader what
you intend to deliver on by its end.

"Aged Josephine looked up at the moon as its silver light called
like a lover's promise in the dark of night. All her life one desire had
never hushed its yearning, never stilled its longing: to find a way to
cross the expanse and stand upon the shimmering surface of the
moon."

That's a statement of Heart's Desire.

4. INCITING INCIDENT AND THE PROBLEM

Once the reader knows what your protagonist desires above all else,
your job is to rip it from them. The Inciting Incident is the initial event
in the opening of your story where the size-sixteen combat boot drops
down on your protagonist's normal world, crushing what they hold
most dear. The Problem is the source of that combat boot, and whatever shape that opposing force takes, it should continue kicking down
your hero every step of the way as they desperately attempt to gain
their Heart's Desire.

5. MAGIC SWORD

Your hero just got their butt kicked—they had no power to stand
against the opposing force because it's stronger than they are. If

they're smart, they'll recognize they can't just rush out and try to take on their adversary again. The definition of insanity is doing the same thing over and over and expecting different results. If they hope to obtain different results, they're going to need to come up with a plan to gain more power.

That talisman of power? I call it the Magic Sword. It has real power to defeat the hero's adversary if they can obtain it and figure out how to wield it. It can be untapped potential within them; it can be a variety of material forms without. It might be hard-won knowledge. It could be learning new skills. It may be a physical item of power but, depending on the story, it could just as easily be achieving an enlightened spiritual state. And yes, it could literally be a preternatural item, even a magic-bearing sword. Whatever the case, the hero goes on a quest to obtain the necessary power to overwhelm their adversary and obtain their Heart's Desire.

～

6. ESCALATING TENSION: THE TRY

A proactive character leaves the comfort of their normal world in order to go forth to solve the Problem and get their Heart's Desire. These attempts are called the Try. Each Try should escalate in difficulty, testing your protagonist to greater degrees. This is how they grow in strength; this is how they prove themselves worthy of ultimately achieving their goal—obtaining their Heart's Desire.

～

7. ESCALATING TENSION: THE FAIL

The Try normally ends in a Fail, and each attempt to push back against the opposing force should make matters worse. "Out of the frying pan and into the fire," sums this up nicely. Each Fail should make it even harder for the protagonist to obtain their ultimate goal. *Things get worse* is the savvy writer's battle cry. The stakes go up, the struggle to succeed heading from the improbable to what looks like the impossible. The succession of Fails should finally make it appear that all is lost.

Make your heroes work for their prize. Put them into the crucible of trials by fire and keep turning up the heat. Learning from our failures is often how we grow—painful lessons are never forgotten. And getting up from our falls is how we ultimately succeed. As in life, so also in our stories.

There is an exception to this rule. A story can also escalate tension through Try/Succeed, as long as the reader knows that with each successful attempt by the protagonist, things are actually getting worse for them behind the scenes. A protagonist climbing the corporate ladder may succeed with each attempt, but the reader should see the antagonist that's looking on move from jealousy, to envy, to hatred, making the reader anticipate a brutal showdown in the end.

Whether it's Try/Fail or Try/Succeed, tension escalates until the ultimate Try is attempted. And that is the …

8. CLIMAX

This is the final showdown by your protagonist against the opposing force. It's a last do-or-die Try where the protagonist risks all to wield the Magic Sword against their adversary in a final attempt to defeat them. In a positive ending story, the hero will defeat or beat back their adversary and obtain their Heart's Desire. In a negative ending story, they will lose to their adversary. Or, even if they win, they will lose their Heart's Desire. That would be tragic, but life does have its tragedies, as well as characters that never seem to learn their lesson. Those stories need to be told, too.

Just remember in Western culture, we do like it when our heroes triumph. We hope they will eventually beat back the bad and get the good they deserve. Those stories need to be told, must be told. As conditions in our world darken, we crave stories of hope. They give us a refuge to escape to where we can see the downtrodden face their trials and win in the end. They fuel our belief that people can change, and that the world can become a better place.

The Climax is the outcome of your opening promise of Heart's Desire and the subsequent quest. Be sure the reader gets a satisfying—even surprising—payoff at the end.

∿

9. DENOUEMENT

Denouement is the French word for untying a knot, and in writing, it refers to untying knotted-up plot twists at the end of a story. I like to think of it as the bow that wraps up the story in a nice, neat package. In short stories, it's a final scene that follows the climax; in a novel, it can be several chapters wrapping the story up. It's also known by the terms Resolution or Validation. It provides emotional space to catch one's breath after an intense climax scene. It resolves any unanswered plot questions. It provides validation that the protagonist defeated their adversary and answers whether or not they obtained their Heart's Desire. It reveals character growth, validating the trials the hero had to overcome. And if it's a positive ending story, it allows the reader to wave goodbye to their beloved hero as they ride off into the sunset.

Well. There it is. All the principles you need to create a howling good story.

The next section of this book is designed to improve your writing craft, which gives your story that sleek, professional gleam that puts readers under your spell. How do we move from apprentice to journeyman to master? By learning our craft and doing the smart practice that makes our work flow flawlessly throughout the entire course of our story.

Master is where it's at. Editors and most readers can immediately sense when they're in the hands of a master. Their stories have all the moves down with skill and finesse. It's as easy to spot as an Olympic slalom skier moving with the masses down a recreational mountain course. You know skill when you see it. It stands out. Mastery of craft becomes an art form in itself.

You don't get there overnight, but you now see what you're supposed to ski. Ready to level up? Turn to the next section and keep those tips up! The powder today is *wicked!*

SECTION TWO

Writing Craft

"So often people are working hard at the wrong thing …. Much more important than working hard is knowing how to find the right thing to work on."

Caterina Fake
Entrepreneur, co-founder of Flickr
Insider, September 28, 2009

12

FROM LUMPY CLAY TO POTTERY MASTERPIECES

N ow that you know or have deepened your understanding of the principles that make stories work, this section will share my Super Secrets of Writing tips designed to help those stories work better. The difference between master and apprentice can readily be seen when comparing works side by side. But it can be harder to discern in writing because no two stories are alike, unlike a master potter that might tell their apprentice, "There. I made you a clay pot I've sold at many markets to serve as an example. Let's see how close you can get to it."

While you might learn a few things from exactly copying a famous story, in the end, you will have that master's story. Do it long enough, and it's quite possible your style will become a very good imitation of the famous author. And there's the problem. It's an imitation. Only that author can create the real thing. No one else can authentically duplicate what they do, despite what the AI doomsayers might tell you. (As for using AI to do any of your writing? Don't!) Originality is king in this business. Just like in music, your unique voice is gold.

That doesn't mean you can't pick up tips and tricks from someone with experience and incorporate them into your work. Isn't that why we take classes, listen to writing podcasts, and yes, buy books on writing? We're hoping to speed up the learning process by absorbing good advice from someone that went through the apprentice phase and figured out how to take their art from wonky to professional. Okay, some gasp when I use the word "professional." They say, "Isn't beauty supposed to be in the eye of the beholder?" (It's funny, but the newer the writer, the more they say things like that.)

Sure. A little child that takes crayons and makes a stick figure of mom standing in front of a crude house will hand it to her mother and say, "Look, Mommy. I made this for you!" She will certainly elicit praise from her mother. It might even make the family art gallery—a cherished spot on the refrigerator right next to the grocery list. But it's unlikely that drawing will sell even at a local market, let alone a famous art gallery. And that's just fine—it came from the heart as a gift to the child's mother. The child had no dreams of pleasing large audiences.

But selling to professional markets requires writing professional-level stories. Editors are like art buyers—they know the difference between a child's rough drawings and a masterful Rembrandt, a Monet, even a Picasso. You see, they are connoisseurs of the writing art, they are widely read, and they can spot both amateur work and work that might fit nicely into their gallery. They can do this quickly. They've usually been at this for years and have a keen eye for quality work.

So, for them to stop and consider your piece of art, they must be able to identify the markers that make for good art, at least for their publication. If you hope to sell to them, you will have to know what a masterful story looks like, you will have to develop the skills to create a masterful story, and you'll have to present it to editors in a way that makes them believe your story has got the goods.

We do this by learning our craft. Learning it to such a level that a connoisseur will look at it and take note, because they can sense we know what we're doing. This writer's got *skills*.

Trust me, that's not hard to spot. And even if we think we can bypass those editors that we believe have their noses in the air, we're going to find in self-publishing that no amount of fancy covers and Facebook ads are going to hide the fact that we failed to learn our craft. Readers may not be able to identify why a story or novel doesn't work, but they do know when they've been had, and they will never read that author again.

We become professional writers by learning our craft. There are two ways to learn. Either we keep throwing clay on the potter's wheel until we finally figure out how to make a clay pot that doesn't look wonky, or we ask an instructor to teach us how to do it. Nothing wrong with learning by trial and error, but it's going to take longer. Could take years longer before we can consistently create a product that sharp-eyed buyers will lay down money to purchase from us.

The faster way to learn is to have a guide. Not someone that says, "It's my way or the highway," but someone who's willing to share all the hard lessons they learned to help you make your pot with your own unique style. Someone that knows how to guide your hands and turn that wheel at just the right speed, the tricks that they learned over time to turn out a decent pot. Then, when they let you have at it, you'll have a good idea of what you're supposed to do.

That's why I wrote these Super Secrets of Writing. To give you a good idea of what you're supposed to do if you want to move from mom's refrigerator into a gallery where the public can see your work. I do know that many who studied these in my online resource and workshop went from unpublished writers to professionally published writers to winning major contests and even launching professional careers. I also know they did it in record time.

I'd like to do the same for you. Now that you know the basics, this section is all about the fine tuning that takes a product from wonky to balanced to sleek. These tips are to help you spot the lump in the clay and to make sure you get it smoothed out. These tips are to help you apply just the right amount of water to your fingers so the clay will shape up as you turn the wheel. And these tips are to help you discern when it's time to stop turning that wheel and call your work done.

There are two aspects to a professionally crafted story: technical craft, and storytelling craft. You can master all the technical aspects but still have a boring story. Likewise, you can have an exciting story idea but lack the technical skills necessary to tell it clearly.

Like everything in life, it's all in the balance.

The following chapters in this section are to help you achieve balance. If your work isn't selling or isn't getting good reviews, there's most likely something in these Super Secrets that can help you pinpoint why. Use these to spot the lumps in the clay and to work them out. Use these to focus your energy on *smart* practice.

My objective? I'd like to see you take your pottery to market—whether that's traditional, indie, or hybrid—and have the satisfaction of selling your pieces to thrilled buyers. Because they're *good*.

13

"WHERE DO YOU GET YOUR IDEAS?"

Go to any panel at a convention or attend a book signing, and when it's opened up for audience questions, you will inevitably hear this question: "Where do you get your ideas?" It's a sincere question by readers and beginning writers alike. The author will smile, maybe even hide a smirk, because they've been asked this question many, many times by family, friends, and fans.

Hopefully, the author gives the sincere attendee a better answer than, "From the air," because they really do want to know how that writer came up with the story seed that grew into the sequoia of a tome they now hold in their hands. Or how the author created that emotion-packed short story they read that won a major contest and helped launch their career. For readers, it's a mystery how writers can create worlds that can transport them like magic out of their own. For aspiring writers, there's one reason they ask the question: They want to figure out how you did it.

∽

THE IDEA

Story ideas may appear to spring from thin air, but they really come from one place—our fertile minds. Life experiences, places we've visited, people we've met, books and articles we've read, movies and documentaries we've watched, it all goes into our labyrinth's treasure trove. Our unconscious mind, what I like to call our kraken, worms through our caverns, running its tentacles over our knowledge hoards, making connections, seeking patterns, analyzing faceted memories from multiple angles and perspectives. When our kraken wraps its tentacles around something it finds particularly shiny, it gets excited, especially if it's got its tentacles wrapped around other treasures in our hoard that it believes could be woven or fused into a pattern.

Those wispy dreams our kraken dangles before us in the morning before sinking back into the unconscious ether? Or that idea that makes us shout "Eureka!" as we stand in the hot shower? (Krakens love water.) That's our primal unconscious mind making wild connections from all the life experiences, data, and images we've absorbed. And when those tentacles give our consciousness a mighty shake and hand us the thing it wrought from our hidden treasures, we shouldn't idly toss it away.

It's telling us it uncovered story gold, and it's offering the raw gift to our conscious mind to fashion into something *wonderful*.

COLLECTING THE RAW MATERIAL

Where do you get *your* ideas from? We are all unique, so the process doesn't work the same for each of us. But for all of us, our lives are a dragnet. Whatever we move through, whatever we see, whatever we taste, whatever we touch, whatever we hear, whatever we feel … all that input feeds into our minds, and at night our unconscious rises up and filters through everything the dragnet collected. Some of it is recognized as important, other things as curious anomalies. Some of it will fit into familiar categories where it can be stored; other things are entirely new and need their own niche in our caverns.

The more stuff of life we gather up and feed into our minds, the more our kraken will have available to wrap its sticky tentacles around. A curious mind watches, listens, analyzes, gathers. It's always taking in knowledge because it's an explorer. It can gather up what others have collected in books and documentaries, but the real gold is in real life experience. We absorb how relationships work because we've been in relationships. We understand heartache because we've had our hearts broken. We know how triumph feels because we've overcome adversity.

This is why stories by youths can at times feel flat, whereas stories by seasoned adults can feel multi-dimensional. Real life experience adds depth the writer can draw upon and infuse into their writing— experience the younger writer might not have had much of yet. Their dragnet is out, their curiosity is active, but it takes time to gather those treasures for the kraken to work with. In time, we'll all have a rich treasure trove to tap into.

How do I gather my favorite treasures? Where do I cast my dragnet? Anywhere, really. I have many interests and hobbies. Of course, I love to read, both fiction and nonfiction. I'm not fond of sitcoms, but I love movies with solid plots and characters—especially science fiction and fantasy—and I'm constantly watching for story fundamentals that make the movie work.

I love to travel, and seek out spots where the locals hang out to get a feel for what their lives are like. Visiting historical places like the Warsaw ghetto, Eastern Germany when it was still behind the Iron Curtain, Auschwitz and the gas chambers where over a million people were executed, Sterling Castle and the site of the Battle of Bannockburn below, Mayan ruins in the Yucatan, Newgrange and the Hill of Slane in Ireland—I hear the echo of the historical events and the people that made them happen as I stand on the very ground where they fought for their lives.

I sail, I fish, I dive, I ski, I paint, I camp, and I love cooking delightful meals for friends. I'm a glass artist and love making glowing, incandescent worlds under my torch. I'm a songwriter and love to sing whenever I get the chance. I'm an aficionado of single malt whisky, and I've been to most of the distilleries I drink spirits from because I am enchanted by the dedication and craft it takes to create such liquid art in a bottle over a decade or more of aging the spirit in seasoned casks.

I've been an entrepreneur since I was twenty, and have had a variety of businesses that have enjoyed both wild success and crushing failures. I've pioneered products that are now universal and that you have certainly used, and I've had accounts with some of the largest corporations in America by burning a lot of shoe leather and never taking no from gatekeepers. I've worked in estate planning and finance and for a time made our living as a day trader. I had a public art studio in a small island village where I taught watercolor to tourists, and had a boutique on a larger island where we hand-picked every item of clothing, shoes, and accessories at market and cared for hundreds of customers each day.

As a kid I've been abandoned by my mother and been beaten repeatedly by my father. I've run away from home to save my life, and I know what living in a heartless foster home is like. I did drugs to kill the pain, and I chose to break free of drugs before they killed me. I've had the real-life knowledge necessary to help others break free from addictions, and I've spent thousands of hours in volunteer work helping my fellow man.

I've fought an $800,000 lawsuit brought against me by one of the most powerful arms of the U.S. government which seized my invested assets. With no funds to hire attorneys, I battled their lawyers by educating myself on applicable statutes and court procedure, and after eight years of court battles I won, only to lose our waterfront island home and business shortly after in the Great Recession.

I've made all the hospital trips for the surgeries and nuclear treatments with my wife as she fought cancer and a misdiagnosed condition that ravaged her body. I spent a year putting cool washcloths on her head and holding her hand every night as we said goodbye in case she didn't wake up in the morning. I know the relief you feel when you finally pass through the storm and can find your way to believe the calm is not an illusion and that normal life can resume again … whatever normal life might be after experiencing near-death trauma.

And yes, I know what it's like to fight to be a writer, and to keep fighting, no matter how many times you've shaken off all the alligators clamped around your arms and legs and neck, only to feel like you're starting from the beginning all over again.

Where do I get my ideas from? The important ones? The ones that matter?

From life. The same as you.

What's in your treasure trove?

~

GO BIG OR GO HOME

Does this mean everything I write is based on something I've personally experienced? Not at all. Some of those memories are too painful for me to write about and I never want to relive them again. It's one thing to read a Grisham court battle where powerful parties with limitless resources use every means at their disposal to destroy the protagonist, it's quite another thing to be the real-life main character running for your life.

For some writers, writing about troubling experiences can be cathartic. For others, it can trigger bad memories and emotions that are hard to shake. In fact, delving too deep into traumatic experiences for extended periods of time—as with a novel—can even be dangerous for some writers. I've seen advice to put your painful experiences on the page, that your deepest and truest feelings will spill into your stories and make them powerful. That can be true. Just be certain you have the tools and support to deal with the monsters if you let them out of the closet.

But I am aware my life experiences shape every idea I have for a story. You should be aware of this, too. It's why having a wide range of interests is good. Readers shouldn't be able to predict what we're going to write about every time they open our work. With diverse ideas and interests to draw upon, our work won't become stale and predictable. P.T. Barnum made a great living surprising his audiences with amazing sights they'd never seen before. Crowds came to his parades and circuses to be dazzled. You and I would do well to do the same. Audiences love to be delightfully surprised.

I've mentioned our kraken likes digging through our treasure troves. For our creative beastie to do its best work, it needs rich hoards to give it abundant raw materials to work with. If we'd like to place the setting for our story in a specific city, region, or country—like Robert Ludlum with his Bourne novels—the best thing we could do would be to travel there and spend time soaking up local details to add authentic seasoning to our stories. Of course, that takes money and vacation time, two things we may have in short supply. But there are plenty of travel shows, online videos, and books on various cities and regions we could fill our minds with. A few well-placed specific details about an area and its people add realism to fiction and make it feel authentic.

Being an avid reader will certainly help with the raw materials that become story ideas, in both fiction and nonfiction. Watching local, national, and international news (I like *BBC News*) can also help writers stay current with what's going on in the world, and the feature stories are often about determined people that triumphed over adversities—great fodder for character creation. And if we write science fiction, it's important to read science journals and listen to respected podcasts to keep up with the latest discoveries.

We could even take classes to farm ideas on a subject we'd like to write about. On a recent interview on *CBS Mornings*, Bonnie Garmus said she taught herself chemistry while writing the book—wait for it, wait for it—*Lessons in Chemistry*. She also made her main character, Elizabeth Zott, a rower. When asked why, she said: "Well, I had to put something in the book I actually knew about." The result? Her debut novel spent fifty-six weeks on bestseller lists at the time of the interview (June 11, 2023), has been translated into forty languages, and is being made into an Apple TV series. Smart ideas woven into the lives of interesting but believable characters for the win!

There are many ideas our dragnet picks up, and our kraken toys with them whenever we are dreaming or daydreaming. It hands us what it's cobbled together and says, "*Easkou chuwa wumpapakka?*" which roughly translates as, "How about this doohickey? Can you make something with it?" Pay attention when it does so. Write those ideas in a notebook. Keep that notebook handy so when the kraken drags its idea back with it into the ether, you've written it down and won't forget it. Many creatives keep a notebook on their nightstand for this very purpose. Or a folder with a collection of restaurant and bar napkins with ideas scribbled across them. Or a notebook file in a smartphone. The point is, capture it quickly with whatever is at hand.

Ideas tend to evaporate in the sun.

When an idea grabs you, play with all the angles. The gold is in the angles no one has written about before. King Solomon wrote that there is nothing new under the sun. Whether you agree with that proverb or not, what is always new is our unique take on an idea. My favorite cartoonist is Gary Larson, creator of *The Far Side*. Poking fun at the oddities of humans through cartoons is nothing new, but mimicking our oddities through bugs and animals as if they were living human lives? That perspective is funny, and he gave his cartoons a twist on the concept that no one could duplicate. Picking up any of *The Far Side* books makes you look at our world and what it means to be human through new eyes, even if they are the compound eyes of a fly or a spider.

The bigger the idea, the better. The fresher the perspective, the better. Weak, pedestrian ideas that follow current trends have been done. Somebody already got in first and cashed in, and everyone else is trying to milk the same cash cow until the udders are dry. Be on the hunt for the fresh, the new, the original. Know what's been done by reading deep into the genre you are writing. Find the original idea that's fresh or that twists the idea in a fresh new way.

One way to discover the twist is to find your big idea and then create the most unlikely, polar opposite character to work with it. Just like in *The Far Side* cartoons, it's the unique angle the idea is told from that makes the concept fresh ... and *interesting*.

In novels, the idea needs to be bigger than life. It's difficult to write a big novel without a big idea. The idea will play out before you get to the end, and the reader will get bored and quit reading if you stuff it with fill to cover the lack. Cloning story? They cloned the first sheep back in 1996, and there have been multitudes of cloning stories since as the process advanced from science fiction to science fact.

But cloning a dinosaur? Hmm. Hadn't been done. What if you could get dinosaur DNA from something? Maybe you read an article about viable cells of extinct animals being preserved in amber. Fascinating, Captain. What if that mosquito trapped in the amber had bitten a dinosaur and the blood contained viable DNA? That could be plausible. Now what application of cloned dinosaurs could fascinate young and old alike? A zoo, yes. But zoos are rather static—watching animals in small enclosures does not create a lot of dynamic story action. Dinosaurs are big, we need this idea to be bigger than life!

How about … a dinosaur *amusement park!* And what if we stretched it across an entire private island! Big idea? You can bet your bottom dollar on that. *Jurassic Park* and all its spinoffs became one of the most popular global franchises of all time, grossing some six billion dollars. Michael Crichton went BIG with his dino idea and was richly rewarded.

And if our big idea doesn't hit the financial stratosphere? Just a fraction of such success is enough to build an author's career. Even if you only write about one singular day, you could make it a fascinating day. Set it in a place many readers have never been but they might be curious about. Like the day in the life of an innocent man sent to prison. That happens all the time, sadly. But have that man accused of being a spy during World War II, and document his grueling day of trying to survive in a freezing Soviet Gulag? Pay dirt. And what if you were able to tap into real-life details from serving years in that Gulag yourself?

Such an idea would have real power, so much so it could defy the restrictions of an oppressive socialistic regime and even undermine the very fabric of its authority. Such was the case with *One Day in the Life of Ivan Denisovich* by Russian writer Aleksandr Solzhenitsyn. His big idea played a major role in Solzhenitsyn being awarded the Nobel Prize in Literature … and a book that many believe formed the wave that became a tsunami that eventually brought down the Soviet Union.

STRIKE WHILE THE IRON IS HOT!

A last word on ideas. Write them down, play with them, but don't allow them to go stale or wither on the vine. Our unconscious mind hands us gifts, we're not pulling them from thin air. But the unconscious mind is primal, it doesn't have the logic to be able to tell whether the idea is big enough to develop or not. What it can tell us is what it's excited about, and if it's jumping up and down and making bells and whistles go off because it thinks it's found story gold, we should listen. Why?

Because it means that deep down inside, we're excited about the idea, it's got our juices flowing. Our conscious mind then evaluates the idea to see if there's enough sizzling steak here to sink our writing chops into it. As mentioned, not all ideas are big enough or fresh enough to develop. So when we see the potential and our spirit is saying *go, go, go*, we should go with it! Don't submit the idea to a committee for peer review, don't tell everyone we meet what a great idea we have, and certainly never ever *ever* tell another writer we have this BIG IDEA that will make lots of money and would you like to write it for me?

As Nike says, *Just do it*. Strike while the iron is hot, because if you don't, all that exciting energy can lose its head of steam. Not *every* time —some ideas do rest in our depths and layer up nacre for awhile like a pearl. But in most cases, wait too long, and the idea will go cold. Your kraken will get a frowny face, drop the idea, and run off to play with something else. Or pout in the cold dark depths because you didn't care. Maybe it will punish you by not bringing you new story ideas for awhile. And when you finally pull that scribbled napkin out of a drawer and decide to work with it, all that creative energy may be gone. Instead of having the benefit of a head of steam and rolling inertia, you're pushing the train from a dead stop. It's going to be hard to get those wheels in motion again. Because you've waited too long.

My advice? Strike while the iron is hot. It's glowing right there, red-hot and ready for you to shape with the radiant coals of your forge. Don't let the idea go cold.

Your fertile mind has given you a gift.

Use it.

14

POINT OF VIEW AND PAST OR PRESENT TENSE

Directors and cinematographers spend a great deal of time determining the angles they plan to film each scene from, including the closeups of the actors. They sit in meetings with artists creating storyboards, they go on location with a director's viewfinder to pre-visualize the framing, they may even hire a CGI studio to create an animated version of the scene to make sure they get the framing right. Why? Because point of view, or POV, is important. They know the choice between a distant shot or a tight closeup will create changes in the emotional impact on the viewer. Much of the art is in whose story they are telling and how each shot will be framed.

It's no different with our stories. Before we write, we need to consider whose story it is, where we'll place the camera operator (narrator), and whether the shot will be a sweeping panorama or a tight closeup. Selecting Point of View is how we do that.

Point of View is who the narrator telling the story is, or what the point of observation is. Who is providing the perspective to this tale? Will your camera be like a mini camera strapped to your protagonist's forehead, capturing only what she sees, or will it be held by a friend or family member like they're recording your protagonist's exploits? Or is it a cinematic god view, hovering over the scene like a drone, taking in the action of all the actors in a scene? These are choices you make *before* you begin writing your story.

There are three types of POVs. Let's list them:

1. **First person**: We see the events of the story and read exposition exclusively through the viewpoint of the person telling the story. "I picked up the gun." Uses *I, me, mine, my*.
2. **Second person**: The narrator is speaking to you, telling you what you see, where you will go, how you will act. "You picked up the gun." Uses *you, your*.
3. **Third person**: An authorial narrative from a viewpoint outside the story, not a character within it. "He picked up the gun." Uses *he, she, they, their*.

When in third person, there are two styles you can use:

1. **Limited**: The narrator only relates what's occurring as experienced by one character—all sensory details, thoughts, and actions are narrated through their lens. *Jake wondered why he had picked up the gun.*
2. **Omniscient**: The narrator sees all like a god hovering over the story, witnessing every event unfold, whether on scene or even off scene, dipping into any character's mind and perspective at will. (There are variations on omniscient narration, but let's keep it simple.) *Jake wondered why he had picked up the gun. Sally wondered why Jake pointed it at her. Their dog wondered who would be left to provide him dinner.*

In third person narrative, you can supply all the information through one character's viewpoint (limited), or through multiple viewpoints or even no character's viewpoint at all (omniscient).

Now that we know the POV tools, what are the pros and cons of each?

~

FIRST PERSON POV

First person has the benefit of the narrator actually being in the story, and the narrator is usually the protagonist. It's their story, and they're telling it to you. If the writer has created a sympathetic character, it's easier to bond with the protagonist because the story is told from the protagonist's perspective, including their thoughts and emotions since the reader is in their head, experiencing the story through their eyes and ears.

The reader experiences the tale through the protagonist's discoveries, and because of the intimate nature of witnessing their reactions to events as they experience them, it can create a strong Reader/Hero Bond. The reader can easily feel they are the ones going on this adventure, or at least are a close companion beside the hero. When the hero is in pain, when the hero experiences doubts, when the hero triumphs over tragedy, the reader is right there, experiencing it all. Many middle grade and young adult stories utilize first person POV.

The cons of first person POV? Bias. Who says the hero's perception of their world and events isn't tainted? A young child could view being wheeled into an operating room as a great evil set on her by her parents, whereas from the parents' point of view, they view committing their child to painful surgery as an act of love, knowing an operation is the only way to save their child's life. A man with schizophrenia telling his story could relate incredible events that happened to him, leaving the reader to wonder if those events actually occurred. A solution to this? Providing the reader with clues that the point-of-view character is naïve, biased, or unreliable can allow the reader to not take everything related by the narrator at face value.

~

SECOND PERSON POV

Second person's strength is that YOU are actually in the story. YOU are being guided through the plot and YOU are told how you will react to events and YOU will receive the boon or bane. This POV reminds me at times of *Dungeons and Dragons* campaigns (but D&D campaigns are far more fun!).

Dungeon master: "You enter a dark cavern, your torchlight flickering on a gilded statue of a goddess set into an alcove within the far wall. You see an altar before the statue, and atop it is your beloved sister, gagged and struggling against the ropes that bind her. A cowled priest lifts a wicked knife over his head, his prayer to the goddess rising to a crescendo ...."

I might not have won a GenCon tournament with that scene (although I did have the privilege of watching the *Dungeons and Dragons* founder Gary Gygax DM at his Lake Geneva headquarters), but you get the point. The narrator places you in the story and takes you on an adventure, serving as your guide through the plot. In story form, you take whatever the narrator gives you, do whatever they tell you. In video games that use this form (and in D&D), you are given the opportunity to interact with the environment and people and objects within it, providing the aspect of choice and the story's outcome.

And there's the con. In a second person POV story, you have no choice, or at best, the illusion of choice. The reader is being told where to go, what to do, how to react. This can be off-putting and even offensive to the reader if they know they would never act or react in the way the narrator is describing. The POV can also insult the reader's sense of individuality and independence. "Who is this narrator to think they can tell me what I would do? I would *never* do such a thing!" Because of these issues, second person POV stories are rare. I know many readers and editors that have a strong aversion to them. But it is a way to narrate a story, a few have been quite successful, and you should know all the tools you have at your disposal.

~

THIRD PERSON POV

Third person POV is the most used perspective in narration. Its advantages are multifold. For one thing, with an omniscient narrator you aren't bound exclusively to one character's knowledge in a story. You can show a mafia thug connecting a bomb to the starter of the informant's car, and later you can show your informant walking up to the car with his keys out, oblivious to what is about to happen. In a murder mystery, you can drop into the killer's mind as the detectives are interrogating him as a suspect, showing his skills of deception as he talks his way out. Third person omniscient allows a writer to show events going on outside of the protagonist's knowledge that will later have a bearing on the story. Many thrillers use third person omniscient.

Cons? Sloppy omniscient. Newer writers tend to do head-hopping, believing they have a free-for-all to drop anything into the story from any character's perspective as they need it. They open their story exclusively from their hero's perspective, so the savvy reader believes they are reading in third person limited. And then the hero joins up with his party to go on an adventure, and the writer drops us into every one of the adventurers' heads to tell their story and why they're going on the adventure as well. As the narrator hops us from head to head, we quickly wonder whose story this is and why we need to know what everyone is thinking.

Another con is that omniscient is distant. It has to be. It's the god view, the wide-angle lens, not the closeup. It can also dilute the main character's story, diminishing the emotional impact on the reader because the plot isn't completely focused on the hero's story—it's taking in a wider perspective of characters. It can be fascinating to see the thoughts of other characters weighing judgment on your main character's actions, or even taking a side trip in a novel with an alternate character, but keep in mind you are giving up story real estate to others that could have been going to your protagonist. In longer fiction forms like novellas and novels, *side trips* with other characters are fine, if they relate to the plot. *Sidetracked* is not.

That leaves us with third person limited, or what I call with a super-close perspective, third person intimate. With limited 3P POV, the story is told completely from one character's point of view, normally the protagonist's. Every sight, every sound, every thought, every feeling—it's all filtered through the character's mind and body. If they can't see it, can't hear it, they can't know something happened. Everything in the story is discovered as the viewpoint character discovers it. This can create an exciting journey when the reader, like the hero, doesn't know what's coming next.

And if you're writing that perspective really close, like right through the viewpoint character's eyes (that mini camera on their forehead), everything in the story is up close and personal. *Intimate.* You can see right into their mind and experience all their thoughts and feelings as they happen because that's where the camera and microphone are. The narrative feeds you the story as though you were wired to the character. Because we're so close to this character and only experience the story through them, it can create a strong Reader to Hero Bond, placing the reader directly into all the action of the story, much like first person does.

The cons? This is a popular style, and a writer would do well to master it. But it can cause problems for newer writers because it can be tough to limit oneself to one character's perspective.

For instance, they may want to increase the excitement for the reader by telling them about that bomb that's wired to the car's ignition, but the protagonist can't know it's there or they would never pull out their keys and get in. Having written themselves into a corner, newer writers might cheat, dropping the narration out of 3P limited and into the POV of another character (or worse, they do authorial intrusion: *Hi there, it's me, the author!*) so that they can feed the reader information that their protagonist does not have. This jump from one head to another after being exclusively in, say, the main character's head, is jarring to the reader. To an experienced editor, it's immediately spotted, and it can easily get a story rejected.

PAST TENSE OR PRESENT TENSE?

There's one more narrative choice you must make before you begin your story. Past tense or present tense? Is the story unfolding in present time as the narrator relates it, or has it already happened, and the narrator is telling us what occurred?

This is another one of those narrative choices that can become extremely complex and confusing. Past tense, present tense, future tense, simple tense, perfect tense, and all the combinations. It can drive you bonkers and keep you from even starting. So, let's make it simple. Simple means you won't get overwhelmed and will start that story!

Past tense is where the action has already happened. "Jake picked up the gun. He pointed it at Sally." The narrator is relating events that have occurred, which, it can be argued, is the reason they know the story in the first place. It has happened, and they're relating it to the reader. This is a common tense used to tell stories. I've listened to famous authors state that it's the only true way to tell a story. I wouldn't go that far. But it's an especially useful tool, and since most stories are told in past tense, editors may raise an eyebrow if you present them with the alternative, because most readers are used to past tense as well. It's a format they've grown accustomed to, and accustomed to means comfortable to read.

The other tense is present. Present tense has the advantage of immediacy because the story is unfolding in real time, right as the characters are experiencing it. "Jake picks up the gun. He points it at Sally." What's going to happen? We don't know, it hasn't happened yet! Present tense can create a faster pace to the story, because it's not old news, it's current, happening now. Every news channel you watch loves to use lines like, "This just in," or, "Happening now," because it creates a sense of urgency. Tension drives plot, so urgency and immediacy in a story's telling can increase reader excitement and anticipation.

Even though most prefer stories in past tense, I have written some stories in present tense. The stories called for it. My story "Super-Duper Moongirl and the Amazing Moon Dawdler" in *Writers of the*

Future, Vol. 35 was written in first person, present tense. I will argue that there was no better way to narrate that story. I challenge you to read it and tell me differently. Writing Dixie's story in present tense created a tremendous amount of energy and tension that funneled into the dramatic ending. It would not have been the same story relating it as if it had already happened.

I've had stories that demanded I write them in a certain way, different from the norm readers and editors tend to expect. I've even tried to change tense or POV to conform, and the story did not work when I did so, and I made myself go back. If you haven't gotten far, this isn't hard to do with short stories. With novels? It's going to be a nightmare to repair. That's a lot of real estate to clean up.

Stories come to me as they are meant to be written, and I've learned to trust that. But I've been writing for a long time. You may be at the start of your writer journey. If that's the case, I have no desire to discourage you from experimenting with these narrative forms. But it's wise to understand current stylistic trends. Your career won't be harmed by writing in a format the majority are comfortable with in the category you write in. Truth be told, it will probably increase your chances of making those early sales that establish your career.

Different is good. Different stands out. But it's risky if you're still learning your craft, because different must be done *well*. It has to work. And the newer we are at our craft, the less likely we are to discern what is working and what is not. That's why I encourage writers to master the basics and branch out from there.

In conclusion, we set the narrative rules when we begin our story. A savvy reader will recognize what POV we have chosen and if we've held true to it. And non-writer readers will still be able to sense something isn't right when we go off the path for the sake of convenience. Whatever choice we make in the POV for our story, we have an obligation to stick with it. A caveat here is that some experienced novelists have done first person and third person POV swaps effectively for different scenes or chapters in their novels. My advice? Save the avant-garde stuff for after you've sold some stories to respectable markets, which provides validation you've likely mastered some of these techniques.

As composer Sir Edward German said: "You must learn the rules before you break them." I know, you probably think Picasso said it more artistically. *Learn the rules like a pro so you can break them like an artist.* Problem is, there is no record of Picasso ever saying that phrase. Just another one of those false attributions flying around the internet. But the premise is valid.

Choose your point of view and as the rebel starfighters said in *Star Wars*, "Stay on target!"

15

THE LOGLINE

Screenwriters call it a logline. Writers call it an elevator pitch. Tomato, tomahto. Well, almost. I'll explain.

A logline is a one or two sentence summary of a television show or movie used to describe what the story is about. Screenwriters also use them as a tool to focus their scripts on the heart of their stories before they write them. Writers call it an elevator pitch, because they practice summing up their stories in one or two sentences to pitch them to agents and editors.

Why is an elevator involved? The thought is if you're at a convention and an editor is riding on an elevator with you and asks you what you're working on, you've only got a sentence or two to capture their interest before the elevator reaches their floor. A fast hook is critical, whether the pitch happens in the opening of a pitch session, in a hallway, at a banquet dinner, at bar con, or yes, riding up an elevator to your room. A well-planned pitch can pique the curiosity of an editor and move them to ask for more details, and hopefully, to give you their card.

I like the term logline because screenwriters use it the way I encourage my masterclass attendees to use it: to provide focus to their stories and novels *before* they write them. An effective logline can keep a writer on track, aiding them to remember why they decided to write the story in the first place. Focused stories are powerful. They don't wander all over the map because the logline acts like a pin in the map that marks the destination. When you know where you're going, it's less likely you'll get lost.

~

ELEMENTS OF A LOGLINE

In several of my masterclasses, I have attendees take their story idea and interesting main character and do a brief stream-of-consciousness session, putting words down on anything that comes to mind. This provides raw material to build their story from. Next, I ask them to sift through that material and create a sentence or two about who and what that story is about. Their logline must include the name of their character and some idea of who they are, where the story is set, what's their Heart's Desire, and who or what is trying to keep it from them. *Boom*. That's a logline.

Now, I don't expect them to go hop on the nearest elevator and pop it on the next editor heading to their suite. I expect them to craft a logline that will tell *the writer* what their story is about. If they can figure out how to sum up their story and the conflict in one or two sentences, they've got their pin in the map. They now know who their story is about, what their name is, where they are at, what they care about dearly, and who or what that's trying to take their Heart's Desire from them.

Pantsers—those writers who like to write by the seat of their pants —will say, "Wait just a minute, Moon! I write by discovery. These things only appear to me after I wander around the map at my leisure until I find the story. Don't tell me I have to *plan* something. I'm not one of *those*."

I have no problem pantsing—I do a lot of it myself. But *not* before I know who my story is about, what my story is about, and where it's supposed to go. Otherwise, that's exactly what my story will do— wander all over the map until it finds itself. And when a story wanders, it's boring. It frustrates readers because they too are wondering *where is this story going? Are we lost?*

A good logline fixes all of that. If you can lock down a character, in a setting, with a Heart's Desire, and the opposing force putting it at risk, all in one or two sentences, it's unlikely you'll forget that as you write. Especially if you jot it on a sticky note and fix it to your monitor. Your story now has a purpose in your mind, and that purpose is going to keep your story on track.

Here's my logline for my story in *Writers of the Future, Vol. 35*. "Super-Duper Moongirl and the Amazing Moon Dawdler is a story about Dixie, a twelve-year-old disabled girl that lives on the moon, and her life support robodog that comes into great danger trying to protect her."

One sentence, right? Note that in that sentence, I named my main character: Dixie. I got in her age: she's twelve years old. I established her condition: she's disabled. I listed that which is most dear to her: her life-support robodog. And I stated that the thing most dear to her will face opposition when it tries to protect her. I could have named who in the story would cause that opposition, but in this case, I don't want to give that away. It's enough that you know Dixie's dear companion that keeps her alive is going to face *great danger*. A girl on the moon with a life-support robodog? And there's danger involved in this story? Yes, please! Count me in.

That's a hook. Not just for an editor that the writer may one day pitch the novel to, but *to hook the writer into the purpose of their story* so that while they're writing it, they keep their plot on track.

I've watched many writers try to describe their novel or story idea in a sentence or two. They can't. You ask them to give you a brief description of their novel, and they'll list every warring faction in their kingdom and start citing off their main character's begats all the way back to the Flood. You've watched the Battle of Wits in *The Princess Bride* where the Man in Black faces off with the Sicilian? I want to say to them, "Truly, you have a dizzying intellect." But I'm afraid they might say back, "Wait till I get going!"

I'll give them this: they certainly know their world. What they don't know is where their story is going, because they can't describe it to me in a few simple sentences. And if they don't have that fixed firmly in mind, their mind can't put it on the page. They haven't forced it to hunker down and figure it out. And until they do, they won't have a story. All they've got is an encyclopedia of their world.

Want to know a great place to study smart loglines? Pick up your TV remote and push *Guide*. Or go to your streaming networks and read those brief descriptions they give you of their movies. Better yet, practice writing a few loglines of your favorite movies, and then go to the streaming channel it's on and read what the pros came up with. See if you can do better. Learning to create strong loglines will help you boil shows down to their essence.

If you can learn to do that with the movies you love, you can learn to do that with the story you're about to write. And *then* you can go galivanting across the map on your pantsing steed.

But at least you'll know where you're going.

16

TITLE IS YOUR FIRST HOOK: A ROSE BY ANY OTHER NAME IS NOT JUST AS SWEET

In Shakespeare's play *Romeo and Juliet*, Juliet opines to Romeo: "What's in a name? That which we call a rose By any other name would smell as sweet." Her premise? That a name doesn't change the person it represents. What matters is who we are, not what we are called—especially when that name is attached to your family's deadly rivals, the Montagues. For her love, Juliet bids Romeo to cast off his title.

But wait! Some roses have cool titles! How about A Whiter Shade of Pale? Absent Friends? Absolutely Fabulous? Atomic Blonde? And that's just starting with the As! Their names make you want to stop and smell the roses (although, as a guy, I'm not sure I want to smell Paul's Himalayan Musk). And how about all those names for shades of color chips at the paint store? You remember a name like Illusive Fawn or Knubby Wool or Apple Crisp. I'm sure there's even an Ala Mode to go with the trim on your Apple Crisp. My point? *Names* matter. *Titles* matter. Don't discard them lightly. Unless you're Juliet and you're doing it for love.

A STORY ABOUT A TITLE'S IMPORTANCE

Ready for a story? I've got one for you! Many moons ago, I spent some time studying the finalist lists for the Hugo and Nebula Awards—these are prestigious awards in the speculative fiction community. (Don't worry, I have something for you romance and historical fiction writers in a moment, promise!) I noticed something about the stories that took the gold. Most of the winners had crazy titles. Imaginative titles, quirky titles, sometimes long titles that read like mini stories in themselves. And when the winners were announced? The winning stories appeared to be the catchiest in the list.

It made me recognize a pattern about many winning stories. Unique titles grab your attention. They don't have to be wild and crazy, but they do have to have that special *something*. They have a ring to them. They sparkle. They are the shiny gift wrap on a present that makes you wonder, *Oooh, what's inside the box?*

You see, title is your first hook.

Since I had been desperately trying to win the Writers of the Future Contest for many years (many of my friends had launched their careers through the contest), I thought a crazy title might just be the trick to achieving my winner. Crazy meaning out of the ordinary—wild in nature, attention grabbing, but not without grounding. I figured what's good for the goose is good for the gander. So I developed the Crazy Title Exercise (I now teach it in my workshops as the Catchy Title Exercise), to see if a wild but relevant title could be my golden ticket to a contest win.

Okay, so who would this story be about? I had recently watched a video on Facebook about a photographer that donated his time to take pictures of disabled children to empower them. How so? Working with their parents, he'd put them in superhero costumes and then photograph them in power settings with fists on their hips or an arm thrust up as if they were about to leap from tall buildings in a single bound. And then, he'd make a big poster for them and do a reveal of it on their living room wall.

Their moms would wheel their disabled child into the room, the photographer would unveil the poster, and there, larger than life, would be that child in costume and cape like any superhero, ready to save the world.

What got me was the moment when the child's mom would crouch next to her child's wheelchair and say, "You see that? That's *you!*" And that little kid would say, "That's me? That's really me?" And their mom would say, "That's really you."

That still gets me in the feels. Maybe because until I had an operation when I was seven years old and had my legs put in casts, I couldn't walk without falling. I spent a long time in a wheelchair and had some idea of what those kids were going through. To see themselves on glossy posters as superheroes, capes flowing in the wind? I bet a lot of those kids could believe anything was possible, that their disability had no power to limit their dreams. As those moms shed tears while their kids grinned from ear to ear, I cried along with them. That photographer was doing a beautiful thing for those children and their moms and dads.

That video report became the genesis of the idea. So who would I base my catchy title on? A disabled girl in a cape, because that was fresh on my mind. Why would she wear a cape? Because it gave her psychological power over her disability. Super-Duper Moongirl was born. I gave her a friendly name you could easily warm up to. Dixie.

Great, I had my main character. I put her on the moon at a moon base because moon bases are cool. I decided she couldn't breathe on her own, so that would be her disability. But unlike the days of the Iron Lung, this would be near future, and she'd be connected to a life support unit that trotted beside her like a dog. Let's make it a robodog! How about a Doberman, because they're tough looking, and she needed someone tough in her life to give her confidence. And then I put a rapper AI personality inside of the talking robodog to make it even tougher, which provided a more interesting companion when contrasted against a twelve-year-old girl.

Now, what to name him? I went into my past. When my parents divorced, my mom placed me and my brother with our grandmother in Spooner, Wisconsin. You might think being taken from your father and then abandoned by your mother would be tough on a boy, but those were the best years of my young life. My grandmother was from the Chippewa/Ojibwe Nation, and she was not only a great oral storyteller that seeded my mind with how stories work, but she was also highly creative in many art mediums, including textiles and music.

One day she rolled out a strange toy she had made for me on a chain, the size of a mid-sized dog. But it was no dog. It was circular with a plywood base, with wooden wheels underneath. She had upholstered the top with foam covered by black innertube rubber. It had a long spring tail, two long eyestalks made from door springs, with star eyes at the top that would waggle in every direction as I pulled the creature by its leash.

"What is it, Grandma?"

"It's a Moon Dawdler. They are shy creatures that live on the moon. This one traveled all the way here to be with you."

I wheeled that Moon Dawdler everywhere, imagining his life on the moon. He talked, too, at least to me, in his own moon language. You see, those wooden wheels made an alien squeaking sound as I pulled him behind me. That was how he spoke, and he only talked about his moon life to me.

Farming memories provided a great name for my robodog, and it came with my special feelings attached to that name. I transferred those feelings over to Dixie for her companion. I put the two characters together and the result of my title exercise became "Super-Duper Moongirl and the Moon Dawdler." No, not snappy enough, and the meter fell flat on the second subject in the line. This robodog was the coolest, especially to Dixie, and the title needed to reflect that. More sprinkles! I put the finishing touch on my title, and it became "Super-Duper Moongirl and the Amazing Moon Dawdler."

That title exercise became the genesis of my story. And yes, that story became my winner in the largest talent search for speculative fiction writers in the world. It was published in the bestselling anthology *Writers of the Future, Volume 35*. The title did exactly what I hoped it would do—get the judges intrigued enough to read the story within, to see its beauty, and to choose it out of thousands of other stories vying to become a winner.

It worked.

How well did it work? While at the award ceremony in Hollywood, the presenter of my award was Dr. Gregory Benford, a famous astrophysicist and science fiction author. He addressed the audience from the stage and read my title. The audience gave a delightful laugh. He smiled and said: "The title alone makes you want to read this story ... at least, it does for me." More delightful laughter. But what no one knew? That was *exactly* what I had designed that title to do. To make you *want* to read my story. In fact, the story only existed *because* I created that title. I'm happy to say it also won a second contest: it went on to win Best Science Fiction and Fantasy Short Story of the year in the Critters Reader's Choice Awards.

Mission accomplished.

Title is your first hook. It's the first thing an editor or contest judge will read, and if they like what's inside, they'll put your story in their stack for final selection. When they go back to choosing which stories are in, which stories are out, your title is the last thing they'll see, and trust me, it's going to help if it's a title they can remember your story by. They don't have time to give those finalists a second read.

The late *New York Times* bestselling author David Farland was an esteemed coordinating judge of the contest. He once said he could guess a contest winner by title alone, and after reading the entries he said it almost always proved true. A compelling title often indicates that what's inside is also compelling. An author that can create a smart title that hooks usually has the skills necessary to write a story that hooks too, all the way through.

THE IMPORTANCE OF A SMART TITLE

I've mentioned I'm a freelance editor. I read a lot of manuscripts for writers. And I've noted many lesser-experienced writers pay little attention to their titles. It usually feels like they just slapped something on without thought, as if they're labeling boxes for a move: *garage, master bedroom, kitchen, torture chamber.* This is a mistake! Well, not the torture chamber label. That sounds unique! As long as I'm not their special guest.

How important is a smart title? Here's the part for you romance writers. See? I didn't leave you out. Ever heard of these novels?

Another Day

Not in Our Stars

Bugles Sang True

Tote the Weary Load

No? I'll bet you read the book those titles were originally attached to.

Gone With the Wind.

Yes, those original titles Margaret Mitchell thought up for what would become her literary masterpiece were lackluster, some even downright depressing. Fortunately, Mitchell kept seeking the perfect title for her novel. While reading "Non Sum Qualis Eram Bonae Sub Regno Cynarae," a poem by Ernest Dowson, she came across a verse that had the far away, faintly sad sound that she had been searching for—*gone with the wind*. The title resonated with readers, and so did the story. It is hard to imagine her book would have done so well had it been named *Tote the Weary Load*.

Here's the one for you historical fiction writers. What would you think of a book titled *A Romance*? Would you get the shivers seeing that title in a bookstore and lunge to grab it from the shelf? Not likely. It intrigues like a bowl of mushy oatmeal.

Yet that is what Nathaniel Hawthorne originally called his work of historical fiction set in the puritan Massachusetts Bay Colony during the 1600s. Fortunately, he changed his title from one that fizzles to one that sizzles. And, I might add, better represented his work about an adulteress and the community shaming inflicted upon her. With three words, *The Scarlet Letter* sets the hook. It compels you to ask, *Why is this book about a letter that's scarlet, the color of passion, the color of blood?* It makes you wonder what secrets lie within, and just like his title, Hawthorne's novel delivers.

For you emerging novelists focused on traditional publishing, will a smart title help you get representation? Madeleine Milburn is the CEO of Madeleine Milburn Literary, TV & Film Agency, a top literary agency in the UK. Note what she said about the importance of titles on her agency's website: "I look for a clear, concise covering letter with a professional yet conversational tone that gets to the heart of the story quickly. Imagine you are pitching your favourite book ... how would you get a reader excited? Look at the blurbs on the backs of books and see how they entice someone to start reading. *I also love a title that stands out, and resonates in some way, before even opening the manuscript or knowing anything about the story.*" (Italics mine.)

Titles *are* your first impression. We do judge a book by its cover because it offers the promise of what is to come. Titles are the complementary amuse-bouche a skilled chef sends out to diners to prime their palates, not only for the savory meal they're about to experience, but for the chef's distinctive style as well.

Don't be bland. Put some spice in that title! A sprinkle of intrigue. A dash of suspense. But even if it's quirky, if you ensure that it nails the mystery that lies within, you'll enjoy the sweet smell of success.

Bon appétit!

CHARACTER NAMES: CHOOSE WISELY

S ince we've been talking about the characters Romeo and Juliet, let's stick with the lovely suicidal couple. Five hundred years after the play was written, we still remember Romeo and Juliet's names. They roll easily off the tongue and have nice meter when spoken together—each name is three syllables long.

But what if Shakespeare had named Juliet Drz'dddgvzbtk? Rashqhashjzkna-ha-ha-ha? Or even something tamer like Billie Bobbess? Her fame in literature would be diminished because household names *need* to roll off the tongue. They need to match the character they represent. Readers need to be able to *pronounce* them, and here's the important part—both from their lips, *and* in their minds. Fortunately, Shakespeare chose the perfect name for the only daughter of Lord Capulet, and the rest, as they say, is history.

Maybe you have a friend that can write as well as Shakespeare. Maybe she's even been published. Maybe her current story is truly brilliant. Maybe she asked you to read it and you loved everything in it, save for this one thing ... she thought it would be sweet to give her protagonist an unpronounceable name.

I get it. We're writers. We make—erm—stuff up. We invent worlds, we create beasts, and yes, from the dust of earth we fashion a body and blow into it the breath of life and bring forth a living soul. We are miracle makers. And then we take our miracle and name it Solazy'me'ear't'w'rkd.

~

THE PROBLEM

The reader opens your story, sees your dashing heroine in her pointy tricorn swinging from a rope off her sloop's yardarm. Yay, she's a pirate captain! She lands on the deck, brandishes her cutlass, and cries out to her bloodthirsty pirates ready to board their prize:

"Chicken dinner with glazed carrots and crème brûlée for dessert to the man that takes their captain alive!" And then, the shocker. The greatest line in the history of literature gets destroyed by the dialogue tag *Solazy'me'ear't'w'rkd said*. <insert scratching vinyl record sound here>

Full stop! The reader backs up. You see their lips move, sounding it out. They put their lips back in drive and try to move forward. They slide into the ditch again. They put their mind into four-wheel drive and back up and take another run at it. Still unnavigable. Do they proceed? The dashing heroine did appear to be able to cook a mean chicken dinner, and your reader does love crème brûlée when the top gets that crusty caramelization, and they get to break it with their spoon and dig into all that creamy vanilla custard goodness. They finally decide to assign your heroine the name Solazy and try not to get stuck in the rut every time they see her referred to throughout the rest of your story.

Alas, in the next paragraph, they discover the heroine's ship is named *Me'uthr'pi-rat-ship'eeza'mer'saydeez*, and the reader throws the book against the wall, forever robbed of their crème brûlée reward they so eagerly anticipated.

Why is it some aspiring writers (and a few famous ones) think unpronounceable names are so cool? I haven't a clue. Even if they provide a secret decoder ring at the back of the book with all the pronunciations to their unintelligible words, I'm not buying. Readers need characters and places with names they can easily hang a hat on. They like complex plots with surprise twists. They DO NOT like convoluted tongue twisters that their minds and lips can't sound out.

Here's why. Names have meaning. Names have power. Look up names in baby name lists and you will see symbolism and history in every name. How about Michael? A household name. It comes from the Hebrew name *Mikha'el,* and it's a given name associated with the challenge *"Who is like God?"* It is also the name of the chief of the angelic armies, Michael the Archangel. We associate the name, even subconsciously, with righteous power.

How about Hannibal? Also easy to pronounce. Also associated with a divinity, Baal, a god at enmity with the Hebrew god. This was the Canaanite "Rider of the Clouds" that brought rain to Canaan's crops and fertility to his worshippers through rituals involving licentious temple acts. In Phoenician, Hannibal means "Grace of Baal." You may not recognize that name at first, but I'll bet you've heard of Beelzebub. Its origin comes from the name Baal-Zebub, the deity worshipped in the Philistine city of Ekron. Today, we associate that name as the chief of the fallen angels.

You see, the name Hannibal has a bit of the devil built within it.

Thomas Harris (*Red Dragon, Silence of the Lambs*) chose it as the name of his fictional cannibalistic serial killer, Dr. Hannibal Lecter. Like Juliet, it's also a household name, but for vastly different reasons. Also note the author's choice of surname. Lecter sounds the same as the word *lector,* which subtly drapes the surname with intelligence—a lector is a reader of scripture in church services, or an academic that lectures at a university.

I'm betting the author fashioned his character's surname to subtly clue the reader in on the level of Hannibal Lecter's intelligence. At the same time—and with the economy of the same simple surname—the author also cued up, at least for me, a subliminal message of perversion. Lector and lecher are not far removed, and I'll bet Harris counted on our brains making the association, even if our unconscious mind chose not to spell it out for us.

Finally, there's the most obvious subliminal message of all. Hannibal rhymes with cannibal. Coincidence? I think not.

Still on the fence? Still holding your hero, the vowelless Lrd Brgv-zldcktkx, tight to your chest? Do you think the wildly successful author J.K. Rowling put much thought into the names of her characters? <Using my best Mr. Rogers' voice> "Can you say Harry Potter? I knew you could."

How easily that name rolls off the tongue. Harry Potter. It's got meter. It's a good thing Rowling didn't call him by his proper name Harold—much too stiff for the portrayal of an orphaned boy living under his aunt and uncle's stairs. But it is the hypocorism—ahem, nickname—of the personal name we all know as Harold. Harold is derived from the Old English name Hereweald, a union of the Germanic elements *here* "army" and *weald* "power, brightness." Do you think that's by chance? You'd have to ask Jo Rowling, but I doubt it, even if it was the unconscious mind offering it to her as a gift. Gotta love our submerged kraken!

Here's what she said about her name choices in a Q&A session in a Boston school in 1999:

Q: *How do you come up with names?*

A: *Some I make up. Some mean something. Dumbledore is olde English for bumblebee. I thought I made up Hogwarts, but recently a friend said, 'Remember we saw lilies in Kew gardens (a garden in London).' Apparently there are lilies there called Hogwarts. I'd forgotten!*—From the video recording: "The Magical World of JK Rowling."

What did she say about her names? *"Some mean something."* That was the understatement of the century. When you look at the names of her characters, it's obvious Rowling put a tremendous amount of creative thought into each one. Pomona Sprout over Hogwarts' Herbology Department? Argus Filch as Hogwarts' seedy caretaker? Bellatrix Lestrange, the mad practitioner of the dark arts from the *Black* family tree? The prim and immaculately dressed *Narcissa* Malfoy? How about her son, Draco Malfoy? Draco is Latin for serpent, from the House of—wait for it—*Slitherin*. It should come as no surprise that every bad apple in her world's history comes from the House of Slitherin.

Do you get any vibes off a name like Severus Snape? Rowling recognized that names have power. They hold meaning. And because she took care to make them easy to pronounce, easy to remember, and then stuffed them with context, Harry Potter and a host of her characters are now household names.

Want more proof? Observe what one of my favorite authors, Terry Brooks, said about names in his book, *Sometimes the Magic Works*:

"...NAMES ARE IMPORTANT. You would think this would be obvious, but I find more often than not that it isn't. Maybe part of the problem comes from not understanding what it is that names should do—because they should definitely do more than act as convenient labels. This is true not only of names of characters, but of places and things, as well. Names should serve two very specific ends. They should feel right for the type of story being told, and they should suggest something about the person, place, or thing they are attached to.

"I am acutely aware of this because of the type of fiction I write. In fantasy, where whole worlds are created from scratch, the writer has to give the reader a sense of both differentness and similarity. Readers have to be able to get a handle on what an imaginary world is like, which means they have to be able to recognize how it resembles our own and at the same time understand why it doesn't. In taste, touch, look, and feel, in language and societal structure, in geography and weather, in any way the writer looks at his own world, he will have to look at his imaginary one. I submit that it all begins with the names you use.

"Even in contemporary fiction, I find that names are important. If a name doesn't feel right, it can bother a reader all the way through the book. The sound of a name, the way it looks on the written page, and the connections we make with it both consciously and subconsciously all play a part in how we feel about it .... You can avoid the lazy writer's approach to slapping something on without giving it any real thought."

Terry Brooks keeps lists of names to use in his stories. So do I. Terry keeps his list on him wherever he goes. I do not, but it's good advice, and it reveals how serious he believes this issue to be.

The names you choose for your characters and creatures and towns and worlds should have meaning and relevance. They should be easy to pronounce. Your readers will use them as filing tags. If your character names are easy to pronounce and, although fictional, hold resonance in the world we live in, they'll stick in the minds of your judges, editors, and most importantly, your readers. They will even have the bonus of, oh, I don't know, being pronounceable. You will bless them with the gift of tongues: the ability to speak the names of your characters so that they might tell others about them.

Maybe enough to make them household names.

May the light through yonder window break. It is the East, and meaningful names that can be pronounced in your story ... are the sun!

THIS SUPER SECRET COMES WITH AN ASSIGNMENT:

1. Keep a Name Notebook. Carry it on you or set up a notepad on your phone or tablet. Watch for interesting names in the books you read, in histories, in street signs, in town, river, and lake designations. My Super Secret name source? Movie credits. They are loaded with interesting names and combinations. WRITE THEM DOWN. Become a collector of names and their meanings. Use them in your stories.

2. Check the names in your existing stories. Are they easy to read, easy to sound out, or did you think it was cool to create an alien language without vowels? Do you know why we can't pronounce ancient Hebrew? THEY DIDN'T USE VOWELS, AND THE PEOPLE THAT KNEW HOW TO SAY THOSE WORDS ARE ALL DEAD. Make it easy to remember your names. Change out those lazy names you plucked from a hat. Your readers and editors and judges will thank you. Maybe with publication and an award. If you're fortunate, maybe one of those characters will become so popular, they'll even become a household name.

Like Wulf Moon.

18

GENRE CUE UP FRONT!

A s a moderator of a popular aspiring writer forum, I know for a fact many newer writers believe that when they submit their baby to a market—oops, I mean *their story*—every word is carefully read by the first reader, and then hand-brushed and gift wrapped and delicately delivered by courier to the editor, where he sits before a roaring fire like Santa in his rocker, musing over each line as he sips a cup of hot cocoa, smiling thoughtfully at the writer's witty prose. *Ho-ho-ho!*

It's a cute image.

And it's wrong.

Let's say in a submission period in a popular publication or writing contest that there are 1,500 submissions. Let's say, on average, that there are 5,000 words in each of those stories. Now do the math ....

There's no way an editor or judge at the big publications and contests can read through every story in each submission period. It's just not possible—they've got their own lives, and usually their own jobs and writing to pay for their editor habit, which is always a labor of love whether they get paid for it or not.

To cope with the volume of submissions, the larger publications have what's called first readers. First readers are the unsung heroes at these publications that make it possible for editors to have a life outside of reading submissions. Most first readers are volunteers. Their job? To sift through the pile of gravel to find any nuggets that appear to be gold. When, *eureka!*, they find that rare story where it appears a writer knows their craft, they may send the story to the editor to consider, or they may read the story to the end, hoping nothing throws them out before they finish. They may even rate it and pass it along to another first reader for a second opinion before a decision is made to pull it from the submissions' stack and send it to the editor.

Another word for this stack of submissions? Slush, or the slush pile. There is no way first readers can read every story in the slush pile (unless they're masochists), nor would they want to. That's not their job. A first reader's job is that of a prospector: to sift through all the gravel assigned to them in order to filter out those shiny nuggets that might be publishable gold. It's the editor's job to sort the pyrite from the gold, even to take the choicest nuggets for themselves and send perfectly good gold back to the submitter. They can't buy everything.

That's the process. It's not pretty, but that's how it is. So how much time do you have to prove that your story is gold? In short stories, a couple of pages, if you're fortunate. In novels, I've heard editors say a few chapters, maybe forty pages if they're feeling generous, but they can usually tell by the first chapter if the story is written well and could be a fit for them. My friend and mentor, bestselling writer and publisher Dean Wesley Smith, once told me he could tell if a story was worth his time just by reading the first paragraph. It doesn't take long to differentiate between the writers that know their craft, and the ones that are still apprenticing.

What's one of the first things first readers and editors ask once they figure out whether you or I can write a good story?

What's the genre?

Why is genre so important? Shouldn't they simply be looking for howling good stories to publish? And what if my writing is so unique, it can't be categorized? I'm *special!*

Sorry, editors have a publication they're buying for. They built its name and reputation as a mystery magazine, a romance magazine, a fantasy magazine, a science fiction magazine. If they're going to devote any more time to reading your story, they need to know one thing immediately: Does this story fit the genres that we publish?

Suppose the editor buys stories for a speculative fiction magazine that publishes science fiction and fantasy. You can have a sizzling title. You can write gorgeous prose. You can open with a cool character, in a dandy setting, with the most intriguing of problems. But if your story is set in what appears to be our mundane world and the magic doesn't happen until page seventeen, no one is going to read that far to find out. And if they're looking for science fiction stories and your future science tech doesn't appear until page six, that's also going to be too late, unless you've dazzled them with your skill and publishing credits. Your story, howling good though it may be, will be returned. Why?

Because they're only going to read a page or two—they don't have time to read more without proof that this story is the kind of story they buy. If you didn't prove to them with a genre cue on the first or second page that this story is their kind of critter, they will move on. They don't have a lot of time to go on the hunt. Like Elmer Fudd, they're hunting *wabbits*. They either see a wabbit when they put their gun sights on your manuscript, or they move on to the next field.

When those readers on the hunt pick up *your* story, make sure it sticks its pointy ears up, munches loudly on a carrot, and says, "What's up, Doc?"

19

OPEN YOUR STORY WITH YOUR PROTAGONIST

Don't get me started about prologues. I never read them, do you? Okay, maybe I sneak back after I've read the story for a bit just to be sure I didn't miss important backstory. Don't tell anyone. And yes, like watching the outtakes on DVD bonus material, I discover I didn't miss much. If the story worked just fine without a scene, you leave it on the cutting room floor.

What I *do* want to find when I open a book is WHO IS THIS STORY ABOUT? And DO I LIKE THEM ENOUGH TO SPEND MY RARE SPARE TIME WITH THEM? Having a moment to read shouldn't be a luxury, but in our busy lives, especially if our eyes are bloodshot and blurred from editing manuscripts all day, any casual reading time is sacred. We want to spend it wisely. And that means our stories should give us what we want PDQ.

Like me, don't you want to find out who this story is about on the opening page? If it's a thriller and we're being shown the heinous act that will bring in our detective, we might be patient and wait until the next chapter because we know this bad guy ain't our detective, but that author better deliver in chapter two or we've got more important things to do, like finding a better book.

We expect to be shown our good guy or good gal in the *opening* of a story, preferably on the first page, maybe even in that first sentence. Why? We know how stories work—mom and dad have been reading them to us since we were babes. There's a good hero, there's a bad villain, and there's going to be a struggle of some sort where it's going to be difficult for our hero, but she'll learn from the experience and rise triumphant, witch's broomstick in hand.

WHY YOU SHOULD OPEN WITH YOUR PROTAGONIST

When we open a story as readers, we seek to hang our white hat on the hero so we can easily track them through the rest of the tale. Because there's such a desperate need to do so before we can settle in and relax, we're going to stick that white hat on the first person we see (although these days, the hat's a whiter shade of pale). Mentally, we dust off our hands and say, *Glad that job's done. Now who's the bad guy bringing on the heat?* Because we've got a black hat just for them, and we're itching to slap it on them (although these days it's more a paler shade of black).

Understanding this reader need is important for writers. When editing, I've read a lot of less-experienced writer manuscripts that fail to lead with their protagonist. I'm reading along, thinking I've got my hero because the story opened with a lady in a checkout line, only to find out in the next scene or chapter that lady was a girl's mother, and perky Jennifer is really the hero of our story.

What? FULL STOP.

I now have to pull my white hat off the middle-aged single mom I thought this story was about, go back, resize the hat, and put it on a feisty teenager in junior high that doesn't like wearing hats! That's a major mental shift, and I know if I'm annoyed, the reader will certainly be annoyed. Unfortunately, I also know the story probably won't have a reader unless it's fixed, because a magazine or book editor is going to be annoyed, too. And editors selecting stories for publication aren't in the business of reading manuscripts that annoy them.

Leading with your protagonist isn't a hard rule, but it is a strong suggestion because of reader expectations at the opening of a story. Think like your readers. A career writer figures out who their readers are, what they expect, and how to please them in surprising and delightful ways. Readers want to see your hero, especially if it's a series and they loved them in the last book. So give them what they want. Get to the hero of your story ASAP. Reader hearts will flutter when they show up on the page.

PROACTIVE PROTAGONISTS

As mentioned in a previous chapter, protagonists need to be proactive. If they're swept along by circumstance and never grab the bull by the horns to solve their problem and take back their Heart's Desire, what basis do readers have to respect them? How will your hero grow if he or she sits back and allows everyone else to do the heavy lifting?

I've already written a chapter on this subject in *The Illustrated Super Secrets of Writing, Vol. 1* workbook titled "Character Agency: I Need a Hero." To be fair to those that supported the workbook, I'm not going to include the chapter here. But I did create the workbook to be a companion to this book, and the lesson is important. I'll put information in the back of this book if you'd like one for yourself to study. If not, no worries. I'll give you the gist of what you need to know:

Passive protagonists swept along by circumstance? *Bad.*

Proactive protagonists that fight to get their Heart's Desire? *Good.*

There. Run with that. It's the secret to an engaging story that makes you respect and cheer for the hero.

Customers come back to stores that give them products that they like. Readers come back to authors that give them stories that they like. That includes a strong opening that engages readers immediately in the plot of your story. They've come to your tale with that white hat in hand, and they're looking for the hero to place it upon. They love it when they spot them holding up their hand at the start, saying, "I'll be your huckleberry."

Give them what they want.

20

START YOUR #$%@! QUEST, WE'RE ON THE CLOCK!

I n the *Illustrated Super Secrets of Writing, Volume 1* workbook, I have a chapter titled, "How Driving to the Story Creates Accidents." I teach a workshop covering this information as well. It's that important. Failure to launch is a critical issue I note in the manuscripts I edit. Writers get bogged down in the setup and forget that the reader desperately wants us to *get to the story.*

The title of this chapter is from my original *The Super Secrets of Writing* online resource. It's far less developed than the chapter in the workbook. As mentioned previously, I'm including some chapters from the workbook in this book, but not all.

The workbook is pretty special. I've been told by savvy publishers and top bestselling authors they've never seen its like. And that's the point. I've got to keep it special, so the workbook gets to keep some special chapters that make it unique. But the information I'm about to tell you is critical, and I wouldn't be doing you justice to leave the guidance out. Especially if you've just begun your writer's journey. You need to know this. At least, the gist of the Super Secret. Get the workbook if you wish to dive deeper.

Almost every manuscript I see by writers in the early stage of their apprenticeship fails to launch. What do I mean by this? They spend all too much time running around the launching pad making sure they show the reader everything related to their rocket has been installed correctly, and they've got all their engineering blueprints and diagrams and math equations to prove it!

If they're a fantasy writer, they'll show us every floor in their castle, or worse, they'll spend days marching an entourage to their castle where we find out—*surprise!*—their waif is really a princess, and this is her home.

Two major violations in that last bit: (1) readers hate it when writers withhold vital information from them (writers think it creates mystery, but all it creates is aggravation), and (2) readers hate it when writers drive to the story. A little setup is necessary, they know this, but they want you to get to the point—which is the plot of the story where all the action happens—as soon as possible.

Let me ask you. When you go on a road trip, what's the fun part? Making all your lists, getting all your clothes and gear packed, meticulously checking each item off and then carrying all that heavy luggage out to the car? Rather, isn't it the part where you've finally loaded it all up and you've checked your map for your first stop and are about to hit the road? Isn't that where the journey truly begins? Because, at last, you're *moving*. You're finally out of the house and on your adventure.

Just like those caravans in Westerns, stories need momentum. There's only so much patience you have as characters are introduced and wagons are hitched up—they've got to get moving. True, the load 'em up part is necessary so we know where the story begins and who is going on the journey, but the sooner we hear the leader shout, "Move 'em out!" the better. We're supposed to be going on an adventure. Reading all the details of how to stock up a chuckwagon gets tedious quickly, even if it's authentic, even if it's for the Donner party.

In Joseph Campbell's Hero's Journey story model, Crossing the First Threshold is where the story truly begins. The Ordinary World where the hero lives (your starting line) has been established, the problem in the form of the Call to Adventure (the Inciting Incident) has taken place, and after a couple of other items are accomplished in that model, the hero commits to the adventure and steps across the threshold from their normal world into the unknown world, what I call the Quest World. That's where the adventure truly begins.

Here's a good example. I bet you've watched *Star Trek: The Next Generation* episodes. Or maybe even the subsequent series, *Picard*. When those original *TNG* episodes started, do you remember how quickly the writers opened with just another day in the life of the *Enterprise*, only to have the ship's mission interrupted by an incident that would take them off course and into the unknown where trouble surely awaited? It was *fast*, because they had to get the crew across the threshold so they could cut to commercials to pay for the show.

Those Starfleet officers would scramble to come up with a plan, Captain Picard would make the final call, and then he'd drop his hand with a finger pointing into the unknown to say that one word every fan thrilled to: *Engage*. I still get goosebumps when I hear him say that, and I bet you do, too. Why?

Because that's where the adventure begins.

So here's the Secret to get your story off to the fastest start possible, while still establishing the necessities to establish your story's baseline: who your protagonist is, where this story is taking place, and why we should care. Figure out when that combat boot—the Inciting Incident—drops into the normal life of your protagonist. When does the genesis of the story problem raise its ugly head, doing its darnedest to keep your protagonist from getting their Heart's Desire (or trying to take it from them). Got it? Take your time, this is important.

Tick, tock. Tick, tock …. (Playing a little *Jeopardy* music for you here.)

Got it? Good. Now back up a little and give us a brief picture of your protagonist and their normal life and what's most important to them *just before this event occurs*. No "driving to the story." Toss away that beginner's wake up scene and get your hero out the door and on to their adventure.

Start your #$%@! quest, we're on the clock! *Move 'em out!*

21

"WRITE SMART DIALOGUE!" MOON EXCLAIMED EMPHATICALLY

*L*ong ago, when one could walk into brick-and-mortar bookstores—yes, young whippersnapper, this was before virtual reality sites—I'd pull a book off the shelf, lick my COVID-free finger, and thumb through gilded pages. What? Yes, yes, books were printed on paper back then. Just cork the questions for a moment and listen!

Okay, where was I? Oh, yes. I'd thumb through those pages, not looking for how the story opened—any writer worth their salt puts the spit shine in the opening. No, what I hunted for was some juicy dialogue in the middle, something I could sink my teeth into. But if that dialogue murmured, mumbled, hissed, inquired, grimaced, gurgled, or growled, I'd spit it right back out and put the book back on the shelf. Mighta' been a few cuss words uttered for the writer, editor, and publisher, too. I'm not saying. But there is one thing I am saying: Write smart dialogue, son!

∽

Said. Said is such a simple verb, it's beautiful. Said is so perfect, nothing else has to be said. It's like the gray man concept of someone walking through a crowd purposely seeking to blend in by becoming bland, unobtrusive, and ultimately, invisible. Only if you stop and study the crowd do you notice he's even there.

That doesn't sit right with aspiring writers. New writers don't like plain clothes. That gray man must be up to something sneaky. They want to spice up that invisible man named Said, put him in some platform shoes, chartreuse lederhosen, a duster with pink polka dots, and a purple pimp hat with a flowing white feather. *Dy-no-mite!* You just shook that invisible dude up and pimped his ride! He's now so pimpalicious, you don't see anyone else in the crowd. Only him.

And that's the problem. In dressing up *said*, said is no longer invisible. Instead of hiding, it jumps out from the text waving its hands and distracts from the dialogue.

Unless your character likes to talk to himself (or a volleyball!), dialogue is the conversational exchange between two or more people. When these people open their mouths to talk, we see what's going on inside of them through the context of the exchange. There is a tempo to dialogue, like an intense tennis match, back and forth, *poing, poing, poing*. The last thing you want during that match is for an announcer to step onto the court and shout through a bullhorn, "See that? Bobbie Jo hit that ball with ferocity! Hear that? Billie Jean rebounded it angrily! Oh no! Bobbie Jo retorted with finality!" Please, please, please, announcer, just get off the court and let us watch the dynamic exchange. You think you are helping by dressing it up, but you are KILLING all the fun!

∾

THE DANGER OF SAIDISMS

Saidisms. These are dialogue tags that replace the word "said" with descriptive verbs and adverbs. Because the writer doesn't trust the reader to grasp the dialogue's context, the writer spices up tags with things like *Jack snorted* or *Jane uttered*. Worse, writers may even stack them, such as *Jack snorted derisively*, or *Jane uttered whimsically*. For one thing, unless you're a horse, snorting is already derisive. Don't restate the obvious. For another thing, to tag a sentence of dialogue with *Jack snorted* means Jack spoke the sentence while snorting. Try snorting as you say this line: *"You're a despicable fool!" Jack snorted.* Can't be done. Not without making a fool of oneself. Let's not make our characters look foolish, either.

This is a common dialogue faux pas for new writers. Even some successful bestselling authors can have a hard time with it. They don't trust the reader to deduce the emotions taking place between the characters as they speak. They HAVE TO TELL YOU through emotive dialogue tags. For readers, this can make them feel that they're being patronized. While the writer thinks they're helping the reader understand the emotional subtext of what's being said, they're actually alienating their readers. So much so, most readers are going to shove that book back on the shelf and never pick up a book by that author again. And if they just happen to be a first reader or editor at a publication, they'll mark it R, slap a form rejection on it, and send it back. Amateur dialogue is the mark of ... surprise! *amateurs* ... and editors are in the business of buying *professionally written stories*.

Wait! Don't throw in the towel! Writing skillful dialogue is easy to learn. And when you learn to write smart dialogue that bounces back and forth like a tennis ball in a match at Wimbledon, it's going to be an exciting game for your readers. You'll create dialogue that reveals the emotional subtext between your characters without ever needing to state it. And that, my friends, is pure magic!

~

HOW TO WRITE SMART DIALOGUE

Smart dialogue does not get bogged down by clunky saidisms. Smart dialogue is lean and mean and *flows*. Here. Let me give you a simple example of some annoying speaker attributions, more commonly called dialogue tags. Why? Because, tag. You're it. Tag, now she's it. In writing, it's like the author holding up a sign that says, *This guy is now talking.* And then another sign. *Now this gal is talking.* Easy. Now here are some badly written tag signs:

"I'm going up that hill to fetch a pail of water!" Jack shouted.

"It's a long way to the top," Jill snorted.

"I don't care. I'm doing it!" Jack retorted emphatically.

"Do you really think you can make it?" Jill queried, doubt in her eyes.

"I'll show you!" Jack exclaimed, stomping up the hill.

"Fool boy," Jill whispered quietly, "you're going to break your crown."

Ever seen dialogue like that? Ever written dialogue like that? "Ahem, ah, no, never in my life, har-har, silly amateurs." Come on, we've all written dialogue like that, once upon a time. But if we're still doing it, we need to stop. It's not professional. And professional all the way is the only way a story wins ... and sells to a respectable market. Well, if we're mere mortals. Some famous writers might get away with this, but usually, they made their name long ago in an era when alternative dialogue tags were tolerated. But no more. Not for you and me.

Go ahead. Get out your red pen. Change that annoying dialogue above into something more palatable. Line out those adverbs and replace them with said. Done? Now doesn't the dialogue read much cleaner? Let's take a look.

"I am going up that hill to fetch a pail of water!" Jack said.

"It's a long way to the top," Jill said.

"I don't care. I'm doing it!" Jack said.

"Do you really think you can make it?" Jill said.

"I'll show you!" Jack said, stomping up the hill.

"Fool boy," Jill whispered, "you're going to break your crown."

Okay, you got me. I kept the saidism *whispered*. You could say "said with a whisper" but "whispered" is simpler. Doesn't this example flow better? See how the dialogue already implies determination, doubt, stubbornness, uncertainty? Do we really need to spell out every emotional implication? No. It's overkill. And your savvy reader will think it's condescending. Also, note the placement of *said*. Said follows the person it attributes. Placing said before the name will date you. Said Jack? Old world. Jack said? Modern world, and we want to be cutting edge new world writers!

However, this piece still has a problem. Said is normally like punctuation—just like a comma or a period, said is practically invisible. But when you start stacking saids in dialogue, said creates an echo. It's no longer the invisible man because it has been repeated too much. Every time the gray man pops his head out of the crowd, he becomes visible. In this mission, he's supposed to be going commando. Or incognito. You choose.

As we look to the edited example, are there any sentences where it's obvious who is speaking? If it's obvious, do we really need to gild the lily? Not if we're lean mean professional writers! Go grab that red pen and line out any tags that are obvious. We don't need them. Done? You sure? Or do you need to use your Phone a Friend? No? Okay, here's what you should have come up with:

~

"I am going up that hill to fetch a pail of water!" Jack said.
"It's a long way to the top," Jill said.
"I don't care. I'm doing it!"
"Do you really think you can make it?"
"I'll show you!" Jack said, stomping up the hill.
"Fool boy," Jill whispered, "you're going to break your crown."

~

So there's the Super Secret. Identify who is talking with a dialogue tag. Identify who replies with another dialogue tag. After that, if it's obvious who is talking—like when there's only two people in the room and one of them has asked a question—we don't need tags anymore. We know who is replying. And you can continue on without tags until it becomes unclear who is speaking. When that happens, you tag again, and on the playful banter goes. Or the lovers' spat. That's always more fun to listen in on.

So, you saw me give out a hall pass on *whispered*. There can be rare exceptions to *said*, but don't push it. The newer the writer, the more one thinks their way is the exception. I recommend you stick like glue to said. But there is another exception I get asked about when teaching dialogue in workshops. If the dialogue ends with a question mark, can you tag with *asked* instead of *said*? After all, said represents a statement, whereas asked does represent a query. Sure. It sounds natural to tag with *asked* after a question. We'll pretend *asked* is the brother of the gray man when you need to tag a question.

ACTION BEATS

There is another secret of attributing dialogue to a character without pasting a string of *saids* onto the page. It's called beats. What's a beat? It's having a character do an action before or after the dialogue that identifies them as the speaker. Like this:

Jack teetered at the top of the peak, hoisting a pail of water. "See? Nailed it!"

Do we need to follow Jack's quoted words with "Jack said"? No. The action beat beforehand clearly shows that it's Jack that's speaking. He's already tagged. We need no more.

Want to see how this works? Here's an example in one of my

stories where I employed beats. It's the opening of "Weep No More for the Willow" published in *Deep Magic, Fall 2019*. The scene opens on the deck of a Spanish galleon sailing through Caribbean waters. While an old sailor named Sanchez dips a ladle into a water cask, Captain Capricho scowls at a storm on the horizon as he consults with his first mate, Salvador ...

~

"There it is again." Capricho pointed at a surreal column that plumed in the distance. It transformed from peaceful blue into wicked flickers of scarlet. He shielded his eyes with a hand, squinted. "Have you ever witnessed its like?"

The burly Salvador hissed when he spotted it. "No. Never."

The column continued shimmering on the horizon in bizarre shades of arterial red.

"Lightning perhaps?"

"No lightning does such things."

"Waterspout?"

"A twister glowing with blood light?"

Capricho lowered his gaze, turned to the old sailor at the water cask. "You, Sanchez? You have traveled this sea longer than any of us."

Sanchez brought the dented dipper to his lips and drained it. He wiped his mouth with the back of his hand, sighed, and squinted a rheumy eye at Capricho. "Thought you didn't want me tellin' my stories."

Capricho frowned. "I said hold your tongue because the men are twitchy from yesterday's squall. They are a superstitious lot."

"By all the saints, they should be after seeing that beast of a storm slice our flotilla apart." Sanchez waved the dipper. "You want to hear about my watch last night?"

Salvador grunted a quick "No" but Capricho held up a hand. "Does it have bearing on this phenomenon?"

"Course it does!"

"Make it brief."

∾

In this excerpt, all dialogue is tagged exclusively by beats. If you were to read on, you'd find only one 'said' in the entire scene between Capricho, Salvador, and Sanchez. The beats aren't contrived. They add motion to the dialogue and convey character and setting details without stopping for lengthy exposition. Using beats in dialogue can kill many birds with one stone, not the least of which is wasting a lot of space with repetitive he saids, she saids. A string of those sound like a kid hammering the same key on a piano over and over. *Painful.*

So you've learned the beauty of that unobtrusive verb *said*, you've weeded out saidisms that can annoy your readers, and you've broken things up by attributing dialogue through action beats. You are now a ninja warrior, your dialogue as sharp as the edge of a katana. You can glide dialogue in and out of prose like a nimble assassin. Ready to scale walls and conquer the publishing industry with your newfound skills?

Not so fast, Grasshopper.

∾

KILL "AS YOU KNOW, BOBS"

Unless you're Tom Clancy or James Michener, lengthy infodumps toss extraneous details into your story that can bog down the pacing of your plot. What's a writer to do, you *need* this information in your tale! I know, what if we get two characters to casually talk about the information our dear reader so desperately needs? I bet no one's ever thought of that before. Brilliant!

Actually, it's been done. So much so, it has its own monikers. It's called *Maid and butler dialogue,* or my personal favorite, *As you know, Bobs.*

What is an "As you know, Bob?" It's when a writer has two or more characters state information they already know for the exclusive benefit of filling in the reader with information the reader may not know. There's no way these characters would normally have such a conversation, but the writer needs to get the information into the scene, so he opens their mouths and makes his puppets do an info-dump. Here, let me present Bob and Bill, two experienced divers topside on a rescue ship:

～

"We need to get that trapped diver to the surface, Bill!"

"Well, as you know, Bob, at that depth, the air in his tank is compressed seventy-five percent by the pressure."

"Right! And as you know, Bill, he's going to have to release air all the way up or his lungs could have an air embolism, or worse, pulmonary barotrauma—the pulmonary overpressurization syndrome that can cause your lungs to burst if you fail to expel the expanding air during your ascent."

"Right you are, Bob. Plus, we also have to worry about nitrogen narcosis."

"Yes, Bill, a drowsy state induced by breathing air under higher than atmospheric pressure. Did you know the nitrogen can be forced into his joints, causing excruciating pain and even death?"

"That I did know, Bob. Good thing we have a hyperbaric chamber on our ship for just such emergencies, Bob."

"Yeah, Bill, we are two smart hombres."

"That we are, Bob."

～

Well, that was fun to write and no doubt painful to read. But it makes the point. Just because you *can* do something doesn't mean you *should*. Writers should not create unnatural conversation just because they feel the need to drop information into the story. This practice was common in the era of science fiction pulp stories. Back then, stories could get published with glaring "As you know, Bobs," often accomplished by having a knowledgeable male scientist lecture an ignorant layperson or reporter. Editors didn't call them out on it. But do this today, you will not pass Go, you will not collect a contract and two-hundred dollars.

This doesn't mean we can't be sneaky and slip a little info in through *naturally occurring conversation*. But there's the danger—if the reader doesn't feel the information would drop naturally, they're going to cry foul even if they don't know what name to call the foul by. And is all that information really necessary? A little dab will do ya. Trust your reader. I say again, *Trust your reader*. Chances are, they know more than you do.

~

FINALIS

One final note to a melody that could go on and on. When out in public, it's important to listen to people as they talk. Be an eavesdropper. A Seattle dock worker will likely speak more colorfully and forcefully than a University of Washington marine biologist. We need to be certain the words and concepts our characters speak accurately reflects their age, their education level, their social circles, the regions they come from, their lifestyles. If not, our characters' dialogues won't ring true, and readers won't believe the words coming out of their mouths.

This can be a challenge for writers because we have an affinity for words, and it can be especially hard for those that are highly educated. They can lean into diction many characters would never use, having them speak in more sophisticated sentence structures than would seem natural for, say, an unassuming Cuban fisherman that's spent his whole life on the sea. Finding good beta readers or a skilled freelance editor can do wonders in weeding out this issue.

If the writer does their job right, the reader should be able to identify who is speaking by the fullness of a character's personality flowing through the words they speak. And when a writer appreciates the simple beauty of the word *said*, annoying saidism tags will be avoided. Beats will do double duty, filling in character actions during the dialogue while silently identifying who is speaking. Clear, naturally flowing dialogue will be the result.

Editors are in the business of buying great stories that will please their readers. They know good dialogue when they see it—it's an essential marker of professionally written stories. Mastering dialogue is critical to being published and enjoying a reader fanbase that gobbles up your work. When that day comes when readers pull your book off the shelf, as they thumb through the pages or that digital sample, they won't be cursing you, they'll be praising you for a job well done. They'll reward you by pulling out their wallet. Why?

"Because you wrote smart dialogue!" Moon said.

22

KYD: KILL YOUR DARLINGS

One of my favorite lines is spoken in the movie *Amadeus*. In the beginning of the movie, the young composer Wulfgang Amadeus Mozart plays for the Holy Roman Emperor, Joseph II. Later in the movie, the Emperor meets with Mozart after a performance, commends his playing, but offers a word of counsel. He tells Mozart his work suffers from "too many notes." As Mozart balks, the Emperor says, "My dear young man, don't take it too hard. Your work is ingenious, it's quality work. And ... there are simply too many notes, that's all. Just cut a few, and it will be *perfect*."

It's a humorous moment, a monarch advising one of the greatest composers of all time that he needs to cut notes from his work to improve it. Had this been any other composer, he may well have benefited from the Emperor's words. But this was Mozart, a composer at the age of five. At six he had already performed before two imperial courts. Musical prodigies are born with a gift, and if they're as fortunate as Mozart, they have a musical family member to help guide that gift to brilliance.

Alas, few in this world are born prodigies. Most of us can become masters, but only if we hone our craft through rigorous practice— hundreds and even thousands of hours of training. Butt in chair, fingers on keyboard, doing our apprenticeship through every word we write, every story we create. If we are fortunate, we will stumble across a mentor, or have the wisdom to seek one out. Hopefully, a qualified mentor that has already put in their thousands of hours, their million words and beyond, with solid proof that they have mastery of their craft. And if we're in the early stages of our writing, it's a good bet that mentor will echo those words of the Emperor. "You have too many notes. Cut some words out, and it will be *perfect*."

And because we are not Mozart, we should take those words to heart.

$$\sim$$

TOO MANY NOTES

My friend, the late Ken Rand, wrote a book called *The 10% Solution*. The premise? Any story could benefit by cutting out ten percent (especially degree adverbs like highly, slightly, quickly, almost, and mostly, although *mostly* can be useful if you're dead, because *mostly* dead means *slightly* alive). Trimming excess makes sense. We all know the saying, "Less is more." Or take my favorite line from Shakespeare's *Hamlet*: "Brevity is the soul of wit." The simpler you can explain something, the easier it is for others to understand.

With story writing, it is no different. Clear tales, clearly written, soar. Bulky tales, densely written, sink. They are hard on the eye, they are hard on the mind, and they are hard to read. Instead of a trimmed path through the plot, the reader must wade through dense undergrowth, a forest of words, hacking their own way through the jungle with their machetes, always wondering where the path lies, and where the trail (if there even is one) is leading them.

Most beginning writers suffer from too many notes. They stuff the melodies of their stories with lyrical words, overblown descriptions, complex scenes, massive infodumps, awkward flashbacks, and tedious movement mechanics. I know. Like all new writers, I once did the same, and even after decades of work, I still do careful pruning. You fall in love with your play on words and beautiful descriptions and the wonderful histories and your mysterious world and soon, you lose track of the fact that you're supposed to be *telling a story*.

I have taught, coached, and edited many aspiring writers. In the beginning, the majority believed they were telling a tight story, and cannot understand why editors and contest judges failed to buy their stories or failed to award them prizes for their work. To cope with the problem, a few take on the mantle of the misunderstood artist. Surely their writing is so brilliant, so beyond the drivel they see being published, the editors must be blind, not ready for their genius. At least *they* are creating art, and not selling out to the unenlightened masses and commercialism.

Sadly, I cannot help those writers. They have built up such a fortress of deception to explain why their work is not selling, I can't get past the front gate. And if I try, I'm told my mother was a hamster, and my father smelt of elderberries. Who likes to be told *that*?

But you're not like that. You're here to learn. You're humble and realize there's always more to be learned, *especially* when we're new at something. You wisely recognize that those who study hard and work hard get ahead. You don't expect good things to drop in your lap without working for them.

Good. You, I can help.

~

THE PROBLEM

Many hopeful writers do not understand the value of economy of words. They love writing and they view every word they write as sacred, because it came from the divine mystery of the creative process within them. Every phrase is a thing of wonder, every story is their beautiful, perfect baby.

To start crafting professional stories that sell—which means they'll get published and be *read*—we have to get past this stage and start viewing our stories as a product. "What?" some may say. "How dare you! I'm not creating a commercial product, I'm creating art!"

But don't we say *the product* of our imagination? We need to recognize that when we're starting out, we're in the apprentice stage, not the craftsman or the master stage. What we turn from our lathes at first will most likely be wonky. What we chisel from stone will most likely not be Michelangelo's David. That first novel we write will most likely not be *The Grapes of Wrath*.

The good news? That wasn't Steinbeck's first novel, either. In fact, his first three novels flopped, no doubt because he was still learning his craft. But Steinbeck stayed the course and actually *wrote* the Great American Novel. You have the potential to do that, too. But first, you must learn to *Kill Your Darlings*.

∼

KYD: KILL YOUR DARLINGS!

New writers try to stuff an oak tree into the space of a bonsai. Instead of *The 10% Solution*, they need *The 30% Solution*, *The 40% Solution*, some even *The 50% Solution*. They can't help themselves because they can't see the issues yet. Their writing runs hither and thither, often including anything that comes to mind. Detailed wake-up scenes, meaningless backstory, endless information on how their science or magic works, the research they did on the armadillo girdled lizard (they're pretty cool!)—it all goes on the page, for page after page. It's a plot killer, because readers don't want to know every minute detail about your world and its history. They came to be taken on a journey, and they expect you to *get to the point and tell them a story*.

So what are some of these writer darlings, and how can you and I terminate them? Knowledge is power! Let's pinpoint a few.

∼

1 - DRIVING TO THE STORY

I've covered this topic in *The Illustrated Super Secrets of Writing, Vol. 1*, in the article "How Driving to the Story Creates Accidents." But it's such a common issue in the works of beginning writers, it should be mentioned here. DON'T drive to the story, which is writer-speak for cutting that opening wakeup scene, the brushing of the teeth, the getting dressed, that look in the full-length mirror so you can describe your character from top to bottom. I know you think it's needed. It's not. Trust me on this! Start your story just before the inciting incident, not when the alarm clock goes off in the morning.

∿

2 - PURPLE PROSE

But Moon, purple is my favorite color! Too bad. What's purple prose? Overblown, extravagant descriptions that become so ornate, the natural flow of the narrative stops. They're like a band playing your favorite melody, and suddenly all the musicians stop harmonizing because the drummer decides it's time for him to show off with a wild drum solo. If you have a vocabulary that can rival the Oxford Dictionary, congratulations on your education, reading, and retention. But the most powerful tales are clear tales, clearly told. Cut excess wordage that is full of itself. There can be places in scenes where it *might* be fitting to describe the bowed iridescent refraction of the sun's piercing beams striking water droplets within the brooding atmosphere casting a nimbus across the horizon, but if the word *rainbow* will suffice, why not use it?

∿

3 - INFODUMPS

The story is hopping along, the game is afoot, and just when you're getting into the plot and your own world slips away, the author hits the breaks and rains down like the God of Thunder an infomercial upon you. Ever had that happen? We all have, and it's not fun.

Apparently, the author thinks it is, because studying the armadillo girdled lizard has been his lifelong passion, and he's finally gotten to the point in his story where one appears, and by God, he's going to share with you everything he knows on the subject, because armadillo girdled lizards are fascinating! And they are, but it's not the time for a ten-page treatise on armadillo girdled lizards when we're reading a novel about a ship captain held for ransom off the coast of South Africa! Now if the captain gets an idea about how to defend himself by watching this unique lizard, a little detail on the creature would be appropriate. Just remember: the more information you drop in that's not directly related to your plot, the more your story wanders off course. Be judicious with the details you share, and be sure they are *essential*.

∽

4 · BACKSTORY/ FLASHBACKS

Just like us, our characters come with a history, often a troubled history. It's what makes them appear real—creating the wounds in their past that give them character flaws to overcome. Backstory is a principal reason characters seem human instead of flat cardboard cutouts. When the world we design has history and milieu, it enhances the realism, creating a solid foundation in our reader's mind because we took the time to work out the details. Backstory is important, even if it's only hinted at. It gives our world and characters *depth*.

But how much backstory should we drop in? This is where hopeful writers often err. They don't trust their readers. Those writers feel they must tell readers everything so they *understand*. The truth is, readers are smart. This story isn't their first rodeo. You take them into the world of *The Lord of the Rings* and show them the immense Arganoth sentinels—statues of Isuldur and Anárion carved in the cliffs along each side of the river Anduin—and they'll get the point. Gondor was once a mighty nation of great power, but with every surrounding edifice crumbling in ruins, the nation must be in great decline. We get it, and we thank Tolkien for not putting the brakes on at that breathtaking point to do an infodump of all the history he had written on Gondor and the Númenor. Instead, he hinted at the past, kept his plot rolling, and the poignant breaking of the Fellowship was not eclipsed by unnecessary information.

Flashbacks can be dangerous darlings as well. Plots become page-turners because the story has tension and it's moving *forward* at a goodly pace. Flashbacks mean the story is looking *backward*, and that always slows the story down because it's a reverse in the timeline. Like all things, flashbacks are a tool in the toolbox, but be careful of their use and how long you keep a reader in the past ... especially in short stories.

And please, please, be clear in the transitions from present to past, and then the return to the present. Clunky flashbacks can make you think you're still in the present when you're not. It's so simple to say, "Kathy remembered that day, four years ago, when the boating accident had happened. The lake had been flat calm, not a sign in the sky of the storm brooding beyond the horizon."

But just as one must downshift gears and take the reader into the past, one must also upshift by doing a clear transition back to the present. Readers need indicators in the text that the story has returned to the current timeline, the point before the flashback occurred. If the transition isn't clear, the writer will create a frustrating experience for the reader, because they're left to puzzle out where they're at in the stream of time, and if they're back to the present now. How easy to say, "Kathy raked back her hair, glanced up at the sky. How she wished she could forget that day, but here she was, on another boat, heading across the same lake."

~

5 - CHARACTER MOVEMENT MECHANICS

I like to call this one unnecessary puppetry. It's not really a darling, it's the result of inexperience, but it must be killed regardless. Inexperienced writers move their characters around their scenes like jerking puppets. Often new puppets will appear on the stage from nowhere, and you're left wondering, "Where did that character come from? I wasn't told anyone else was in the living room. Is the *Enterprise's* transporter beaming people into this scene?"

A larger problem often occurs in the mechanics of moving a character through a scene. The writer supplies layers upon layers of unnecessary detail as they work out on the page how their astronaut is going to enter their rocket's capsule, or how their wizard will perform the movements associated with their spell, or even how someone will enter their own house!

Here's a *slightly* exaggerated example of what I often see when editing stories from new writers:

Jonas walked up to the door of his three-bedroom rambler. He reached into his pocket and pulled out his key chain. He selected the right key for the door. He inserted it into the lock. He turned it to the left. Hearing the click, he turned it back to the vertical position and pulled it out and put the keychain in his pocket. Turning the brass handle with his right hand, he pushed open the door inward. Fully open, he stepped past the threshold and into the room. He turned around and with the palm of his left hand gently pushed the door until it closed.

If you've done this, don't feel bad. We all started out doing things like this. But is there an easier way to say that paragraph above with less words? How about *Jonas entered his house?* We use such shorthand in our everyday lives. Why not in our stories? Get to the point. Kill those tedious descriptions with smarter coding. Your readers will thank you.

So will editors considering your story for purchase and publication.

~

PRACTICE MAKES PERFECT

There are many other ways to streamline a story. Instead of saying a character started to do an action, be decisive, just have them *do* the action. And why say "he ran quickly" when you could say "he raced"? Some writers believe melodrama adds tension, but continually dropping similes and metaphors like "Her heart pumped like a fire engine at a five-alarm fire!" and "Her blood burned hot as ore in a blacksmith's fully stoked forge!" actually *diminishes* tension.

Sometimes you'll discover entire scenes can be cut, just like you see in the outtakes from your favorite movies. Many a movie director will tell you that the difference between a box office blockbuster and a box office bust is what is left on the cutting room floor. No matter how much you love your scenes or chapters, anything that does not contribute directly to your plot must go.

Whether William Faulkner, Anton Chekhov, or Arthur Quiller-Couch said it first, Stephen King phrased it best. Here it is, from his book, *On Writing*: "Kill your darlings, kill your darlings, even when it breaks your egocentric little scribbler's heart, kill your darlings."

We need to be ruthless with our work—every word we write is not sacred. Get your words on the page, but be sure to go back in and give them a cold hard stare, knife in hand. Writing flash fiction can really help, because it trains one to write with an economy of words, trimming the fat.

I teach a masterclass on KYD, which is my flash fiction training system to teach economy of words. I developed this system to help me win a year-long flash fiction contest that had around 30,000 entries. Two of my stories placed in the top ten, one winning the grand prize. When I spotted this issue of bloated prose by most aspiring writers in my workshops, I taught them my exercise. The more they practiced it, the clearer their stories became. Many went from unpublished writers to published writers to winning major contests and launching professional careers in record time.

The majority said practicing my KYD exercise taught them how to write tighter stories, creating a shortcut on their path to being published.

I wasn't surprised. The KYD exercise transformed my writing. I knew it would do so for them—that's why I had them drilling in it. The more you practice clear, concise writing, the more it will flow that way from your mind onto the page. Practice the skills regularly, and your first drafts become final drafts. You won't need to do heavy editing, because you trained in lean writing, becoming a lean writing machine.

If you work hard to kill your darlings, one day when the Emperor waves his hand and tells you, "There are simply too many notes, just cut a few and it will be perfect," you can smile and confidently say, "There are just as many notes as I require, sire, neither more, nor less."

For then *you* will be the maestro. *Rock on!*

23

TRUST YOUR READER

M y father loved horses, but he loved good deals even more. When someone had a horse with issues, he'd buy the horse on the cheap, and then tell me to train it and make it rideable.

I was a scrawny teenager then. I had to pit my 135 pounds soaking wet against an easily spooked beast weighing a thousand pounds or more. These horses would go wild at any loud sound, or if you lifted your hand too fast, or if a horsefly bit them. There was a black Morgan gelding I had lunged and worked with for a week that I thought I had figured out. So, I took him out on a ride with friends feeling pretty proud of myself.

When we turned back home I discovered his real issue and why Dad had gotten him so cheap. Barn sour. Worst I'd ever seen. Most horses like the comfort of the barn, but some go crazy to get back to it. This one galloped flat out like he was at the Kentucky Derby, and no matter how much I shouted whoa or pulled those reins, he wouldn't let up. I finally cranked the right rein around the saddle horn and had his head winched in so far his neck was bent to where I could stare him in the eye, and he in mine. He still galloped flat out as if he could see the path ahead.

I couldn't stop him. I figured it might be better for both of us if I gave him his head so he could at least see where he was going—there were several fences we needed to navigate around. Thankfully, I made it back alive and in the saddle with only a bruised leg where he slammed into a fence post as he turned into the barn. Some of those turns were at such high speeds they should have thrown me, but I never let go.

That horse was Charlie. I gave him a new name that day. From then on, he was Charlie Horse, the most dangerous horse I've ever ridden and trained. He wasn't as big as Dad's Quarter Horse, but he had a fire in him and couldn't stand to be in second place when we raced with friends—I just had to be sure that race always pointed *away* from the direction of the barn.

Dad gave him to me and forbid anyone else from riding Charlie Horse. You could only ride him if you understood his triggers, and you could only know those triggers if you had ridden him and had a deep understanding of his issues. He could have injured or killed someone else.

Why share a bit of my horse history with you? Because there's a couple of Super Secrets here you should know.

~

TRUST YOUR READER

Ever had someone puff up their chest and explain something to you that you already knew? It usually starts with a preamble: "Well, actually, it's not like that, it's like this." Perhaps they talked down to you because they believed you weren't quite as knowledgeable as they were on the subject. Worse, as they continued their lecture, it may have become obvious they believed you knew nothing on the subject. As it continued, you might have bristled—the tone of the conversation made you feel like they were calling you ignorant.

If a woman knows cars and a car salesman tries to pull the wool over her eyes, she's likely to tell him off. If a mother gets lectured about childbirth by a single man because the guy read a book on it, she's probably going to give him a piece of her mind. No one enjoys being told how things work by someone that has never experienced what we have experienced. Nor do we like being talked down to. We might put up with false assumptions for a little bit, but if the lecture continues on, we're likely going to speak up and set matters straight.

Women call this mansplaining, or a funnier term, correctile dysfunction. It's patronizing, even condescending. When women do something similar to men, men call it womansplaining or femsplaining. In either case, one party is saying to the other party that they have superior knowledge of a subject, and that the one of the opposite sex that they're explaining it to has inferior knowledge. They presume they know more, and presumptuousness is not a becoming look. Especially if you have a PhD in childbirth by right of bringing seven children into this world, and the single man does not.

Writers can unknowingly do the same thing. They may assume their readers know nothing of the subject they are writing about, and so they go into great detail *writersplaining* to their readers. (I do believe I just coined a new word.) Perhaps they are writing a diver story, and although they've never been on a dive, they've just done all the research, and they're going to work all that information into their novel for your benefit.

This often drops in the form of infodumps (or worse, What About Bobs) because the writer believes you don't know this information and they need to fill you in. Perhaps you do need the information, perhaps you don't, but nobody likes to be lectured as if they're an ignoramus. Worse, the writer could be giving all these textbook details to someone like me, that was PADI certified on the island of Cozumel, that's been on shark dives in the Bahamas, cavern dives in the Yucatan, wreck dives in the British Virgin Islands, and spearfishing with buddies miles off the California and Oregon coast. The more the writer drops in their textbook knowledge, the more likely I'll recognize they've never been diving in their life. It won't take long for me to get annoyed by the *writersplaining*, because I'm going to feel talked down to. Why?

Because the writer failed to recognize that they'll have readers that know more about their subject than they do.

I opened with a snippet of my horse history, and here's the reason.

If you're writing a Western or a weird Western or an epic fantasy with knights on horses or a Montana romance with lots of riding and you've never been on a horse, I'm going to spot you as a greenhorn from a mile off. Can't be helped. Riders know other riders, just as sure as they can recognize someone trying to get up in the saddle for the first time. No amount of book research will be able to hide inexperience. There are telltales that will give you away. Sorry.

This will always be the case. There's always a bigger fish. There's always someone that knows more than we do. We should assume this, even if we do have expert knowledge on a subject. Likewise, there will be readers that have little to no knowledge on that subject, and they will need some information from the writer to understand important plot points. Damned if you do, damned if you don't. What's a writer to do?

You could just write what you know. Some writers advise that, and while you'll have all those nifty inside details that prove you have authentic knowledge, you'll also be limited as to what you can write. There's a big world out there—none of us can experience it all. And there are historical events we've never lived through, and future events and cultures and scientific advancements that we can imagine but that haven't yet occurred. At the time of this writing, no one has been to Mars. That didn't stop Edgar Rice Burroughs and Ray Bradbury and Andy Weir from writing stories about people living on it.

But how do we keep it *real*?

Solid research from reliable sources is a great start. Many experts share their knowledge in books and articles, and we can absorb much by doing a deep dive on a subject—the trick will be in remembering most of that research is for our benefit, not the reader. It doesn't go on the page.

But there is a problem with book knowledge and trying to work from other people's expertise and experience instead of our own. It's never going to ring as authentic as actually having experienced the thing ourselves. Reading about sailboats is quite different from actually sailing one in a storm. Reading about horses and horseback riding is quite different from getting on one yourself. And reading a dive manual to write about a cavern dive is quite different from doing one in the Yucatan and watching your buddy vanish like they turned on a cloaking device as they entered the halocline.

Solution? Get out more and experience life. Soak up all those fascinating real-life details that can make our stories come to life. If we're going to write tall ship stories, perhaps we could go to some ship festivals, book a day trip on one, or even take sailing lessons. If we're going to set a story in the San Juan Islands, how about visiting them and getting a feel for island life? Writing a Western set in the time period of, oh, I don't know, maybe 1883? We can't go back in time, but how about visiting a museum in the area we're writing about, or taking some riding lessons so we don't sound so *green*?

"But, Moon," someone might say, "I live in New York City and don't have the time nor the money to travel to Montana. And how can I take riding lessons—I've never even seen a stable in Manhattan." Fair point. So just wing it. Maybe no one will notice. Or … you could phone a friend. You may not be a horseback rider, but maybe you have a friend that is. They could look over the horsey parts in your book and tell you if they sound authentic, and how to fix them if they don't.

Don't have a friend that has real-life experience on the subject you need? How about joining an Internet group that has experts on the subject and ask them for help? People like talking about themselves and what they do, and if you tell them you're writing a story, screenplay, or book on their subject of expertise? Many are happy to oblige.

Years ago, I emailed a surgeon in the UK, told him I was writing a story for *Star Trek*, and would he be so kind as to verify that I had used the proper terminology when detailing a critical blow to the spine? He wrote back and confirmed I was correct, gave me technical reasons as to why (which I didn't use but I appreciated his expertise), and he invited me to contact him with any future medical questions I had. That story, "Seventh Heaven," was a winner in Paramount's *Star Trek: Strange New Worlds II* anthology contest. A borg love story. What could be sweeter? And I had the comfort of knowing my anatomical statement wouldn't cause a kerfuffle with any doctors that read my story.

But here's a simpler way to keep from annoying readers. Don't pretend to be an expert on something you are not. Instead, trust your reader. Even if a reader may have zero knowledge about a subject, they are smart. They can put two and two together. They know how to connect the dots. In addition to a wealth of life experience, they are widely read. They're readers! They'll appreciate it if you show them respect and don't talk down to them by lecturing them via the page on all that research you just did. It's likely they don't need it.

And if they do? Keep it brief. Trust your reader.

You can also bypass an area where you lack knowledge by getting out of that area as fast as you can so you don't expose yourself. Don't know horses? *They mounted up and headed for the village* works nicely. Dropping in all that whinnying and snorting and nickering on the ride can expose you, and if you're already in your nickers, you can get caught with your pants down. Don't know sailing? Make your adventurers landlubbers, and when the captain says a sail is footloose, make them dance like Kevin Bacon.

But seriously, folks, the point is, keep it brief. Lack of experience is hard to catch if we don't dally in areas we know little to nothing about.

~

THE STORY DOESN'T HAPPEN ON THE PAGE

Where does the story occur? When I was a newer writer, I believed the story occurred on the page. I felt I had to describe people and objects and scenes in detail for readers to *see* my imaginative world. It was my vision, after all. I wanted them to see *exactly* what was in my head, because the vision in my head was beautiful.

And then someone shared one of their own Secrets, a concept I had never considered before. This was decades ago, and I believe science fiction writer Algis Budrys was the instructor that shared it with me. It was one of those light bulb moments; it transformed how I wrote stories. I should assume you know this Secret after what I've just written in this chapter. But what if you don't? Then I need to share this, because it was a monumental thought for me, and it may become a monumental concept for you.

The story does not occur on the page.

It happens in the reader's head.

"What?" someone will say. "I have this visionary concept that I took great pains to carefully transcribe onto the page. I'm seeking a wise publisher to see its lofty merit so they can pay me good money for those pages, and you're trying to tell me my story is *not* on the page?"

That's exactly what I'm saying. Here, let me show you:

Clown riding around a circus stage.

When you read the word clown, what came to mind? Take a moment and draw a picture of what a clown looks like in your mind, riding around on a stage. Got it? Great.

As I wrote that phrase, I saw a clown with a red rubber ball nose, an obnoxious red wig, white-faced with an exaggerated red face-paint smile, a white ruffled collar, a white jump suit with pink polka dots, enormous black hobo shoes, and he's riding a giant tricycle with a brass bicycle horn that goes *oogah, oogah* whenever he squeezes it. He's still squeezing it. *Oogah, oogah, oogah.* It's getting quite annoying. Someone turn off that clown!

But what picture came to *your* mind when you read the word *clown*? Your clown might have had a sad face, even a scary face. *He* might have been *she*, and she had a bowler hat on instead of the wild wig. She could have been riding a little scooter around the main stage, a monkey in a policeman's suit chasing her with a billy club. I don't know, it's your clown that got in trouble with the monkey police. You bail her out.

Well, there it is. My experiences bring up what I think a clown riding around on a stage looks like, your experiences bring up what you think a clown riding around on a stage looks like. The code word *clown*, written down on the page, won't bring up the same clown that's in my head for yours. Your clown will be different. That's because you draw from *your own memories and experiences* to visualize what that word means. I can't put my brain into yours. All I can do is use my coding on the page to ignite a vision in your mind from your own personal experience that I hope will be close enough.

But what if *clown* doesn't make you envision my happy clown? What if you see an evil clown, perhaps like the one on the *It* movie posters. *Brrrr.* This is a happy story; I don't want you to envision an evil clown! I'll have to do better, give you more definitive coding.

Happy smiling clown.

Much better. Now you see—*wait!* Your clown is riding a minibike, my clown is riding a giant tricycle. This won't do—that bicycle horn is critical in the climax of my story! I'll have to make my coding more specific.

Happy smiling clown riding a giant tricycle around a circus stage, honking his bicycle horn.

There! Now you know the clown of my story is happy, he's riding a giant tricycle, he's in a circus, he's honking a horn, and the pronoun *his* means that he is male. You've now gotten enough description— what I call coding—to have my code on the page run like a program, generating the proper images in your mind.

But wait! My clown has an outlandish red wig on, your clown is wearing a bowler hat. And my bicycle horn is brass, and I see you've made yours shiny chrome! We don't have the same vision, even after I made my coding more specific. Why aren't you seeing the phrase the way I've written it down on the page?

Because words have meaning, but we supply the images from our own life experiences that we tag those words to in order to define them. No matter how much detail I add to my clown on the tricycle, my clown is going to look different than your clown. The scene is happening in your head, not on the page. I can force the issue, adding detail after detail so YOU SEE MY EXACT CLOWN, but the more I do that, the slower the scene gets, and the more annoyed you're going to be.

Because I'm not trusting you, my dear reader.

My job as a writer is to give you just enough coding on the page to activate an approximation of what I'd like you to envision. No more, no less. You're going to fill in the blanks, and truthfully, that's part of the fun. If I can ignite your mind to bring up your own wondrous imagery while still guiding you down the path of my tale without losing you, we both win. I don't have to tell you to get rid of that bowler hat, or to put some pink polka dots on your clown. It's not critical to my plot. I'm going to trust that you can draw up your own good version of a clown for the sake of my story. But he does need to be male for this story, and he does need that horn.

I'll let you color in the rest.

Trust your reader. Remember that the story happens in their head, not on the page. Don't force them to see your exact vision, because it won't be exact, no matter how much information you give them. Give readers enough information to get the gist of the picture, the essential elements, and move on. They'll fill in the rest.

Try to get real-life experience, but if you can't, do your research. Get those important details in the coding on the page without dropping Wikipedia infodumps. No *writersplaining*. Respect your readers' good judgment, and they'll respect yours.

The story happens in their heads, and they've got good ones.

24

YOU HAVE FIVE SENSES—WHY AREN'T THEY ON THE PAGE?

After teaching my Super Secrets of Writing masterclasses at a convention this year, I returned home with a cold. The COVID-19 pandemic had mainly run its course through the population and I'd been vaccinated three times for all the latest variants. I have damaged lungs from whooping cough and with the crowds at conventions, all someone sick needs to do is look at me and I come down with con crud. I'm used to it. Par for the course. And with this particular con crud, the flu seemed milder than those prior that had made me cough up a lung.

I opened an excellent brand of strawberry Greek yogurt for breakfast. Yeah, all the fat, the five percent stuff—I'm all about rich flavor and can't stand skimmed down versions of *anything*. (You'll thank me if you ever come to our home and enjoy one of my special recipes, like *Moon's Seafood Chowder*.) I scooped out a helping, my mouth watering as I anticipated the tartness of the yogurt playing against the sweetness of strawberry. I don't even mind crunching down on those little seeds because it means real strawberries are in the mix. I placed that creamy goodness into my mouth and let it melt across my palette, awaiting the snap, crackle, and pop of contrasting flavors.

No sizzle. Not even fizzle. I was eating glue, but even glue has flavor (hey, we all find that out in kindergarten). My delicious blend of sweet and tart yogurt tasted like a viscous blob of nothingness, a mass of flavorless goo. I took another bite. Nothing registered, just gooey texture. What? Had I mistakenly purchased plain yogurt? Because I could easily fix that with strawberry jam. I checked the label. Nope. I bought strawberry yogurt, all right.

Then it dawned on me.

Duh. I had COVID-19.

A test kit confirmed it, and I isolated. It took several weeks for my sense of taste to return (whew, for some it never does), and even longer for my lungs and brain fog to clear. Recovery delayed the timeline on this book's production. But it did give me a good talking point for this chapter. Sometimes there are silver linings in those black clouds.

We have five sensory modalities. They enrich our lives. Take any of them away, and the sensory experiences of our world that are a major part of our human experience flattens. We experience a multi-dimensional world because of these sensory inputs. Each stacks on its own unique enhancements, enriching even the simplest of items. Like yogurt—even the sour smack to our tastebuds of plain yogurt is preferable to tasteless paste.

The same is true in writing. If our prose only codes up visual images in our readers' minds, we lose dimension to our imagined world, and will cheat our readers of a richer sensory experience. We have five sparkling senses: taste, touch, smell, hearing, and sight. Some even say a sixth sense or an x sense—an inexplicable perception of realities beyond our natural awareness. I can't deny that I have personally sensed unseen things and took immediate action that I know saved my life and my wife's. I'll bet many of you have experienced sensory perceptions beyond the norm as well.

And yet, with all this richness that can add beautiful depth to our prose, many writers—especially emerging writers—fixate on coding strictly visual cues in their writing. They forget that to build a world that might come close to mirroring our own, they'll create a less colorful tapestry utilizing only one sensory thread, when they could be weaving with four more modalities that will make an imagined world feel complete.

When readers say, "I love that author's world. It feels so real, like I'm right there," you can bet the writer placed vivid sensory cues into their coding on the page. They know the power of giving their readers a full sensory experience. That's because they're tapping into the entire array of sensory inputs stored in the reader's noggin over the course of their life. These memories are powerful—they are how we define our world, how we remember important life moments, and how we compare and categorize new experiences against the old. The more skilled we become at igniting a full array of sensory memories in our reader through our coding, the richer the reading experience becomes, the richer our created world becomes.

Vivid sensory details don't simply enchant readers. They entrance them. They ignite their minds within our creative vision by unlocking all those magical sensory drawers filed away in their neural pathways. Our coding is the key to those neural drawers. Unlocked, sensory memory mists spill out in the reader's mind, enwrapping them in the spell of our tale. True masters can make a reader's real world bleed away, transporting them across reality's threshold and into the illusory reality of the dream world.

Through immersive writing, writers' careers have been made by creating worlds so real and vivid, readers never want to leave them. They long to remain in those worlds, experiencing regret when they see the book ending, and they'll eagerly anticipate the next book in the series so they can dive back into those waters and float along in the author's vibrant current.

Immersive writing is refreshing. Immersive writing is potent. Immersive writing is addictive. The more immersive our writing becomes, the more we build our fanbase, because our readers will crave the unique flavor and immersive experience that only we can produce. Frank Herbert did it with *Dune*. J.R.R. Tolkien did it with *The Lord of the Rings*. Margaret Mitchell did it with *Gone With the Wind*.

We can do it, too.

~

WEAVING WITH THE FULL SENSORY ARRAY

There are many aspects to immersive writing. I define immersive writing as engaging the reader's mind *and emotions* so completely, they cross the threshold from their reality and enter the imagined world we've coded on the page for them to experience. I've already given you many of the ingredients of immersive writing in this book: writing in first person or third person *intimate* POV; creating a flawed but interesting protagonist with likeable qualities the reader can quickly attach to; revealing the hero's Heart's Desire and then crushing it with a powerful opposing force; building escalating tension through the protagonist's attempts to push back at the opposition; killing infodumps, unnecessary backstory, and purple prose that make the story drag like a snail; and coming up with fresh takes and big ideas and interesting twists that will fully engage the reader's mind.

What I haven't told you yet is that a major aspect of immersive writing is weaving a full array of sensory details consistently throughout your work. Do you want your world to become multidimensional to the reader? You have to go beyond visual storytelling, which is merely describing scenes and interactions within them. Unless your protagonist is deaf, they're going to hear sounds in that scene, like songbirds singing or children squealing as they play outside. Unless they've lost all sense of touch, they're going to feel the cool sweating glass when they pick up a Scotch on the rocks. Does your detective buy a hotdog from a street vendor in New York? You have a wealth of flavors you could spark up in your reader's mind depending on the condiments chosen.

And how about smells? The human olfactory system can detect around 10,000 distinct scents. That Scotch in the glass? It's not just going to go down with a bite. The olfactory receptors will detect notes of fruits or burnt sugar or peat smoke or even tobacco or seaweed, depending on the distiller, whether the barley was smoked, the type of casks it was aged in, even where it was stored. But please, if it's a nice single malt whisky, don't add ice. Have your aficionado take it neat, or better, with a little distilled water both to curb the concentrated alcohol burn to the nostrils and to release the complex aromatics.

Ever open a bottle of cheap champagne or sparkling wine? Pop the plastic cork, pour it in the glass, and the bubbles rush up like a mushroom cloud and quickly fizzle out. You're left with glorified sugar water. But fine champagne? Pop the real cork, pour it in the glass, and watch tiny bubbles rise continuously through this nectar of grapes, tickling your palette and even your nose with notes of vanilla, pear, apple, or citrus, until the last sparkling sip twirls its final ballet across your tongue.

Like great champagne, we want our sensory details to rise continuously through our prose and release bubbles of delightful thought and emotion in our readers. Consistent bubbles of evocative sensations throughout our tale create a sparkling experience all the way to the finish. But if those bubbles fizzle out like cheap champagne or are not there at all, the story becomes flat and lifeless.

Many manuscripts I edit suffer from this flatness, something I call single sensory weaving. It's all visual, the story coded primarily in the sensation of sight alone. Here's an example of single sensory weaving with the sense of sight.

Sally saw the motorcycle coming toward her. She jumped into the bushes and looked out. She saw the killer drive by. Good. He hadn't seen her.

The description holds drama—looks like a killer is hunting Sally, and we're probably glad the killer didn't see her. But what's missing? All those sensory details that could enrich this moment and make it come alive. So let's add specific sensations of sight and sound and see if we can turn up the heat.

Sally heard a rumble like an approaching thunderstorm and looked up the busy street. The biker on the Harley chopper in a German half-helmet halted at the intersection's stoplight and revved the engine. The killer! Had he spotted her? She crouched behind bushes lining the sidewalk as the light turned green. The biker rolled by, the Harley going pop-pop-pop *as he continued down the street. Thank God. He hadn't seen her.*

There, we got in some motorcycle sounds that alerted Sally to the man hunting her so that she could hide before he got there. And by stating it was a Harley, many readers will hear the Harley's distinct rumble as it idles at that intersection. More realism! Can we layer in taste and smells? Taste is one of the hardest sensory details to get into scenes, but adds another layer of depth to our prose when we can judiciously work it in. Let's see if we can do so without bogging the scene down.

Sally stepped out of the coffee shop, glad for the warmth in her hands as she took a cautious sip of her triple-shot mocha. She had added so much cream it tasted more like hot chocolate than coffee—just the way she liked it.

She lifted the cup to take another sip when a rumble like a thunderstorm sounded up the street. A biker on a Harley chopper in a German half-helmet halted at the intersection's stoplight and revved the engine. The killer! Had he spotted her? She crouched behind bushes lining the sidewalk as the light turned green. The biker rolled by, the Harley going pop-pop-pop *as he continued down the road, trailing a cloud of oily blue smoke that stung her nostrils when she finally took a breath.*

Thank God. He hadn't seen her.

There you go. Sight, touch, taste, sound, scent. All five senses worked into a short scene. Isn't the prose more evocative than the first clipped description based solely on sight? The added sensory details not only enhance the scene, they add depth to Sally's character and deepen her fear.

Does this mean you should have your characters running around licking and sniffing everything in sight? No, that would be a dog. Like everything in life, perfection is in the balance. Not too much, not too little. Just enough to add depth, not so much that it bogs your story down.

I don't advocate writing systems designed to layer in sensory texture through line-by-line formulas. If you're following a pattern, it's like doing a paint-by-number painting—the writing can appear stiff and manufactured, even as you're attempting to achieve a more natural feel to your world. Writing should be organic—emotive writing flows effortlessly while weaving in sensory details. But there's nothing wrong with going back after we've finished a section and making sure we've woven in enough sensory details to add that richness to our prose. If we discover the scene is primarily visuals and we can't count off any inputs of sound, scent, taste, and touch, we're painting from an extremely limited palette. Our stories will be less likely to stir our readers' imaginations, let alone immerse them in our world so they forget about theirs. Their world has all of these sensations, and we're competing against it for their attention. If ours is flat, we will lose.

We have five sensory modalities. They enrich the fullness of our lives. They brand our memories with vivid highlights. When thoughtfully woven into our prose, they'll enrich our tales and make them come alive. They'll be tasty delights, not bland globs of paste.

Care for some strawberry yogurt?

25

MAKE IT WORK!

We've now discussed a solid set of writing craft elements that make stories work. Executing them with finesse takes practice, for which there is no substitute—practice makes perfect. Practice creates skill over time, but focused *smart* practice will reduce the time to become skilled. This is why I created the Super Secrets of Writing—to help you see what to focus your efforts on so that you're not blindly striking the air, but are instead aiming for specific targets. Smart, focused practice makes perfect *faster*.

There are four final Super Secrets in this section I must share with you. I saved the most important for last. These will determine whether you become a writer or not. Ready? Are you taking notes? Good. Put these on a sticky note or card and tape them to your monitor so you don't forget them.

1. **You must finish what you write.**
2. **You must finish what you write.**
3. **You must finish what you write.**

This principle goes back to the first story ever told. A story (or a screenplay) has a beginning, a middle, *and an end*. A story is not the idea. A story is not the cool character. A story is not the dazzling fight scene. A story is not the beginning. A story is not the middle. A story is not the beginning and the middle. A story is the beginning, the middle, and the end. It's not complete without finishing all three components.

Beginning. Middle. End. To get there, quit telling your friends and family and game store clerk about the cool story you are going to write. Talking about your idea to everyone uses up all the steam you could have used to write your story. Don't be that person. Just do it! Like anything that is challenging in this world, the more you do it, the easier it gets. But it will never get easier if you don't …

Do. The. Thing.

You must finish what you write. You cannot sell an unfinished story or novel. Okay, some Big-Name authors can, and Big-Name screenwriters can, too. But that's because they're not just selling a proposal or a treatment, they're selling on their reputation that they finish what they write and deliver quality product. They built that reputation by delivering the goods time and time again to their publishers and producers.

New writers have no such reputation. Truth is, most aspiring writers never finish the stories they start. They discover—*surprise!*—reading is easy, writing is hard. So, when you finish what you write, you cross an important milestone in your writer's journey. You prove you can do it; you can finish a story. Not only are you ahead of the hopeful writer pack, you now have a finished product you can send to market, or market yourself. That's how you get published! And getting them published is how your stories get read!

Of course, those early works won't always be pretty. Odds are, they'll be wonky. But at least they'll be done. Done is beautiful, because done means you can move on to the next, and that's where you build your skills. Completing one work, moving on to the next. Over and over, learning as you go, until you move from apprentice, to journeyman, to master. Because you did the work. And you finished the work. And you got better at it over time.

You may get frustrated if you're just starting out, trying to finish your first story. There are many elements you'll need to figure out and get a grip on to make a story work from start to finish, but don't throw in the towel. You have all the tools that you need right here in this book to accomplish the task. The more you work on a challenging task, the easier it gets. Neural pathways grow, understanding dawns, skills are developed, shortcuts are discovered—if we keep pushing through the gray matter permafrost and finish what we have begun.

I will add a fourth Super Secret here, and it's not mine. Fashion mentor Tim Gunn said it on many *Project Runway* episodes when an aspiring apparel designer had a hot mess on their hands and the clock to finish was running out. I say it now to you:

4. **Make it work.**

26

SECTION TWO REVIEW

We began this section talking about pottery. Go to a local craft fair and you'll find all types of artisan products. For instance, you're in the market for some handcrafted soup bowls, so you head to the booths that sell pottery.

One booth has a table covered in wonky bowls made from lumpy clay the crafter didn't wedge sufficiently before throwing it on the wheel. You pick a piece up to inspect it. It feels rough in the hand. The glaze is poorly applied—there are several bare spots in the finish. Oh, they're bowls, all right. They'll hold soup. But it's obvious this artisan is still learning their craft, and you want something special that will impress your dinner guests. You smile at the seller in the back corner, but they've got their nose in a book, hoping you'll throw money at them without talking to you.

You put the bowl back and move on.

At the next booth, the artisan looks up, smiles, and says, "Good morning. Look around and let me know if I can answer any questions." There are lots of people milling around, several holding pottery pieces close to their chest. Oooh, there's a beautiful set of hand-turned bowls, the surfaces smooth, the rims round and balanced. The turquoise glaze shimmers, perfectly coating the bowl, no bare spots revealing the fired clay underneath. These bowls are things of refined beauty, the work of a craftsman. They even scalloped the rims! You'd be proud to serve special guests with these. Suddenly, you're the one holding pottery close to your chest. You're not letting these get away.

The great thing about handcrafted works created by those that have worked hard to master their craft? They don't have that sterile machined feel. There's personality to the pieces—you can sense the artisan within the work, reflecting their heart and love for their art. You also sense that everything that happened to create that piece occurred by careful design. Their skills guided the raw material to become an appealing representation of their mastery over the craft. The lump of clay now speaks because the artist knew, from years of training and practice, how to breathe life into it and make it sing with their own unique voice.

How did the artisan get to such a level? They learned all they could. They went through many lumps of clay and created many, many wonky pots and bowls. But at some point, they got all of the elements just right, and some of those pieces coming out of the kiln were of such high quality, they could take them to market and people were willing to pay money for them. As they continued to perfect their craft and got comfortable with their skills and worked their own style into the medium, they stood out from others and built their own following. Their work became recognizable as unique to them, special in its craftsmanship. Some no longer viewed the artisan's work as product. They called it art because the piece both reached a pinnacle of mastery and it spoke to their soul.

To me, that's what professional work is ultimately about. Hitting such a high level of mastery with so much heart within it, a work can be called art with a capital A. We won't hit that level all the time; we don't need to hit that level all the time. People need sturdy bowls. Filling that need will pay the bills. But when we create works that are a cut above the rest, others will take note. And if it's got that special something that resonates with the emotions of many, our work will be in demand. Some will even call it a work of art.

Those works will stand the test of time.

I can't share every Super Secret with you in one book to get you there, nor do I know them all. Nor will those that I use to speak through my writing with my voice necessarily work for you to speak through your works with your voice.

But I do believe the ones I've given you in this section will certainly help. Both in making good quality bowls that will sell at market and pay the bills, and in creating those special works that will rise above the norm and make a name for yourself. The art is not in the perfection, because as imperfect people, perfection is impossible to create. The art is in mastering the balance.

When you master your craft to such a high degree, the structure is no longer seen; there is only you shining through your glorious work, moving the minds and hearts of others with what appears to be effortless grace. When you accomplish that, they're going to become collectors, and they'll line up at your booth to get your latest work for their own, holding your art close to their chest.

You don't have to tell them how much work you had to do to get to that point. Let them think you were born with it. That's part of the mystique around all creatives that have built a name for themselves. But you and I know how they got there. And if we study hard, focus on what matters, and put in the work, we'll get there, too.

Now where's the review I promised of the fine-tuning points in Section Two that help us create the balance?

You do it this time. Go back through the chapters in this section. Pick one that you feel you're wonky in, whether it's intriguing titles, original ideas, mastery of POV, writing smart dialogue, killing your darlings, or weaving with all five senses. Review the points in that chapter. Jot them down and apply them to the next piece you write.

And the next.

And the next.

I've shown you a few of the bullseyes that can significantly improve your writing. This is what smart practice is all about. Identify an issue. Work on the issue. Master the issue.

You're going to go through a lot of clay, but trust me, some of those works will start to sell. It's going to happen.

Because you focused on your craft, did smart practice, and stayed the course.

SECTION THREE

Belief Determines Reality

"Confidence is going after Moby Dick in a rowboat
and taking the tartar sauce with you."

Zig Ziglar
Author, salesman, and motivational speaker

27

SHARING YOUR WORKS WITH THE WORLD

L eonard Nimoy, the actor best known as *Star Trek*'s Spock, said: "The miracle is this: The more we share the more we have."[1] There is a deep application of Nimoy's philosophy to writing. For the miracle to take place, the share must happen. We must get our stories out of our own hands and into the hands, minds, and hearts of others. Getting our works published is the way we make the miracle happen.

Believe me, writers *are* miracle workers. We weave worlds and people and inventions and escape realities out of thin air, the cosmic twinkles in our minds, dancing across our synaptic pathways. And then we code it on the page to be absorbed by others through their fingers (the blind), their ears, their eyes, so that those cosmic twinkles will be transmitted into their minds, igniting the dance across *their* synaptic pathways. The process of writing, getting published, and being read (or listened to through audio or watched through visual media) is a magic transmission system unique to the human experience. For a writer, there is nothing better than seeing your stories in print, being paid for those stories, and then having a reader approach you on the internet or in person to say how much your story moved them. Sometimes, they have tears in their eyes. Sometimes, they're trembling as they hand you your book to sign. They can't believe they're meeting the actual creator of worlds and characters that have touched their hearts and transformed their lives. And sometimes, on a most monumental moment, a reader will tell you that they were in a dark place, and your story saved their life. You helped them escape; you gave them hope.

I'm telling you if you stay the course, it's going to happen. All of it. But none of it will happen if you don't package your finished story up and get it published. Motivational speaker Zig Ziglar said: "You don't have to be great to start, but you have to start to be great."* I've designed this final section of *How to Write a Howling Good Story* to make sure you start. The magic show won't happen without a stage, an audience, and sharing those tricks you've been working on that make it appear you're pulling live animals and silver dollars out of thin air.

You have the power. You have the knowledge. Now you must do. Here's where I use my Yoda voice on you. *"Try not. Do ... or do not. There is no try."*

You say you're not afraid? *"Oh, you will be. You will be."*

Everyone's afraid when they first send a story to an editor, an agent, a publisher. Everyone's afraid when they first publish a story on an online retail platform. Everyone's afraid when they first push *launch* on their Kickstarter campaign to crowdfund their novel. Everyone's afraid when they first stand in front of producers or studio executives pitching their screenplay.

Face it. The unknown is scary. We hope for the best, but negative results are possible, even likely if we're in our early apprenticing stage. Those that push past that fear do so because they have an ardent desire to communicate, and they long for the next part of the equation—they want their words be read. Or heard in the case of audiobooks. Or produced in the case of screenplays. The desire to communicate with an audience is so strong, writers push past their fear and send that story out. Remember what I said in the opening of this book?

Everything worth achieving is on the other side of fear.

In Section One you learned the fundamentals of how to write a story. In Section Two you learned how to execute those fundamentals with technical proficiency. You now have a handle on writing craft. If you followed the advice to, ahem, FINISH WHAT YOU WRITE, you now have a completed working story. It's okay if you haven't finished quite yet. I have faith that you will. You've gotten this far. THE END IS NEAR!

While that may sound apocalyptic, quite the contrary! When you type THE END, you now have a product. Oh, I know many aspiring writers hate that term. Their writing is not a product, it's ART, created through years of busking on street corners and living in homeless camps so they can then transcribe for posterity the suffering of the common man in one pristine tale.

Well and good! The world needs such stories. We could all use a little more empathy for those who have come upon misfortune. But whether we've created a laugh-out-loud comedy about clowns or a tear-your-heart-out exposé about a mom addicted to opioids, if you want the public to read your tale, you'll need to package it up and showcase it somewhere to get it into the hands of others. Or send it off to a publisher that will do some of the work for you. Either way, it's still a product.

And now it's time to sell it.

~

QUALITY CONTROL

Conscientious companies do quality inspection of their products to make sure the consumer is getting the best value for their dollar. Their name is on the product. Their brand is involved. No one wants to be known for shoddy merchandise. Consumers feel cheated when a product falls far short of what is advertised. They expect good value for their money and time invested.

This is why it's important for a writer to learn their craft, and why I've spent a large portion of this book discussing the subject. If we'd like to be published and enjoy not only having readers but being paid for our time entertaining them, we need to learn how to write a story, and how to write it *well*. Well sells.

This is especially true when self-publishing, or what's better known today as indie publishing. Indie authors retain the rights to their work and self-publish with the hope of profiting and even earning their living from their writing. But no amount of fancy covers or slick ad campaigns can compensate for poor quality within. Consumers live by the maxim: *Fool me once, shame on you. Fool me twice, shame on me.* Your story must deliver the goods. It's the only way those readers will come back for more.

Good news! If you're an aspiring writer and you studied this book up to this point, you are now ahead of *ninety percent or more* of all the emerging writers submitting stories to markets or publishing them on their own! In fact, some of these Super Secrets I've taught you are unique to me, meaning no one else knows them because *no one else is teaching them.* Unlike most of the aspiring writers thrashing about in the dark, you have just had a clear path cut for you and a spotlight shining the way in the form of this book. Knowledge is power. Knowledge and smart implementation of that knowledge is what takes a writer from apprentice to master. You are now ahead of the pack.

Don't believe me? You think my numbers are bloated? Um, have you ever read slush? Those stories that get sent to editors en masse when they make open calls? Those novels agents and editors receive when they take a chance on a query? Trust me, you're going to feel worlds better about your chances if you volunteer to read submissions for a magazine. Most writers know how to put words on a page. That doesn't mean they know how to write a coherent story.

Still don't trust me? Don't believe you're now ahead of ninety percent of other writers trying to make it out there? I forgive you. After all, you just learned all this stuff. But I know it's true because I have data that you don't.

I've been training writers in these Super Secrets for close to five years now at the time of publication. Almost everyone studying them were unpublished writers when they began. I encouraged my workshop members to submit to the number one writing contest for emerging speculative fiction writers in the world—the Writers of the Future Contest. During that first year, virtually everyone achieved honorable mention or higher—one even won the contest studying the early set of Super Secrets I posted. Thousands enter from around the world every quarter. The contest states that when you get an honorable mention, you are in the top ten percent of all submissions. My Super Secrets' writers regularly accomplished that and more. In fact, so many have become finalists—the top eight out of thousands each quarter that the three quarterly winners are selected from—I no longer keep count anymore.

Want more proof? I encourage my writers to submit to the professional speculative fiction professional magazine, *DreamForge*. It's a beautiful full-color, fully illustrated print magazine. Not only is it a gorgeous showcase for a writer's work, but a custom illustration is also crafted for every published story. It's a rare privilege of seeing your work published with custom art, which makes a sale to *Dream-Forge* all the more special. The editor, Scot Noel, has told me every time he does an open call for stories, the Wulf Pack Writers group is always in the top ten percent of all submissions. Many of my writers and clients studying these Super Secrets have achieved their first sale and publication in this professional magazine.

Still a skeptic? I did a challenge for our writers, encouraging them to write fresh, original stories and then submit them to a professional anthology's open call for stories. Most of our writers submitting stories had never been published, let alone paid pro-rate for their work. They not only rose to the top ten percent in this anthology call, they made the top one percent that got accepted, paid, and published!

Here, don't take my word for it, take the editor's word. She knows —she's the one that bought their stories! Here's Juli Rew from her foreword in *After the Gold Rush* by Third Flatiron Publishing, Book 31, Summer/Fall 2022: "We are especially grateful to Wulf Moon, who leads his "Super Secrets" workshop that he began in the Writers of the Future Forum. He encouraged writers to submit to our latest call, and by our count, seven "Wulf Pack" authors of the twenty-one in this anthology are new to our pages."

I started these anthology submission challenges last year with my writers, and in several anthologies we targeted, half the stories accepted were written by those trained in the Super Secrets. And that international writing contest, Writers of the Future, that receives thousands of blind submissions every quarter? At least a dozen winners and published finalists came from my Super Secrets Workshop or told me studying and applying the Super Secrets was critical in helping them write their winners. In fact, as I write this, we're at the halfway point of results from the contest's Volume 40 year. *Half* of the current winners are from my Wulf Pack Writers group.

Writers and Illustrators of the Future is a blind contest. There are no names on the manuscripts; I have no pull there. And the contest is judged by some of the brightest stars in the science fiction and fantasy firmament—Brandon Sanderson (*The Stormlight Archive*), Kevin J. Anderson (*The Saga of the Seven Suns, Dune* prequels), Larry Niven (*Ringworld*), Nnedi Okorafor (*The Binti Series*), to name just a few. They don't know these are Super Secrets' writers, but they do know good writing when they see it. Understanding story fundamentals and how to apply them makes your writing stand out and rise to the top.

But for that to happen, you've got to screw up your courage and send them out.

∿

SENDING YOUR STORIES TO MARKETS

In Section Three, we'll talk about ways you can train yourself to become an excellent quality control inspector for your brand, how you can get your own team of free inspectors should you choose, and how you can even hire professional help to enhance your product to be all it can be.

If your goal is to be traditionally published, your product needs to be of excellent quality, it still needs to be properly packaged, and it needs to be sent to a publisher in order for you to see it in print. Contrary to what some might say (who are likely speaking from inse-curity over their work not selling), you are not "selling out your art" nor have you "gone commercial" by seeking to be paid for your work. The truth is, if a publisher is willing to pay you a fair wage for your work, they have subscribers or a paying distribution channel—that's where they get the money to pay you. This means they've got readers!

Customers! People paying good money to read good stories and novels by good writers like you!

And because you now know how to serve up a solid story by learning your craft, editors are going to take a chance on you, put you in their kitchen, and put your dish on their menu. And when customers clamor for more, critics will show up to see what all the fuss is about. They'll write about you—they might even recommend your creation for an award.

And as your name as an accomplished chef grows, you might even open your own establishment. That's what indie writers are doing. They've built up a list of happy customers that will follow them anywhere they go. Just as there's a love affair with good cooking and the chef that makes those out-of-this-world dishes, the same is true for great writers. They've made a name for themselves by consistently delivering tasty, quality product.

We'll talk about how to build your list of clientele and how to stay the course for the long haul. Finally, I'll share what the difference is between success and failure. And I'm giving you one last power Super Secret at the end that has changed the fate of many.

Ready to plate up your creation and send it out to those hungry customers? Let's roll out the awning and turn on the OPEN sign. You are ready for business!

Order up!

28

BABY STEPS

E ven with the power of the Super Secrets behind you, you're going to have to write. A LOT. There is no substitute for diligent work, even though it appears that's what many wannabe writers want. I recall a meme of an owl teaching her child the violin. The little owl, violin base to her cheek, asks, "Why can't I just skip to the part where I'm brilliant?"

Wouldn't that be nice.

Inventor Thomas Edison states the truth here: "Genius is one percent inspiration, ninety-nine percent perspiration."[1]

Is your goal to move beyond hobby writer? You'll need to increase your output so you can get the necessary practice in. Would you like to start as a short story writer? Learning your craft in short form is an excellent way to train for long form. Or would you rather cut to the chase and become a full-time writer? What does full-time mean? Going to work when the mood moves you? Or putting in a healthy workday with a productive output day in, day out?

Let's take a look at short story writers, novelists, and writing goals.

~

SHORT STORIES

Short stories are an excellent way to learn one's craft. They're short, so they can be easier for the mind to wrap around. They are sprints—you can see the finish line from the starting line. Many experienced writers can finish a short story in a week or less, but don't let that scare you. Newer writers can take a month or more to complete a short story— they're still building up their writing muscles. The important thing is to start at your pace, not at someone else's. You build from your present baseline.

Q. How does one get to the top of the mountain?

A. One step at a time.

This is how it works for all of us. Everyone started with that first step, and built from there. Even the ones that like to pretend they never were in your shoes or never had any help. They were. They did. We all had our humble beginnings. And hopefully have stayed humble. The thing about humility? The moment we cry out that we've achieved it, we've lost it. It takes humility and a recognition that we don't know it all to keep learning. This is how we grow.

We also grow by doing the work. You can't become proficient in a thing without doing the thing. A LOT. Did I say that already? Why yes, yes I did. I've watched a lot of writers pass through my workshops. The ones that knuckled down, studied hard, and did the work? They skyrocketed to the top and now have writing careers, or are well on their way. Others are working to get there, it's just taking them more time because they may have different circumstances, greater outside demands on their time, or they may have to unlearn some of the things they've learned that haven't been helping them. They're doing the work at a different pace, but it's still forward, and they know they'll get there by staying the course.

But the ones that thought they'd get a magic edit or learn the secret handshake to instant success? They're off chasing that next shiny butterfly that will sprinkle the magic fairy dust of success on them. Writing at a professional level—moving from apprentice to journeyman to master—takes weeks, months, and yes, years of practice, practice, practice. There is no substitute for practice. There's only shortening the time it takes through smart practice, training and learning with others, and if you're really fortunate, finding a master to mentor you.

There's a whole chapter in *The Illustrated Super Secrets of Writing* workbook, the companion to this book, on mentors. I encourage you to get it. Finding a mentor is the fastest way to level up. You'll still have to do the work, but the work will move faster. That's because they're lending their own years of experience to your training. A skilled mentor can spot what you need to do to advance, and can share knowledge they learned through the school of hard knocks so you don't have to knock about.

Back to the short form of fiction writing. I've seen a lot of confusion over what constitutes a short story, what length a novelette should be, what's a novella, and what's a good length to write stories in. While there's some debate about lengths, here's some guidelines. And the thing about guidelines? If a publisher defines the limit for their publication, it doesn't matter what the industry says. Follow the publishers' guidelines if you hope to sell to them. It's their house; they make the rules.

Here's some general industry guidelines.

- **Microfiction**: like the name suggests, little fiction pieces of varying lengths under 300 words.
- **Flash fiction**: short pieces of 1,500 words or less, although some publications and contests limit flash to 1,000 words.
- **Short Stories**: stories that run 1,500 to 7,500 words.
- **Novelettes**: stories that run 7,500 to 17,500 words.
- **Novellas**: stories that run 17,500 to 40,000 words

Whether the contest or publication counts each category inclusive or exclusive of these high and low marks? You'll have to read their guidelines. It varies.

So what length should your story be? I always say a story needs to be exactly as long as it takes to tell it. No more, no less. The problem is, the newer a writer is, the more likely they'll use more words to tell the story than is necessary. Less is more. They simply haven't figured out they don't need as much as they think they do.

The vast majority of writers start out like this. They discover how to write tighter as they do smart practice. It takes time to figure this out. This is why writing flash stories regularly can accelerate a writer's progress. I train writers in a program I've named KYD, or Kill Your Darlings—a system that teaches them how to trim the fat and write lean stories. The system works—most of my writers swear by it, and indeed, many of their first published stories and contest winners came from this exercise. But you'll get there too if you practice flash. It's the best way to eliminate one of the most common issues that holds emerging writers back.

A word of advice, and it's only that. Stories do need to be as long as you need to tell them. But if you hope to sell those stories, the longer a story is, the harder it's going to be to sell. There are limited markets in traditional publishing for the long end of novelettes, and for novellas it's even more challenging. It's easy to understand why. Big stories like this take up a lot of space in a publication, and if a publisher is going to give up that much real estate, they need a mighty good reason. It needs to be a superlative story, and usually written by a Big-Name Author.

Many magazines and anthologies even limit their short story lengths to 5,000 words and under—in fact, there are a lot of markets that limit stories to 3,000 words and under. I'm not saying to write to word count—I'd hate to have that stifle your creativity. But it is prudent to be aware of current market conditions and what lengths publishers are buying.

$\sim$

NOVELS

If short stories are sprints where you can see the finish line, novels are marathons over a long and winding road. A novel has a finish line, but it's off in the distance. I recall my mentor David Farland (*Runelords*) once saying novels are simply a series of short stories tied together, and it's an uncomplicated way to look at novels. I've also been taught by Orson Scott Card (*Ender's Game*), and he said short stories are like taking a speedboat across the lake, whereas novels are like taking a wandering pleasure cruise on a pontoon. Both have a destination they'll end up at, but novels take their time getting there.

Do you wish to be a novelist? Most writers do. How many words does it take to write a novel in the genre you're writing in? Do you write for a middle grade (8- to 12-year-old) audience? An MG novel might run 25,000 to 50,000 words (yes, I know I said novellas run up to 40,000 words, but let's face it, it's not a perfect world). Is your protagonist a teenager? Then you're likely writing a young adult book. A YA novel runs anywhere from 40,000 to 80,000 words. Are you writing a novel for adults? What genre are you writing in? Historical fiction, romance, science fiction, epic fantasy?

Here's a quote from Dave Chesson's website, the *Kindlepreneur*. After doing extensive in-house research on novels in the top 15 Amazon Kindle categories, here's their takeaway:

"While a book only needs 40,000 words to make the threshold for a novel, best-selling authors are writing closer to 90,000 words on average. Readers might expect yours to fit that mold as well.

"Fantasy, historical fiction, and horror novels are about 15% longer than other genres.

"In one case, a fantasy book was in the top 25 best sellers with approximately 42,000 words (less than half of the average length for this category). Word count matters, but rules can still be broken!

"To answer the commonly asked question: Are 70,000 words enough for a novel? 70,000 words would be enough for a standard religious fiction or erotica novel. However, most authors today are averaging 90,000 words in a novel, so you may want to increase the length."—*Kindlepreneur.com*, March 24, 2022.

Again, story determines length, but if you're writing an epic fantasy weighing in at 454,000 words thinking you'll be the next Brandon Sanderson, you might want to put a pin in that until you've built up your name and following first. Don't let me steal your thunder, but it's wise to be realistic and to know the average word length of novels selling in your chosen category.

~

BABY STEPS

I love the movie *What About Bob*. Bill Murray plays Bob, a lonely man with only one friend—a goldfish named Gill. Bob makes it to his new psychiatrist's office and claims to have every phobia known to man. The psychiatrist, Dr. Leo Marvin, hands Bob a "groundbreaking new book" he's written called *Baby Steps*. Bob takes the title literally, moving everywhere with tiny steps to accomplish big things. He even uses the concept to get himself on a bus and travels all the way from New York City to Lake Winnipesaukee in New Hampshire. It's a desperate attempt to get more therapy sessions from Dr. Marvin while he's on vacation at his lake home with his family.

It's a humorous story, but the concept behind it is true. Lots of baby steps equal great big steps, and every journey begins with the first step. French author Antoine de Saint-Exupéry stated in *The Little Prince*: "A goal without a plan is just a wish." We must plan and *engage* to obtain the future we desire. Even if it starts with baby steps.

So what's your goal? To write every week? Then pull out your planner or calendar and make squares on the days you'll write for one month. Baby steps. Give yourself permission to write on those days, let it be without judgment, and put a check in the square on the day you wrote. You're a writer. Writing makes writers happy. It's when we allow our critical voice to judge our writing that we become unhappy. Write for the joy of it, even if it's as simple as writing in a journal. The rest will follow.

After a month, you'll know your writing days and even the time you write. You will have built a habit. Now, you can up your game. Those baby steps need to become bigger steps, aimed toward your destination. "To reach your full potential, you have to set goals that will stretch you."—Zig Ziglar, *Born to Win: Find Your Success Code*

Let's say you're new to writing. You have the desire, but you've never really finished a story. Set a goal you'll write a *fresh story* using the things you've learned in these Super Secrets in three months. Mark it three months out on your calendar; check it off when you've accomplished it. Once you've done that, you've got a new habit started. Expand this habit out to a year, marking these goals ahead on your calendar. That's an original story every three months, or four new stories a year.

I've started many aspiring writers on this program. Simple, achievable goals don't frustrate us. Trust me, this and so much more is within your reach. You are a bundle of limitless potential. But first, you have to plumb those depths.

You can add word count goals if you like. Start easy with a goal that's reachable and doesn't stress you out. I know one teacher that writes for one hour every night after she's put her kids to bed. Her goal is 500 words. She can write that in an hour, and often gets energized by the writing and gets in even more. But she keeps the goal at 500 words, making it easy to fulfill, but having that number keeps her accountable to her writing.

Add up the result. In a week, writing five days a week and taking the weekend off, she's got 2,500 words. That's a novel chapter, maybe even a short story. In a year taking every weekend off? 130,000 words. More than enough to write a novel a year as we saw by the previous study, or to create a slew of short stories, like twenty-six 5,000-word stories.

Baby steps. Bigger steps. Set reasonable goals. These are goals according to *your* abilities and circumstances, *not* someone else's. When your writing muscles build up from these workouts, you can enhance your goals, stretching your abilities. You'll have created more product than you ever could have imagined when you first began. Baby steps will have led you up the mountain. Or at least to Lake Winnipesaukee. I hear they've got great psychiatrists.

Now it's time to do a quality check on your product and you're ready to package it up to go to market! Your destiny awaits! Just don't forget—Gill's lovin' all that fresh air up there, but he needs some water.

29

TO EDIT OR NOT TO EDIT, THAT IS THE QUESTION

I wrote my winning story in *Writers of the Future, Volume 35* in the last thirty-two hours of the contest year. It's all the time I had. My wife had been recovering from cancer surgery and nuclear treatment and as her caregiver, there had been no time for me to write a fresh story for the contest that last quarter.

I asked her that fateful late afternoon if she'd be okay while I wrote something for the contest. She said yes. Great. Now what should I write? She said, "Why don't you write that Moongirl story? I've always wondered what happened to Dixie."

Perfect. I'd forgotten about her. "Super-Duper Moongirl and the Amazing Moon Dawdler" was the result of a title exercise I created for myself a good six months before because I'd noticed stories that won some of the speculative fiction industry's most prestigious awards often had outlandish but intriguing titles. I decided to try my hand at it, worked up a crazy title, and after writing that Moongirl doozy, I asked myself, *Now who is this girl in the story?*

My Wulf Pack Writers group know I do an exercise called KYD, or the Kill Your Darlings Exercise. Most have taken the masterclass. To grossly oversimplify the exercise, you end up with 250 potent words that become your story seed. I named my protagonist Dixie and had her tell me who she is and what she cared most about—her Heart's Desire—all in 250 words. (If you read the story, the result of this exercise is the same opening you see in the book, I didn't change a thing.) I handed the piece to my wife to read, she loved the result, but I had no time to expand the story seed and filed it away.

Until she reminded me about it. Thirty-two hours before the contest closed for the year. That late afternoon and evening, I wrote 1,000 words. Most of the time was spent researching current theory in moon base construction so I'd get the science right. The next morning, I saw my ending as if I had just sat beside Dixie in her spacesuit with her robodog on the dark side of the Moon. My vision of the ending was so vivid, I could see the light shining on her face inside her helmet as she sat on the edge of a crater in the dark. I watched her breath fog on the faceplate as she spoke to Moonie beside her.

I wrote like a madman to get to that ending, another 5,000 words, building the necessary scenes to lead the reader there. At 11:15 p.m., I typed the last line. I hadn't eaten all day—not good for a diabetic—so I rushed into the bedroom and asked my wife if she could read the story while I made myself something to eat. At 11:45 p.m., I came back into the bedroom. Clock's ticking. Time's up.

My wife was *bawling*, sobbing her heart out.

I laughed hysterically.

She said, "Why are you laughing? I'm *crying!*"

"Because it worked!"

I snatched the manuscript out of her hand, ran back to my office, corrected the marked typos, and loaded it into the contest's online submission portal. The time stamp said 11:56 p.m.—a slim four minutes before the year's cutoff.

I took a deep breath and immediately began writing my acceptance speech. I knew I had written my winner.

And then remembered my crying wife. I went back into the bedroom to apologize. It had been a manic rush to get that story written. I had been trying to win that contest for a *very* long time. And I did have only minutes to get it in or it would have been another long year.

She forgave me.

I submitted a story to the largest talent search for speculative fiction writers in the world that had been written in thirty-two hours, eight hours of that time spent sleeping. A first draft I had never even gone back through to read just to see if it was coherent. A pure work of Flow state, with no editing besides a ten-minute race to correct typos my wife had marked and answering questions on the contest's portal form. That's all the time I had.

And it won.

I've had a few wonderful mentors in my life. One advocated this very system—write a first draft and never look back. Write fast, write fresh, move on to the next. Another advocated going back and *rewriting* however many times is necessary to get the story just right. Two diametrically opposed methods. Both were right for them, each bestselling authors with multitudes of followers.

To edit or not to edit. To write or to rewrite. *That* is the question.

I've tried both ways. But instead of A, instead of B, I'm going to give you C.

You decide what works for you.

∿

EDITING YOUR MANUSCRIPT

First, let me be clear. Anyone taking my workshops or who's a member of my Wulf Pack Writers group knows I advocate writing fresh, original stories. I believe editing the same story or novel over and over again is a trap for many writers, especially aspiring writers still learning their craft. There are many famous writers that would agree with me. And there are some that don't. In the end, you'll settle on what works best for you. But if a writer hides behind trying to create the perfect story or novel, oftentimes they never send it out, because it will never be perfect.

I've seen some work on a single story for years trying to get their story exactly right. Some screw up their courage and do send it out to markets, but every time it comes back, they believe something is wrong with it and work on it again, perhaps totally rewriting it. Sometimes, this method actually works, and it gets published or even wins an award. And then I see the writer get stuck, because they fixated on the story for so long, their creative muscles atrophied. They can't write anything else. And without fresh work, it's unlikely you'll have a career and you certainly won't see anything new of yours published.

There are exceptions, and I'll give you one of the biggest. Dean Koontz. In an interview on April 19th, 2004, Dean Koontz shared his revision system: "I write one page at a time, revising and polishing it until I can't make it better. That can mean 20, 30, or even more drafts. Then I move on to the next page. Slowly, I work my way through the book. At the end of each chapter, I do a printout, which I pencil because I see possibilities for improvements on the printed page that I am not able to see on the screen. After three or four pencilings, I move on to the next chapter. When I reach the end of the novel, it is done—except for whatever editorial notes inspire me to make changes. Those usually take a couple of days."

Obviously, this system works for Dean Koontz, so it could work for you. Just be sure you're willing and able to dedicate the amount of time necessary to write and edit like this. In the interview he stated he works sixty hours a week drafting stories and often longer. Without a spouse to support you or an independent source of income, it can be difficult to find that kind of time.

So we'll call this type of editing **System A: The Multiple Draft System**. Write and rewrite until you get the story just right, however many times it takes.

Another way is to write one draft, but the writer cycles through the material, doing the edit on the fly. Shut off your cognitive mind, let the unconscious mind take control to create the raw material, and after a few pages loop back and let the cognitive take over, filling in missing details, correcting typos, checking the flow of the narrative. Satisfied, you repeat the process all the way to the end, and your first draft is your only draft. It has actually already been edited once—you just did the editing while you were writing, moving through the story like the loop-the-loop maneuver with a stunt plane or a rollercoaster track at an amusement park.

These writers don't rewrite, they may not even reread what they wrote. For them, the story is done when they type The End and they send it off to a market (or self-publish it) and move to their next. Cycle editing can allow the writer to produce a large body of work quickly because less editing is involved. And it is true the more you write, the better you get at writing over time. This is why I could write a professional story straight through from beginning to end without any edits, cycling or otherwise. I had been writing for many decades. You develop skills over that much time, and in the rush of Flow state, your mind can tap into power and knowledge it doesn't have in your slower cognitive state.

But normally, these writers cycle as they write, doing their edit on the fly. We'll call this type of editing **System B: The Single Draft System**. Get some pages down, circle back and edit, then move to the next, cycling forward and back like this all the way to the end. One draft, edited as it was written. No looking back, no endless rewrites. Trust the process, send it out, and on to the next. The goal is volume, trusting your craft will improve over time with experience. It does, and this system has worked well for many writers. Especially indie writers that make their living by creating many new titles for their series readers. Some of what's called "whale readers" won't even buy a novel in a series until they know the series is completed. Fast writing with lots of output solves this issue.

~

MOON'S HYBRID FLOW SYSTEM

Me? I'm a hybrid of the two, somewhere in the middle. We'll call this **System C: Moon's Hybrid Flow System**.

First, let me say there's nothing wrong with System A or System B. They work for multitudes of writers, some extremely successful, yet totally opposite of each other. If you've been working in these systems and they work for you, great, you're producing work, and that's what it's all about. Keep doing what you're doing if the method is productive for you and you're achieving sales or receiving signs you're about to. You've obviously found your sweet spot. *Godspeed*. I'm happy for you.

I have my own philosophy. It may not work for you, but it does work for me, and this book IS about my Super Secrets of Writing. I get to share my beliefs and philosophies; you get to decide if they make sense and will work for you. So here's my belief: *Don't worship word count; make each word count.*

Don't get me wrong. I believe in producing a healthy body of work. It's tough to have a career without creating fresh product for your consumers to buy. But I also believe that for those works to have deeper meaning, to stand the test of time, to resonate with humanity, something more than output must be in the equation. *Art takes heart.* Making money is secondary to that. And to create art, Deep Thought must be involved. Some of those stories have to come from deep within you to have lasting meaning. But you don't need to take 7.5 million years to calculate the answer to the ultimate question. There's a way to dredge the depths for writing gold while still having nice output to create your writing career that will ultimately pay for life's necessities so you can be fulfilled by doing what you love. Writing.

My goal at every writing session is to enter Flow state. If you'd like to understand the science behind Flow state better and how to access it, I do teach a masterclass on it, and there's an entire chapter on it in my workbook *The Illustrated Super Secrets of Writing*. The basic premise of Flow for writers is to remove all external influence so you can enter the dream state, allowing an inversion to take place where the conscious mind submerges and the unconscious mind emerges. Your best writing comes from this state. It takes around fifteen minutes of continual writing without being interrupted by external influences before the unconscious can take the wheel away from your conscious, analytical mind and start driving. And it does take practice to engage this powerful hyperdrive. It doesn't happen overnight.

Understanding Flow is key to my system. You don't set a timer, because it takes time to enter Flow state, and once you're in it, if you stop, it takes even longer to enter Flow state a second time. When you enter Flow, your unconscious super brain takes over, what I like to call your kraken, because it lives in the great depths of your mind and has tentacles reaching into every bit of knowledge you have. It can even make intuitive leaps into knowledge you don't yet have. You'll see lightning-fast visions of your story, and your fingers will fly on those keys trying to get everything down. It's like your unconscious mind is dictating a story to you, and you are its humble servant, recording it as fast as you can for posterity.

Alas, at some point we're going to get interrupted, and our kraken is going to say, "Oh, bother," and sink back into those dark depths. It's sensitive and does not like to be interrupted, and its nemesis is our conscious, analytical mind. The analytical mind gnaws away at its power, saying things like, "Let me take the wheel, you're a crazy driver," or try to speak in your father's voice: "You're writing crap, you're writing crap, you'll never make a living doing this." But the conscious mind is not all bad. Even as it's idling in the background, it's also our guardian that watches over us when we're in this state. It will interrupt to say, "Hey, buddy, you need to eat, your blood sugar is low," or, "You feel that? That's called your bladder and it's about to explode," or, "Feel that explosion that just tried to take your house off its foundation? That was your neighbor's house that just blew sky high. You might want to see if you need to evacuate." Yes, that happened a few houses away while I was writing this manuscript. Sometimes you must listen to that voice in your head. It's there to protect you.

So, Moon's Hybrid Flow System. Protect my writing environment. Use my Flow triggers (I have several) at the start of my session to tease my kraken up from its depths. To fire up the writing synapses, I circle back to the last section I wrote, which not only primes the mind with what needs to follow, it also allows me to edit the previous free-flow writing session. By the time I've moved to the blank space on the page, I've got a head of steam. I now know where I'm at on the map, and the unexplored waters shimmer before me. My kraken loves seeing that unexplored area on the map that says, "Here be dragons." The kraken takes over and I write like hell transcribing what the kraken shows me. Eventually, the head of steam will be used up and the kraken will tell me, "Let's take a break." More often, my office cat will jump between me and the keyboard, or my back will ache and I'll need to get up and stretch, or I'll realize it's time to take care of my body's needs. When I return, I read the last section I wrote, touch up what is necessary, and I'm off to sea again.

I repeat the process all the way to the end of my story. I'm not a plotter, and I'm not a pantser. I'm a hybrid. I know my opening and I know my destination before I start my stories. I usually have points on the map I'm heading for because my writing will wander if I don't. What happens in between those markers is the mystery for me, and where all the fun is in writing. I've given my kraken some guidelines so I'll have a coherent story when I'm done. It doesn't run all over the map—I point it in the right direction, but let it have free rein to run.

Often my kraken gives me my last killer line, a line that drops like a judge's gavel at the end of a trial. Sometimes my kraken says, "I got nuttin'. You're on your own, buddy." So I engage my analytical mind, go back to the beginning, and hunt for my statement of Heart's Desire —after all, that's what the story was all about. And then I fashion my ending line to ring the bell for the reader that resonates on that opening promise, the protagonist's journey, whether they received what I promised the story would be about, and possibly, where the protagonist will go with the new power and knowledge they've gained (or the loss if it's a negative outcome story). At last, my work here is done.

Not so fast! My kraken is good, even deadly at times, and I did check on its work throughout my manuscript. I know the story works the way I wrote it because I trust my super brain, and I let it have its head. But the real question is, *Did I get the coding right on the page for the reader?* You see, my kraken showed me all the details of the vision, I was in the writing trance. I saw worlds within worlds. There's no way I can transcribe all that information on the page, nor would I want to. I need just enough to light up the reader's imagination and yet guide them down the path I wish them to take.

And I won't know if I accomplished that until I reread my completed story.

In the first read, I'm going in as if I'm the reader. To accomplish this, it's best if I can let the story rest so my original vision isn't quite so vivid, tricking my reader experience by filling in the gaps. Some like letting their work sit a week or two before returning to it for this very purpose. I'm always writing to deadlines, so I don't have this luxury. But I do let the completed story or chapter sit overnight before I give it this read. I have a fresher reader eye by doing this.

As I proceed with this reading, I ask questions. Did I mark the path for the reader to take so it's easy for them to follow? Are there enough details to allow them to feel the ship lunging over strong waves? Can they sense the mood I've set for the scene from the environment? Do they feel that salt spray hit their face, smell the ozone in the air as lightning strikes? Can they see the distant shore the ship is desperately trying to reach, or is my prose wandering, allowing the reader to take a side journey (or worse, a yawn and a trip to the fridge) that I never intended?

You won't know these answers until you give the story a careful read, not with your writer hat on, but with your reader hat. One of the best editing tips I can give you is to *read your story out loud*. Your eyes can fool you, filling in missing words. Your ears will not. They'll hear when a word is missing, or when your prose clunks like an engine that's misfiring. When sentences are so awkward in construction that they're hard to speak, take note! If the flow tripped up for you, it's going to trip your reader as well. I make marks along the way, judicious marks, because I trust my kraken knows its business. I'm just cleaning up some spots where the kraken piddled on the deck while it was engrossed in telling me its tale.

Great! I've touched up the story and the prose flows nicely. Now I'm ready to send it off to a respectable market or publish it meself, matey!

Not so fast, Moon, ye swaggering swab! Even though I read the finished piece as if I were a reader coming upon it for the first time, I'm not really coming upon it for the first time. I know what's in those scenes and where the plot will lead. I might think I've provided all the necessary coding to get the reader there, but the mind is a tricky thing. It can think you put something on the page that isn't really there. The newer we are at writing, the more likely this will be true. Let me repeat that. *The newer we are at writing, the more likely this will be true.*

This is why you need a wise reader. They don't need to be a writer, in fact, using a writer as your wise reader may not always be a good idea. You see, a writer is going to tell you how to fix it, and they can easily push their voice and style onto your style. If you're not careful, a writer can take your story off course, offering suggestions to destinations you never intended the story to take. *Danger!*

Instead, I like my wise reader to be someone well-read in multiple genres, but not a writer. After I've read the finished story and fine-tuned any spots I thought were loosie goosey, I hand that copy to my wife to read. She's an avid reader, in all kinds of genres. She's not aware of why some novels and short stories don't work for her, she simply knows they don't work and where she stopped reading or plowed ahead, but with difficulty.

For me, that's a perfect wise reader, also known as your alpha reader. They aren't editors, and probably shouldn't be writers. They're readers first and foremost. Their job is to tell you if the story worked, if they were hooked and entranced at the beginning, and if your story engaged their mind and heart all the way to the end without having to stop and puzzle anything out. If they hit a speed bump and got knocked out of the enchantment for any reason, you want them to mark the spot and jot a note why. They will illuminate code that's missing so you can fix the issue for the next reader. Or expose where you put in so much code, they got bored (the most common new writer mistake). And yes, they're going to spot some typos or missing words. And mannerisms and what's called "echo" words. We might not discern we've used a word multiple times, but the wise reader is listening to the score and can pick up on the same note hit twice or more on the page, sometimes in the same paragraph. These create annoying "echoes" for the reader. Catching them will keep issues like these from annoying the next reader, which will likely be a first reader or editor at the publication you send it to. Annoying the prospective buyer is never a good idea.

I hear you saying, "Okay, Moon. Now that I addressed the issues my first reader uncovered, can I send the story off to be published?"

Yes, you can. You've doublechecked your work after writing it, and you've tested the result with an experienced reader. If you've worked on learning your craft you'll now be sending your best work out *at the level you are currently writing at.* You've done what I call quality control. The raw product came off your assembly line. You checked it over to make sure there weren't any wonky bits, and then you handed it to an experienced consumer to see what they thought about the product. They might make a few suggestions on improvement; you decide if they're right.

Your product is now as good as you can make it. Time to take it to market to see what others think. If it sells, you've done your job right. If it doesn't, you take it to the next market. And the next, until it sells. You don't rewrite it (a total gutting of the house), you don't edit it again (wouldn't a sunroom or skylight be nice here?). You leave it alone, cycle it through the markets or put it on your favorite online retail platforms, and move on to the next.

Done is beautiful. If you keep grinding away on the story every time it comes back, not only are you not creating new product that gets better with experience and innovation, you are stuck in the past, endlessly polishing the old. The best thing a writer has is their original voice. No one can duplicate your voice, it's unique to you. Your writing will stand out from all others because there is only one you. Your career will be based on whether your voice shines through. But if you're constantly rubbing down the paint job thinking you're buffing it out, you can actually strip away the paint. All that uniqueness that shined with your personality vanishes.

Know when to walk away from a work. Keep those grubby paws off it!

I will add one last point on this topic. After years of writing and taking in new knowledge, I know stories written in my past that have gone the circuit might have something wrong with them that I couldn't spot during my apprenticing period. Not always. I shopped my story "Beast of the Month" around for twenty years before finding a respectable home for it, and didn't change a thing during that time. I knew it was good. I believed in that story and trusted it was just a matter of finding one editor that had a taste for what I was serving up.

But on a few stories that are very old, I still believed in them (I love all my baby krakens), but I've reread them to see if my knowledge and experience gained over the years might now uncover something that's not working right. I actually apply my own Super Secrets to them as a litmus test. If I find the fool in the gold, I go back to refining and skim the excess out. Sometimes, it's not removing the dross—I actually need to add in a missing critical element. Guess what? I now have the knowledge and experience necessary to fix the story instead of screwing it up by messing with it. And it often sells to the next market I send it to.

Note that I only do such an analysis after my skills and knowledge have grown over many years. When we tinker with complex creations without knowledge of what makes them tick, we can unknowingly break stuff. Yes, failure is another way to learn. The problem is the newer we are, the less likely we'll know if our "fix" actually damaged our product. We could send those stories out to markets for years without knowing we broke them while tinkering around with their parts.

There are ways for writers, especially newer writers, to find a workaround for this issue. Some have had tremendous success using them, but each way has its pros and cons. You should know them. Want to find out?

Turn the page.

30

BETA READERS, WRITING GROUPS, FREELANCE EDITORS

C hilean-American actress Cote de Pablo said: "It wasn't until I found my tribe of artists—people who were outspoken and not afraid to say what they thought, whether in a song or a dance or a piece of classical music—that I found a refuge."[1]

It's important to find your pack, or as I tell my writers, your Wulf Pack. Lone wolves get slaughtered; wolves that run in a pack thrive. That's because there's strength in numbers. Power and knowledge get shared, skills are exchanged, and your pack is ready to howl for you when you succeed. Writing can be lonely and even painful work as rejections pour in through the apprenticing stage. Sharing frustration with trusted allies can lift some of the burden off our shoulders. Our pack understands. They're our people.

They are also a great group to level up with, because they are striving for similar goals.

~

BETA READERS

After addressing first reader (alpha reader) concerns, many writers, especially aspiring writers, use beta readers for additional editing before sending a story out to markets. The thinking is if one reader is good, two or more will be better!

This can certainly be true. I've seen small groups of writers with similar goals level up together by critique swapping and sharing knowledge. When they're small, they're called writer circles. I've even helped form a few, always trying to get at least one experienced writer in the group to help the lesser-experienced writers. Some have been phenomenally successful, others, less so. Not all writers with professional sales have the skills necessary to translate their knowledge to others. Teaching is a gift.

The pros of having beta readers? By having multiple eyes on your work, one writer might catch something another will not. Nobody is perfect, but by submitting your work to the collective, there are fewer chances errors will slip through the cracks. Beta readers are also good for spotting plot holes and logic issues. They're writers, so there's a good chance they'll know when something is missing. And if a deadline is fast approaching but your alpha reader is busy, beta readers can be your ace in the hole. Just be ready to return the favor so it's an equitable system.

The cons? In tight writing circles, the members can start writing like one another. When a small group thinks like a hive mind, one's voice can easily be assimilated. Voice, as I've said before, is the most precious commodity you have. Skilled writers that shine with unique voice become their own brand; a brand readers can only get by reading that writer's work. Careers are built off voice. Some readers will buy anything a writer writes, no matter what genre or age group that work is written for. These superfans will say, "I just like what they write." What they're really saying is they love *how* they write, and that's a writer's unique voice and style. But if a writer blends their voice to please members of the group, they can lose their uniqueness and become homogenized.

Members of writing circles can also fan egos instead of telling it like it is. Some of these become social support groups and chattering kaffeeklatsches instead of circles devoted to advancing the skills of their writers. Note actress Cote de Pablo's quote at the opening. She found her tribe not because they told her what she wanted to hear, but because they were *honest* in their comments, people who were outspoken and not afraid to say what they thought. The only way a writing circle will help one another improve is if the members strive to improve and say it like it is. When comments are seasoned with salt and offered as suggestions, not absolutes, writers in the circle can feel safe sharing their stories and chapters, knowing everyone in the circle has their best interests at heart, even if truthful commentary can sometimes sting.

Writers like Brandon Sanderson often have long lists of beta readers they thank in their acknowledgments. With sizeable novels with multiple characters, it's easy to make a mistake as to what color someone's eyes were, what apparel they wore in an earlier scene, whether fictional words and character names stayed consistent throughout, and so forth. And if you're writing something more technical or period based—like science fiction or historical fiction—it's smart to have someone that's knowledgeable in that field double-check your details. It's better for you to catch those errors than your readers. Smart beta readers really help with these issues.

Beta readers can offer benefits, but be aware of the pitfalls. Especially when we're new and haven't gotten grounded in our voice yet.

~

WRITING GROUPS

Another way to advance in our writing skills is to join a writing group. If we live in a large community, there's a real possibility a group meets regularly in our area, perhaps even specializing in the genre we write in. Often talking to bookstore owners will cue you in on a local group. Sometimes, the owner makes available a room or even their store for the group to meet in after hours. Bookstore owners love books, and they love the writers that make them.

There are also multitudes of writing groups on the Internet. Here is a way you can find your tribe—there's so many, you can find groups specializing in the exact genre, subgenre, and age category you write in. Often these groups are quite large, sometimes numbering into the thousands. Again, being part of a large collective can have advantages —there is usually someone that has an answer to the questions you ask, and multiple viewpoints can give you a more informed understanding of a topic. In many of these groups, there are professional writers and editors, giving their time to help others. And if they like who you are, some will reach out, offering a helping hand or even an opportunity to be a part of their next project. Networking does go on in such groups.

The pros of writing groups? You can find your people in such groups, even in the large ones where you might feel like you are drowned out by the numbers. Watch those posting and sharing, and like and comment on posts that speak to you. Friendships can be built this way, and you can even reach out in private messaging to build more personal relationships. It is very helpful to have a tribe, both large and small, to tap into. The only people that truly understand what we go through for our craft and art are other writers.

The cons of writing groups? Like any group, if you haven't hand-picked and created the group yourself, there will be all kinds of personality types in it. Some writers have good social skills, some do not. Some can be kind and nurturing; others can be haughty and abrasive. If the group offers critique sessions, be sure to sit in on a few before sharing your work. Know what you're getting into.

I was a member for ten years in one of the power groups in speculative fiction. We met every week in a bookstore after hours for round-table critique sessions. Many bestselling writers were members of this group—Hugo winners, Nebula winners, Stoker winners, Writers of the Future winners, even a writer that had written *Star Trek: The Next Generation* episodes. They were an open and welcoming group, and after sitting in and taking part in several critique sessions, I knew what I was getting into and submitted my first manuscript to be critiqued.

It can be shocking, even devastating for a newer writer to have their manuscript critiqued by professional writers the first time. They don't mince words. Some know how to season their words with salt, making their comments palatable, and some are quite blunt. It's not for the faint of heart, but good writers really are trying to help. Truth can hurt. Be prepared for the truth, do your best to check your emotions at the door, and look for commonalities in the critiques. If several writers that know what they're doing say something isn't working right in your story, they're probably correct. Listen and learn. In time, you'll toughen up, and the critiques won't sting so bad. In fact, you'll welcome the input.

Here's some thoughts from the perspective of watching my own online writing group, the Wulf Pack Writers. Our members have a great work ethic—the results they're achieving prove it. While they love talking about books and writing techniques, they are not a kaffeeklatsch group. They do the work. They write. They are serious about getting published and advancing their careers, but not by crushing others around them to get there. Groups with a generous, helpful spirit like that thrive.

Another advantage I've noted in my group. Working with a focused team of writers and stating goals to the group helps keep everyone accountable. Sometimes we need that accountability, especially when everything in our world can appear to be trying to sabotage us. Runners in a marathon get tired, but having your fellow teammates and even the crowd cheering you on can help you find energy you never knew you had to run the course to the finish.

As Rudyard Kipling said in The Jungle Book: "For the strength of the Pack is the Wolf, and the strength of the Wolf is the Pack."

Find your pack.

~

FREELANCE EDITORS

There's another way to get expert help with your manuscript. Freelance editors.

A freelance editor is somebody who works for writers to get their content ready for publication. Instead of working for a publisher, they work independently. There are many types of edits a freelance editor may specialize in. To list a few, there's developmental or content edits, line edits, copy edits, and proofreading. Each type of edit carries a different fee depending on the skills involved and the labor intensity, which equates to hours of the editor's time to do the work. A good place online to find median rates is the Editorial Freelancers Association. Again, these are average rates. Less-experienced editors charge less, experienced editors with solid credentials and successful clients charge more.

It's good to understand the category terms, and what the purpose of each edit is. It's also good to remember labor intensity on a project goes up with newer writers, goes down with experienced writers. This is especially true with large projects, such as novels. If your project is a novel, a freelance editor will likely request to see a sample chapter before quoting you a rate.

In my own editing business, I do both the line edit and the developmental edit—normally charged separately—under one combined rate. My goal when editing is to keep a writer's voice intact while suggesting improvements to help increase the manuscript's chance at selling to respected markets or winning awards. Many projects I have edited have subsequently sold to respected markets, have won multiple prestigious contests, or have become a #1 Amazon Best Seller novel in a major category.

True, some projects I've worked on did not hit these high marks. I can only help the author make the work they've delivered into my care shine in its best light possible. And it's up to the author to decide what portions of the edit they'll apply. But I have noted in the majority of cases, even if that particular story didn't have immediate success (it takes time to find the right home for a project), the writer had success with the subsequent stories they wrote. That's because even one professional edit will reveal what a writer needs help with, exposing blind spots they cannot see on their own. We all have our blind spots. We do need help to spot them so that we can work on them—we won't level up until we do.

What's troubling to me in the industry is that there are many freelance editors hanging out their shingle that have no professional sales, no contest wins, nothing they can point to to prove they've actually done what they are promising they will do for their prospective client. And yet, writers by the droves throw their money at them to get that magic edit that they believe will get their manuscript professionally published or win a major contest award.

I'm not saying they're all bad actors. I have deep respect for editors that have worked at major publishing houses for years that have worked on multitudes of successful projects and are now freelancing —they have the experience and credentials to prove their edits will be helpful. What I'm saying is, *be careful*. There are many scammers out there preying on your desire to get published, with zero credentials to prove they actually know what they are doing.

Why would you pay a contractor to help you build a house that has no proof they've ever built a house? You want expert advice, you hire someone that has done what you hope to accomplish, and has references you can verify to prove it. Watch Olympic competition categories, like figure skating. Who do teams hire for coaches to train their amateur athletes? Other amateurs that have never won a single championship in their life? Or retired athletes that have won the Olympic gold medal? You know the answer. Why? They've got the goods. They've proven they have the skills necessary to win at the highest level, and if they're good trainers, they can pass those skills on to others. No wonder some teams consistently produce gold medalists. They hired gold-medalist coaches.

Conscientious edits take a lot of time on an editor's part. Before hiring a freelance editor, be sure they have solid credentials. This often means two things: (1) They've accomplished what you hope to accomplish, and (2) They have a long list of clients that have had verifiable results by working with that editor.

Anyone can post a list of testimonials. For the scammers, they'll likely be fake. Or they'll be by clients that these editors intentionally fluffed up to feed their egos so they'll keep coming back to hand them money. But what have those clients sold? Where were they published? What contests have they won? How have their novels done? Sadly, some editors know they'll get repeat business by tickling the ears of their clients instead of telling them like it is. I've seen some of those edits. They are surface fluff that will not help a writer get published.

I get it. It's nice to have an editor praise your work. They should praise the things in your manuscript that you did right. But if they don't give you actionable direction, don't show you how much you need to do to get a manuscript into shape so it can sell, you're paying for therapy, not an edit.

I was on a panel of freelance editors at a convention, and a writer in the audience asked us how they could tell the good editors from the bad. After the others had spoken, I said the way you tell is to see if they've succeeded at doing the thing you are trying to do, and if they've proven they can teach that thing by checking on the results of their clients. I thought it was very telling when one of the editors that had already spoken immediately raised her hand and said, "Well, that's not true. Some of us might not have been willing to put in the time it takes to learn the skills of a professional writer—that can take at least five to ten years!"

I rest my case.

Yes, we can go it alone. We can sit in our man caves and she-sheds and isolate ourselves from the world and keep telling ourselves what we're writing is brilliant. And it might be, with time and practice. Or we can step into the light, see what's going on in the real world. We can do some friendly sparring with other writers, learn the skills necessary to win, get a helping hand when we get knocked down. We can even hire a personal trainer, giving us a custom program so that our blows are not striking the air.

Writing is a solitary business, but you don't have to go it alone. There's strength in numbers. Iron sharpens iron.

Find your tribe. Run with your pack. Give as much as you get, and you'll find refuge.

31

PROPER MANUSCRIPT FORMAT FOR THE WIN!

You've written your story (product), you've used the system you have in place to check it for errors (quality control). It's time to stop tinkering with it and call it good. You've got quality product to send to market! Let's go!

Um, did you format your manuscript properly?

Oh yes, you say! Single-spaced with .25-inch margins with a new font you discovered named Curlicue Cuticles in blood-red. It's *perfect* for your horror story, you know it's going to stand out in that pile of pasty-white manuscripts.

It's going to stand out, all right. And not in a good way. For some reason, the newer a writer is, the more they feel the need to spice up their manuscript. Perhaps they have a desktop publishing program, or they've seen some fancy blogs, and they think slick is how manuscripts should look. Stylish formatting. Cool fonts. Raised caps. Your manuscript will be dressed for success!

That couldn't be further from the truth. Professional manuscript format has been standardized. It's not a Gucci look—it's as plain Jane as dressing a manuscript can be. All professional writers follow it. And if you want your story to look professional and walk into that editor's office with its best foot forward, you should follow it, too.

PROFESSIONAL MANUSCRIPT FORMAT

On Year One of my Super Secrets Workshop, I numbered each Super Secret in a forum topic to make it easier for writers to locate and remember. I had already posted seventeen of them when I noted a recurring issue in the stories I had been editing for workshop members. No one knew how to format their manuscripts properly. Not one. They'd all been writing for some time, but their manuscript formatting was off, some drastically so.

What I had thought was basic knowledge proved to be elusive to emerging writers. Even when I showed them an example and encouraged them to make standardized manuscript templates, the next manuscript they sent me would still be two or three beads off center. What they didn't realize is that if a manuscript doesn't follow proper manuscript format, it looks off-kilter to first readers and editors. If it's significantly off, it will mark the story as amateurish without one word being read.

With so many stories in the submission pile vying for an editor's attention, the last thing you want to do is to irritate the editor with a funky font or an odd page setup. Or worse, long blocks of single-spaced text. Best foot forward is looking like all the other pros that have their stories in that pile. Editors' submission guidelines normally ask writers to *please* follow proper manuscript format.

You should know the elements necessary to ensure your manuscript follows that format. It will keep a smile on that tired editor's face as they pluck your story out of the pile to be read.

I was surprised to discover my workshop members—most having written for many years—did not know this. I needed to take them back to the basics. So I called it "Super Secret #0: Proper Manuscript Format For the Win." I gave them the guidelines that showed them what a pro manuscript is supposed to look like.

Done deal, right?

No way. They still kept sending me funky manuscripts. And I was editing all of their manuscripts for free, but they needed to get this right if they wanted my help. So I sent their manuscripts back until they got it right. For some, it took three tries.

It's not only a problem with newer writers. In my editing business, I've had to go over proper manuscript format many times with the same client. It's like they're looking at those plates of colored dots in the Ishihara test at the optometrist office. If you're color blind, you can't see the number hiding in the dots no matter how hard you look at the plate. And when you can't see the issue, you can't fix it.

I've talked to other editors, and they've noted the same issue with their clients. It is difficult for many writers to *see* that their manuscript doesn't match the proper format—it's like it's a cognitive impairment. Maybe doing it for years the wrong way makes it difficult to see the right way. Maybe it's just too darn plain to satisfy the colorful nature of creatives. Whatever the case may be, until we get our manuscript formatted properly, our stories will look like they're wearing Hare Krishna sandals to a black-tie and Oxford's event. We want our *story* to stand out, not the packaging.

Please study the sample I've provided. Check my manuscript against yours. Go back to the sample. Check again. When you're sure you've got it right, make a template and use it whenever you start a story. If you don't, I'm betting you'll creep back into old habits.

Forewarned is forearmed.

∿

"LAST WORDS"

The following is a brief sample for you to study. This is a story based off a KYD 250-word flash piece I wrote that was a winner in a year-long flash fiction contest I entered that ended up having some 30,000 entries. This story is not based on my Grand Prize winner—this is based on my other Top 10 winner. One of the twenty professional judges in that contest was the editor of *The Rose and Thorn Literary Ezine,* a respected online literary magazine in the day. She invited me to expand "Last Words" into a 1,000-word flash fiction story for her magazine and published it in 1996. Have a look.

Wulf Moon
123 Moonbeam Road
Olympic Peninsula, WA 12345
(123) 456-7891
moon@myemail.com

1000 words

Last Words

by Wulf Moon

I sat in a hard plastic hospital chair, fingers touching the book inside my jacket while I watched my father die. Dad rested in bed, eyes closed, eyelids twitching, lips grayish blue. The room's window was etched in frost, streetlights glowing upon the crystals, illuminating patterns like stained glass in a chapel. The air smelled of pine solvent and rubbing alcohol, and the divider curtain was drawn, giving the illusion of privacy.

I ran my fingers along the binding of the tome, felt the impression of stamped letters. My book. The latest collection of poems. My lifelong secret. My last chance to let Dad know. Becoming a poet had always been his dream, and I didn't know if I could tell him.

Dad had known success. He'd won Realtor of the Year for Century 21 in Minnesota, had the view office in Stillwater overlooking the St. Croix River, yachts cruising past like fat swans. Everyone in town knew Dad, but it wasn't his successful career that gave him joy.

Just writing those damnable sing-songy poems.

When I'd stop to visit at his office, he'd have me pull up a chair, ask his assistant to bring me some coffee. Awful stuff, tasted like brewed charcoal briquettes. We'd talk about his new listings and pending closings, about how I was doing after the divorce, how my teaching was going at Carleton, how the girls were doing in school. And every time, before we'd head for ribs at Brian's Meat Market, he'd reach in a drawer and toss me that worn leather binder.

"Penned some new ones, kid. Try these on for size."

I'd give up the view of the yachts, lean back in my chair and read his poems, sweating to find something good I could comment on. Then I'd smile, because, hey, they were from his heart.

"Hmmm. 'Snowfall' is good. I like this verse: 'The snow falls in time with memories of my mind as I chew on the rind of forsaken mankind.' Reminds me of Frost." It did remind me of Robert Frost. Thought a lot of his works were sing-songy too, repetitive rhyme and meter, but that didn't seem to harm his career. Success is hard to argue with.

Dad always smiled when I likened his work to famous poets. "Damn right it's good. But do you think the Poetry Society of America would think so?" He'd flash the latest. "Form rejection. Not even personal."

"Do not go gentle into that good night. Proud of you for not giving up. There's something to be said for our stubborn German blood."

"*Jawohl,*" he'd say, thumping his fist against the desk. "You hungry? Let's go eat."

I remembered Dad's comments on my works when I was a kid. I'd be lying in bed, staring at the glittering bits in the ceiling texture, words pouring into my mind like songs from seductive sirens. No way they'd grant me sleep unless I rose to their call and danced.

I'd hunch over a typewriter in the basement until two or three in the morning. As the night flowed on, the keys striking the platen would sound like volleys of thunder. I'd set a pillow under the base, wrap a towel around the sides, hope Dad wouldn't hear, and immerse in verse again.

It didn't work. Inevitably, Dad would hear and come lumbering down the stairs. I'd swim up from the hazy depths, float on the surface of the muse as Dad drew up alongside, scratching the stubble on his chin. He'd stand there in his sagging underwear in a silence as long as the sea. He didn't have to speak--I knew what his verdict would be.

"Rhythm seems off. Doesn't flow. Good ideas, son, but you won't make money at it. Trust me, I've tried. You'd make a great Realtor though--got my name to carry you in town. Get to bed now, you've got school in the morning."

I started winning awards in national student contests. Now he'd be proud. Now Dad would know the fire burning in my heart was true. But every time I'd show him a certificate, he'd ask to see the poem, make some comment about how it didn't rhyme or the metaphors were off, and his words would rip the wind from my sails. I quit telling him about them. And as I'd head to bed after he had finished his spiel about my wonderful future in real estate, I'd think, yeah, just what I want in life, to wear a baby-crap-yellow jacket to work every day.

Years later--many rejection slips later--when *The New Yorker* took my first poem, it was published under a pseudonym. I never told him. Then *The Atlantic*. Then some chapbooks through good university presses. Then St. Martin's Press bought my collection. I never told him. I had sold. Dad hadn't.

And now here I was, sitting by his side, holding his blue-veined hand, oxygen hissing like serpents through pale green tubes at his nose. The air was winter dry, and the chair had a

227

deep slant that forced me to balance on the edge of the seat. The book in my coat felt heavy as a brick as I mulled over the best way to tell him.

I jerked as Dad sat up. "Michael, it's you. Good. Want you to do something for me."

"Sure, Dad. Just sit back."

"Hell with the doctors! Listen to me, kid."

I leaned forward.

"All my life, only thing besides family that meant anything to me were my poems."

My throat caught. "I know, Dad."

"Only thing I didn't succeed in, getting published." He coughed furiously. "Take my stuff. You're the only one who understands. Keep sending them out for me."

I rubbed his weathered hand, my stomach twisting like a ball of baler twine. "I will."

"They were good, weren't they?"

A hot tear wandered down my cheek. I shifted my coat, tugged the zipper a little higher.

"They were great, Dad."

The End

~

SHUNN'S GUIDE

As you've probably gathered, there's more truth than fiction in that story. If you're going to plagiarize something, plagiarize your life. It's full of crazier twists than you'll ever find in fiction. I wrote that story wondering how the situation with my writing and my father might end one day. Turns out the real-life version had quite a different ending. In a good way. Maybe I'll share it in the next book. It still chokes me up too much to write about it at the moment.

The go-to for professional short story manuscript format on the Internet is William Shunn's *Proper Manuscript Format*, often referred to as Shunn's Guide. Choose the modern version. Review it from time to time to stay on track. https://www.shunn.net/format/story/

The format looks plain so you might be tempted to dress it up. Don't. There are many reasons editors prefer this format, especially double-spacing and one-inch margins so they can mark corrections. And all that white space between the contact information and the title? It gives editors space to write notes. Stick to the format and your manuscript will be dressed for success. To an editor, this makes your story look like it's wearing Armani instead of a hobo suit.

Here's the basics. One-inch margins left, right, top, and bottom. Set alignment to the *left*, not *justify*—you're not doing layout for magazine columns, that's the typesetter's job. Black color for your type should go without saying, but editors have reported so many crazy things, it needs to be said. Set paragraphs to double-spaced with the first line at 0.5 inches (don't tab those in when you type). Don't add spacing before or after paragraphs. Just the standard double-spacing is all you need.

As for font, Courier used to be the font of choice because it looked like the output from a typewriter and it's monospaced, making it easier to spot typographical errors. Today, many feel using Courier dates a writer, and I've seen some editor's guidelines state not to use Courier, one even saying "it makes my eyes bleed." Times New

Roman is now standard, or something similar. Font size should be set to 12 points.

After you get all of this down, you'll still need to check the guidelines of every publisher you send your manuscript to. Many have their own adjustments to these standards, such as an editor with bad eyes that would like your type in 14 points, please. Don't give an editor a reason to get annoyed with your formatting. Follow their guidelines. Make them happy and they might make you happy with a sale.

Insert top headers in your document, and select "Different First Page." This allows you to set up your legal name and contact information on the left side, your word count on the right. I know some say differently, but don't put any professional organizations that you're a member of on the manuscript. If you feel it's important, save that for your cover letter.

In the old days, we didn't have word processors with the word count feature, we had typewriters, and had to do fuzzy math. That's why you see "about X words" or "approximately X words" on manuscripts. Today, we know exactly how many words are in that manuscript (although it does vary slightly depending on which word processing program you use). I recommend you state the exact word count instead of rounding up or down. Some writers actually cheat on their word count to make it under a publisher's or contest's guidelines —sometimes massively so! Don't be that person. Editors and judges didn't get those jobs by being stupid.

You're not going to be paid on an approximate, nor will you be paid more for rounding your number higher. State the exact word count in the upper right corner as you see in my sample (yes, it's exactly 1,000 words), and you'll have the number the editor will likely pay you from when he or she buys your story. It's time for word counts to enter the reality of the 21st century. I'm not alone in stating this—I've seen some editors say the same thing in their publication's guidelines.

While you're still in that separate first page header, after you've entered your contact information and word count, hit Return (Enter) several times until you've dropped down the page one-third to one-half. Center your title like you see in my example, hit Return once and you'll have a double-space where you'll enter your centered byline (make sure your 0.5-inch indent is turned off here or your title and byline will look wonky—off-center). If you write under a pseudonym, the byline is where you enter it. When your story gets published, this is the name your story will be attributed to. Hit Return twice, and that's where the text of your story begins.

Now that you've got your first page header set up, go to your next page's header. As long as you already selected Different First Page, when you set up this next page, it won't reset your first page. In the upper right of the header, insert Page Numbers. The editor will also need your name and title Aligned Right in the header (in a shortened form if it's a long title). As for my sample story, it should look like this in the upper right corner: Moon / Last Words / 2

Now exit your headers and go back to your first page to start your story. Make sure your paragraph settings and line spacing are set properly. I always check my first page to be sure it has twelve or thirteen lines of the story on it. That always gets my title and byline in just the right spot. Why twelve *or* thirteen lines?

I'm strategic. After the first paragraph or two where I set my stage, I usually have a kicker line, a line that jumps out and hooks the reader. I don't want it to be on the second page. Many first readers and editors only flip to the second page if the first page grabs them. I don't leave this to random chance if I can help it. I'm hooking them on page one, and I'll do a slight adjustment to my first page to make sure that happens. There's a Super-Duper Secret tip for you. I'm giving you a vial of *Felix Filicis*, like the one Professor Slughorn gave to Harry Potter. Your reward for reading to the end of this book. *Congratulations. Use it well.*

When it comes time to start the next scene in your story, hit Return, dropping one double-spaced line, type the hashtag # symbol, center it (turn off your 0.5-inch indent only for this), then hit Return again, and start your next scene. That hashtag symbol represents what's known as a *scene break*—it tells the editor the extra space is intentional, and they know they're now entering the next scene in your story. The typesetter will also take note of those hashtags, removing them but setting the necessary space in their formatting for publication.

When you get to the end of your story, you have the option of simply ending on your last line, or hitting Return and centering The End on the next line (I like dropping two lines just to make it clear this is not part of the story text). Some endings can be ambiguous, so typing The End makes it obvious this is where you intended the story to end.

There are other little things, like using Italic to italicize your text instead of underlining the text like it was done in days of old. You'll figure it out. Look at manuscript samples if in doubt.

I have one final thing to say in this chapter: *The End is here!*

And just in case my ending is too ambiguous …

The End

32

COVER LETTERS

Did you see the movie *A Knight's Tale* with the late Heath Ledger? I love that movie. After the cold open (teaser scene) and title card, the movie begins at a medieval jousting tournament. Just when you think this is going to be another chivalric period piece, Queen's "We Will Rock You" plays and the spectators in the stands go *stomp—stomp—clap, stomp—stomp—clap* to make the pounding percussion for the song. Whoa! What an opening!

It's an immediate cue to the viewing audience that while the movie is set in the milieu of The Hundred Years' War, it's a twist from the traditional medieval knight genre. The musical segue becomes a superlative transition, informing the audience this will be a *modern* telling of this tale of chivalry.

My favorite parts in the movie? The scenes where the heralds stand in the jousting arena to announce the patents of nobility of their knights—credentials that gave knights the noble right to compete in the tournaments. Heath Ledger's character has no patent document— he's a starving squire who reaches beyond his station in order to joust for fame and fortune. By chance, he meets a destitute writer on the road who can forge patents of nobility, and Sir Ulrich von Liechten- stein from the obscure province of Gelderland is born.

The destitute writer? None other than Geoffery Chaucer, played by Paul Bettany. You might know Paul Bettany as the AI Jarvis from the Marvel movies, but *A Knight's Tale* is where Bettany's acting truly shines. He reveals his wondrous talent in this role, and he steals the show with his outlandish heralding for his would-be knight.

Cover letters. These have parallels to patents of nobility. They introduce a writer's credentials to editors, reminding them to pay attention to the deeds of this noble knight—er, ignoble writer—before them. But are cover letters as important as some might believe? Do we need to trace our writing lineage back to Charlemagne and beyond for editors to take notice?

Just what are short story cover letters, why do we use them, and why should we be careful not to gild the lily?

~

COVER LETTERS: WHAT'S THEIR PURPOSE?

A cover letter is a letter addressed to the editor to give them information about you and your story when you submit it. Some publishers have several anthologies or multiple submission calls going on simultaneously, so a cover letter can guide your manuscript to the correct one. It notifies first readers and editors of your story's title, genre, and word count. If you've been published in respected publications, listing a few is a good idea. And if your story relies upon unique expertise—like you wrote a tale about an undercover FBI Special Agent and you actually *are* a retired FBI Special Agent—this is the place you let the editorial staff know.

A cover letter is *not* the place to list your patent of nobility back to Charlemagne and beyond. What do I mean by that? A cover letter is not a bibliography of your published works. A cover letter is not a summary of your story, nor is it a place to include testimonials from your mother on what a great writer you are. A cover letter is not a place to get cute with the editor and share anecdotes about your cat or dog.

There is one rule about cover letters: Keep it simple.

WHAT GOES IN A COVER LETTER?

The term *cover letter* is actually a misnomer today. In the ancient days of old when writers mailed their stories out to editors, a letter was placed atop the manuscript being submitted, thus the *cover* on the manuscript. Today, most publishers have submission portals that require many of these details to be placed in their form fields, or they ask writers to email their submissions with specific keywords to be placed in the subject line so they can sort out submissions. No paper letter atop a manuscript is involved. It really should be called a *submission letter* now, but old habits die hard.

If the publisher doesn't require a blind submission (no name or contact information on the manuscript), your name and address should already be on the manuscript—there's no need to add it to your cover letter. If you entered the word count and genre in the submission portal's fields, why include that information in your submission letter? In this case, the portal already has it.

Do open your letter with a salutation and the editor's name, but get it right—it won't do you any favors with the editor if you mess up the spelling! You can address them as "Dear Editor" if you can't find their name—most won't take offense. Then, it's just a matter of pasting your adjusted submission letter in the designated area in the portal, attaching your manuscript file, pushing submit, and you're good to go.

If you're submitting via email, you'll need to provide helpful information to the editor in the body of your email. After the salutation, your submission letter should include the title of your story, the genre it fits within, and the word count—all just a line that becomes the first paragraph of the letter. In the second paragraph, you list a few publication credits if you have them. In the third paragraph, you list any special qualifications you have *if they're pertinent to the story*. If you've written a story about Moon landings and you've been to the Moon, by all means, let the editor know! Finally, close with thanks for their consideration, then a complimentary closing like sincerely, your name, and you're good to go. Simple, right?

Right. Unless we can't help ourselves and feel the need to include our patent of nobility. A long list of honorable mentions in contests, every place we've been published or not-so-published, and maybe we should include that comment a famous writer made about our writing prowess when we took her workshop. Surely heaping such highlights from our writing lives in our submission letter will dazzle the editor and get our story published!

Um, are we forgetting that editors are *very* busy people? That the last thing they want to turn their bloodshot eyes upon is a cover letter longer than the flash story we're submitting? Instead of helping our story get read, long cover letters do the opposite. They can annoy the editor. And when an editor's eyes are blurring late at night from trying to get through hundreds of submissions, the last thing you want to do is irritate them.

Less is more. Nowhere is that truer than in cover letters.

WHAT DOES A PROPER SHORT STORY COVER LETTER LOOK LIKE?

I'm glad you asked. I'll give you one of mine as a sample. If you've been published in respected markets that first readers or editors would recognize, list a few. If you've won a significant contest the editor would recognize, list that, too. Having professional sales won't bamboozle an editor into buying a bad story. But they do notify first readers and editors that your story likely has merit due to your experience, and they'll probably give it closer consideration. If a first reader feels a story is on the edge, seeing strong credentials will likely move them to bump it up to the editor to make the call. And if you've been published in the publication before, by all means, get that in the cover letter. Editors love seeing fresh stories from writers "in their stable."

What if you have no sales? No biggie! Editors love publishing new authors in their pages. I know it may not look like it, but it's true! The problem is many aspiring writers aren't writing at a publishable level yet—they're still in their apprentice stage. And even when they do write publishable stories, editors may have just published a similar story, or don't have room in their publication for a longer story by an unknown writer. They still want to see a new writer's work. When editors see an unpublished writer trying to break in, they'll take note. As they see their stories level-up with each submission, they'll even hope. It's an editor's greatest joy to discover a new writer. Why shouldn't that writer be you?

So here's how a standard submission letter looks when sent via email. Let's send this story to the editor at *DreamForge Magazine*. We'll pretend *DreamForge* doesn't have a submission portal, and yes, Scot spells his first name with one T, not two. Gotta get it right!

Dear Scot Noel,

Please find attached my story "Shaken, Not Stirred" (SF, 5149 words).

My stories have appeared in numerous publications including *Writers of the Future Vol. 35, Galaxy's Edge*, and *Star Trek: Strange New Worlds 2*.

Thank you for your consideration.

Sincerely,

Wulf Moon

There, short and sweet. I actually list some of my awards as well, but I don't want to confuse you. That's really all you need for a short story submission letter, and the editor will appreciate your brevity. They're looking for an introduction to you and your work, not your life's history.

Save your patent of nobility for when you go jousting.

33

NEVER LET GO

Barnacle glue, or barnacle cement, is one of the strongest adhesives known to man. Its tensile strength is five thousand pounds per square inch. It bonds so strong to boat hulls that after you shear the barnacle off, you're still going to have to grind away its cement to be rid of it. A barnacle NEVER lets go.

Nor does a professional writer. You're reading this book, so there must be questions like this on your mind: Why does one writer become a pro writer, and another does not? Why does one writer talk about writing year after year, and another gets their work published year after year?

I'll tell you why. It's because one writer never truly attaches to their dream of becoming a professional writer, while the other writer grabs onto the dream and never lets go. That's because it's not a dream for them. It's their destiny, and they know it. And, I might add, they are willing to do the diligent work to achieve that dream.

∽

THE LARVAL STAGE

In barnacles, the first stage, called the nauplius, is where the larva matures as part of ocean plankton. It hasn't fully developed at this point, so it floats wherever the wind, waves, and tides may take it. The nauplius literally goes with the flow.

Just like the barnacle, every writer in existence has had their larval stage. Aspiring writers get tossed about in this stage, swept up in currents of conflicting misinformation, often generated by those that have no professional credits to their name. Worse, larval writers may be devoured by predators—disreputable editors and agents and contests that charge exorbitant fees with the promise of promoting or publishing their work, but in truth are just there to fleece desperate writers trying to navigate the overwhelming currents that seem to keep them from their destiny.

There are also storms and rocks that can not only take an aspiring writer off course, they can dash their writing time to bits: fighting real life battles to survive such things as job loss, severe health dilemmas, relationship issues, childcare—the list goes on and on. And finally, there is the toughest battle of all—wrestling with our inner self. Are we worthy? Do we have what it takes? Will our writing efforts ever pan out? Will we even get to that successful sale and enjoy that glorious dawn of self-fulfillment as we see our work published and shared with the world?

The difference between storm-tossed plankton and the resolute barnacle is that one kept floating about the currents, while the other vigorously sought the next level of its existence—attaching to something solid and never letting go. The difference between a novice and a break-out writer is the same. If we wish to become a professional writer, we must keep seeking that goal. We must find a way to lock onto it and never let go. We must hold fast to that belief and do the necessary work required until belief becomes reality.

∾

WRITING CONTESTS

My story of how I got published, of how I *continued* to get published, and what I learned along the way is indeed a tale of *never letting go....*

I've been writing fiction for over fifty years, and had my first professional sale forty-six years ago at the time of this writing.

That sale came as the result of a writing contest. When I was fifteen, I won the national Scholastic Art & Writing Awards—the same contest that first discovered Stephen King, Peter S. Beagle, Truman Capote, John Updike, Joyce Carol Oates, and a host of iconic names in the arts. The editor at *Science World* saw my winning entry and published my science fiction story "The Last Ray of Light" in 1978. With professional pay beyond even today's standard and with a circulation of 500,000 copies per issue, this was my first professional sale.

So here is the first lesson I learned, and I learned it young. *Amateur contests are an excellent way to get published.* How so? You're competing on a level playing field. When you submit to professional magazines, you are not. Competition is extremely tough at pro markets because your story is up against those written by seasoned veterans, many with tremendous skill and prestigious awards to prove it! It should be a no-brainer that professional magazines are going to be hard to sell to for a new writer, while winning contests that restrict entries to amateur writers is going to be easier.

Plus, winning a contest is a great ego boost, and in that battle against self-doubt—our worst enemy—having acknowledgment from a respected contest judged by bestselling professionals can help cement our belief that we can indeed become professional writers. In the case of the winners of Scholastic Corporation's contest, it's been said that these writers—by winning this prestigious young adult contest at the national level in their developmental stage—got the validation they needed to solidify their belief that they could make a successful career out of writing. With such powerful proof to stand on in their formative years, they went to work in earnest and turned belief into reality as adults.

Belief is a powerful thing. We must believe before we can accomplish. *Fake it till you make it* is a common phrase. But belief is something you don't fake. It's a fire in your gut you can't put out. You know you can do it; you just haven't had the full opportunity to prove it yet. When a newspaper reporter asked George Mallory, "Why did you want to climb Mount Everest?" he replied, "Because it's there." But I believe the true answer is, *"Because I knew I could."* He had climbed and trained on many mountains before he climbed Mt. Everest. He had proof positive he could do this thing. He had reached the pinnacle of other summits successfully. With proof positive he had the necessary skill set, he had the confidence to take on greater challenges. Winning writing contests will help you believe in your abilities, and with that proof, you can more easily forge ahead toward higher peaks in publishing.

Winning contests can also provide an aspiring writer with credits for cover/submission letters, especially if the contest is respected for helping writers, not fleecing them with expensive fees. I've won many such contests, including one sponsored by bestselling author Nora Roberts, where I had the privilege of writing the conclusion to her online novella. I'm a professionally published Star Trek author now because I entered Pocket Books Strange New Worlds Contest for aspiring writers and was a winner in Volume 2. Do things like that look good on the submission letter you send with your story? Certainly! As stated in the last chapter, if credits are significant, they can act like a Sherpa to guide your story from of the hands of first readers up to the editor-in-chief who has the power to buy and publish your story or novel.

Want me to recommend a contest? I've got one for you. *Writers of the Future.* It's a speculative fiction contest, so if you write science fiction, fantasy, and soft horror, this contest is for you! This contest has been around for almost forty years at time of writing, there is no fee to enter, the judging is by some of the biggest bestselling authors in the industry (like Brandon Sanderson), and submissions are restricted to amateur writers. If you have no more than three professionally published stories, you can enter this contest.

Don't get me wrong, there is serious competition, as thousands from around the world enter every quarter trying to win. But the benefits to an emerging writer make this the number one market you should be submitting to. Winners receive substantial prize and publication money, an expense-paid trip to Hollywood from anywhere in the world, a week-long workshop with top names in speculative fiction writing, massive media promotion, and their stories get published in an international bestselling anthology.

There are many other benefits even if you don't win the contest. Setting a goal of entering every quarter teaches you how to meet deadlines—a vital skill to learn for those planning a professional career in writing. And as your writing rises toward professional standards, you'll receive honor certificates that let you know how close your writing is to the mark. Semifinalists get comments on their story from the coordinating judge—this is a personalized critique from a bestselling author. The contest's quarterly deadlines also help you create new stories—and even if they don't win, you'll have more stories to send to other markets. I've sold several stories I wrote for this contest to professionally paying markets, and several have been reprinted—one in a best of the year anthology ("Muzik Man" in *Best of Deep Magic, Anthology 2*).

On top of that, there's the Writers of the Future Forum, an online forum where novice writers gather to discuss tips to help win the contest and to write professionally. It's a social forum where writers swap stories, share resources, and encourage one another to fuse themselves to their dream and never let go. In fact, I first created *Wulf Moon's Super Secrets of Writing* within that forum as an online resource and workshop for aspiring writers. What motivated me to do this? I noticed that a lot of novice writers rewrite and rework the same story over and over again, thinking they will perfect it. In truth, as I read these rewrites, I discovered they often ruined their stories. So, I established a challenge to get members to write and submit four fresh, original stories in a year. I also posted writing tips and exercises, writing resources, and books to help aspiring writers craft professionally written stories that would sell and win contests.

It worked. In a little over four years since I started this program, over a dozen writers that I've worked with through my Super Secrets of Writing have either won the contest, been published finalists (which gets them the same treatment as the winners), or both. Others have written to me privately in thanks, telling me their study of the Super Secrets helped them achieve their win. Several even wrote to tell me my Super Secrets posts helped them take up writing, and they achieved their first professional sales by following the lessons. One of these was a fifteen-year-old from Taiwan that said she wanted to become a novelist. She's now eighteen and has published twenty-two novels, many of them award winners in multiple contests. My *Super Secrets of Writing* topic has logged around 850,000 views at time of writing; I'm happy this resource has given solid footing to so many trying to find their way.

∾

BROADWAY VS OFF-BROADWAY

I'm going to let you in on another secret, and *no one* is going to tell you this. I've had professional writers tell me to only send stories to professionally accredited markets, such as those approved by organizations like the Science Fiction and Fantasy Writers of America. Start at the top paying markets on their list, stop at the lowest paying market still vetted by such organizations as a professional sale. On the surface, this sounds logical. Who doesn't want the most money for their work, with the highest readership to broadcast their story out to? But for new writers, there can be a pitfall here. I'll give you my advice, since I'm supposed to be telling you What *I* Learned Along the Way.

Here's the deal. Top tier professional publications need well-known authors to help sell their books, magazines, and e-zines. When they publish a new, unheard-of author, do you see their name as a headliner? Not often. Why not? Because novice writers' names don't sell magazines. They have no following so it's unlikely the publisher will put them on the cover. Editors need to buy good stories from well-known writers to sell their publications to stay in business. They love discovering new writers, don't get me wrong, but it's a business, and they need to sell copies to stay in business.

Reality check. There are very few openings in magazines and professional anthologies for novice writers, and you are always competing against writers that have a good track record and proven professional skills. These publications already have a stable of professional writers they're buying from, many of them currently or previously on top industry bestseller lists. Even when publishers do open call anthologies—meaning anyone can submit stories—many have already filled the bulk of the anthology with private invites to proven writers, leaving only a few spots for everyone else to compete over. And who is in that mix? All the pro writers that didn't get the private invite but want that juicy sale. This is why it is so difficult for new writers to break into top-tier markets. The apex predators are always up there feeding, and you're not a big fish yet.

Does this mean you should surrender, swim away from the battle and send your writing to token or non-paying markets instead? Not if your goal is to become a professionally published writer! I don't believe writers should sell themselves short, nor give their hard work away—except for worthy causes, like charity anthologies. But I don't believe we should limit ourselves to SFWA qualified (or HWA, RWA, etc.) markets only, as if the gold standard is the only currency. Silver pays the bills as well, and performing on some of those slightly lesser stages can be the gateway to the fancy theaters. You build a good resumé, and you keep trading up if your Broadway auditions aren't panning out. Yes, you still go to those Broadway auditions as you're able, but you are not above acting in a play just around the corner. In fact, I believe the more you play on those stages *close* to Broadway, the more likely that famous Broadway director will pay attention when you try out for their next production.

Some have scoffed when seeing me give this advice, even though I've proven the theory both in my own case, and in the case of many I coach in my Wulf Pack Writers group. This article has been published for years now, but something serendipitous happened right when I was converting it to a chapter for this book. I watched a piece on CBS Sunday Morning (June 11, 2023) where writer and comedian Alex Edelman explained how he got his show on Broadway. Take a look.

"Here's how I got mine there. First, I put up the show in a pub behind a London shoe store. Then, I worked it out in smaller venues and at festivals. That step took about three years. The thing about getting your show to Broadway if you really want to get it there? You have to think it's never going to get there. You have to love your show and be happy to perform it anywhere you can. Unless you're Andrew Lloyd Weber—he needs a big stage. All of those cats aren't going to fit in a pub behind a shoe store, are they? Anyhow, the show went up *off* Broadway, and believe it or not, it sold out like a hundred-and-sixty shows in a row. Mostly because the *New York Times* and Sarah Jessica Parker said nice things. A year, I found out I was going on Broadway, and I thought, 'Maybe now my uncle will stop asking me about law school.'"

So, there you have my theoretical off-Broadway analogy proven. You *can* work your way up. Most actors do. Most writers do, too. You have to get your work out there in venues for it to be seen. And you must refine your craft so that it's worthy of appearing on those top-tier stages. Alex Edelman did it. You can, too. Maybe your sites aren't set on Broadway, but you get the picture. You don't have to have an all-or-nothing approach to writing. You don't have to start at the top. Build up your successes and top editors and publishers will take notice.

I didn't always think this way. I came from a famous writing work-shop filled with Nebula and Hugo and World Fantasy and Stoker winners. Almost all of them established pros, telling you to send your work to SFWA approved markets, because you build your career by selling to the big-name magazines and winning the prestigious awards. That message was right for them. They were already performing on those Broadway stages, why would they step down? But I don't believe it's the right message to give to new writers. The novice writer is still learning their craft. Like a novice actor, it's going to be rough getting work if you decide the only place you're willing to audition is on a well-known Broadway stage.

And I still hear this rhetoric today. When I tell SFWA members my work is dancing across these stages, some automatically respond: "I don't submit to any markets that aren't SFWA listed. My work should be worthy of professional pay." I bite my tongue, but still get out: "They PAID me pro pay."

It's not like my story is a busker holding out a cup on Skid Row.

These are off-Broadway productions, just around the corner from Big Name Theater. Truth is, I shopped many of these stories for years to every SFWA accredited pro market. I got back wonderful personal rejections, but rejections and holds aren't sales. So, with my new "Off-Broadway, just around the block" thinking, I decided to step my search down to the next tier—pro-pay but *not* on an organization's list of accredited markets.

I made sale after sale after I did so.

Guess what? These magazines and anthologies are in no way slumming. They have famous authors in every issue—why would top authors on the industry's prestigious bestseller lists send their stories to markets they felt would detract from their sterling reputations? Truth is, it's a way for these name authors to net up more fans. And I don't mind netting up more of those fans myself.

Such "accredited market only" rhetoric can be damaging to new writers. I know it held me back; I have changed that thinking now. I know precisely when I did, and I had immediate results when I did so. Walk with me.

~

MY BREAKOUT MOMENT

It was a dark and stormy night. After hundreds of rejections on my stories and about seventeen years since my last sale, I said, "Why don't I lower my search engine parameters to pro paying markets, but *not* SFWA qualified? (I use Diabolical Plots' *The Submission Grinder* as my market search engine.) Lo and behold, the first name that popped up was an anthology called *Strange Beasties*. I had a story called, "Beast of the Month." The publisher, Third Flatiron, had a long history of creating anthologies that garnered great reviews, they paid the professional rate, and I had the perfect story to match their theme.

Guess what? It sold. Then, they hired me to narrate it for a podcast. And then I used that podcast as my demo reel, submitted it, and got approved as a narrator at Escape Artists, Apex Publications, and

Gallery of Curiosities. The latter has hired me to narrate many stories for them.

But wait! There's more! Third Flatiron paid me to reprint "Beast of the Month" in their Best of the Year anthology as well. And then the editor bought my story "War Dog" for another anthology. And hired me to narrate it. And that story went on to win Critters Readers' Choice Award for *Best Science Fiction and Fantasy Short Story of 2018*. And then editor Alex Shvartsman of UFO Publishing fame heard some of these podcasts and hired me to be his podcast director at his new professional magazine—*Future Science Fiction Digest*. I had a story published there as well. And because of the reputation I built there, I landed a job with a *Wall Street Journal* bestselling author that paid thousands of dollars.

All because I changed my thinking, sent a story to a respected *mid-level* publisher ... and worked my way up. That decision to change my standards and submit to semi-pro publishers paying pro rate or just under changed *everything* for me. And guess what? It just keeps going up. Once you sell a story to an editor, they watch for your work for future issues and anthologies. You've broken the ice, you've made a good impression, and they enjoy welcoming you back to their stage. You can build a career with an editor that loves your work. And as your visibility grows, other professional editors take note. The next story you send them might get more than just a first-pages glance. It might get you a sale, and on to that Broadway-level stage you go.

~

NEVER LET GO

I know the startup is hard. It can take many years to get professionally published with little to nothing to give you signs you're going to make it along the way. That's because those early stories are where you apprentice, they're your practice sessions where you learn your craft. Some writers don't survive the process—they take the volume of rejections as proof that they cannot write. The truth is, virtually every famous writer you know had to pass through this trial by fire. They had to learn their craft by doing the work. Why should it be any different for you or me?

Here is where you have to be that barnacle, resolutely fused to your goal, allowing nothing to shear you away. I have seen those writers cling to their dream, holding on through thick and thin. I have seen them battling the elements and fighting their own self-doubt. But I have also seen their breakout moment. They go for years selling nothing and then, *Bam!*, out of nowhere they sell everywhere. To pro markets, winning awards, making a steady string of sales. I'm happy for them. I know they exerted themselves with Herculean effort to get there.

Still, it's only natural to wonder, "When will *my* breakout moment come?"

Well, it does come if you're studying hard and doing the diligent work, usually when you least expect it. In my case, my breakout moment (actually my Phoenix moment) began with four remarkable things in a two-week span. I was awarded the Superstars Writing Seminar Scholarship, the best writing conference I have ever attended. I sold "War Dog" to the *Terra Tara Terror* anthology, and it went on to win Critters' best short story of the year award. I won the international speculative fiction talent search *Writers of the Future* with my story "Super-Duper Moongirl and the Amazing Moon Dawdler." And Alex Shvartsman asked me to be an editor at a new professional magazine, *Future Science Fiction Digest*.

All in a two-week period. All because I started thinking outside the box.

I had my breakout moment. I metamorphosed from amateur to professional writer. And it can come for you as well. But to get there, you must never stop writing fresh stories, and you must never stop learning your craft, and you must never stop believing you are a writer. You must cling to your dream to become a professional writer just like a barnacle ... and *never* let go.

~

BULLET POINTS FOR EMERGING WRITERS

- Enter *reputable,* no-fee amateur writing contests, like the Writers of the Future Contest and The Mike Resnick Memorial Award.
- Subscribe to and read the publications of the markets you submit to.
- Take writing courses by experts in the craft.
- Attend *professional* writing seminars where you can learn from real pros that know what they're doing, like the Superstars Writing Seminar.
- Stop reworking old stories, thinking you can make them better. Write fresh stories! We grow with every fresh story we write.
- Write full time. Pro writers write full time, meaning a regular weekly writing schedule. If that's not possible at present (you've got to pay the bills), schedule *fresh story* or *novel writing time* (not writing chat, not rewriting, not editing) each day if possible. Set an achievable word count if it helps motivate you—500 words a day is a good starter one —and *stick to your goal.*
- Send stories out. They will never get published if you don't send them out. When they come back—and they will—send them back out and write your next story. In time, they won't come back. They'll sell and get published and be read by your adoring fans!
- If your goal is to be a successful indie author, first learn your craft. No amount of marketing skill can cover up bad product. In fact, having some awards and traditional sales to respected markets will notify prospective readers that you are bona fide.
- Establish a *friendly* and *positive* social media presence focused on both your interests and your writing. Start a website and build your fanbase through a blog and a newsletter. Publishers need to know you have an active

social media presence and will promote their publication if they choose to publish your work.

- Hire a professional editor at least once to edit a short story, or a chapter from your book. Be sure to hire a reputable editor that has accomplished what you're trying to do and has proven they get results for their clients. They will help you see your blind spots so that you can eliminate problem areas and advance your skills.

34

DEALING WITH CRITICISM, PART ONE:

The Good, The Bad . . .

"*There is only one way to avoid criticism: Do nothing, say nothing, and be nothing.*"

This quote is often attributed to Aristotle, but that's a fallacy. The man that spoke the closest approximation to this adage was American writer Elbert Hubbard: "For the man who doesn't want to be knocked and laughed at I give this recipe: Do nothing, say nothing, be nothing."[1]

The point? There's only one way to avoid criticism. Hide in the reef from the rest of the fish in the sea. No one can criticize you if they don't know you or your work exists. You'll be safe from predators—both the armchair critics and the professional ones. You'll never be read beyond a few family members and friends, but anonymity is the price your security demands. You may even have a plan in this scenario—that your work will be discovered after you die. It's happened to a few writers in history. Why not you?

Why not? Because it's as unlikely as winning one of those billion-dollar lotteries with the hundreds of millions to one odds. Let's face it. If you want your tales to be read beyond your circle of trusted friends, you're going to have to find a way to get them into the hands of the public. You now know how to accomplish this. And when you do, the public will have something to say about your works. Hopefully good things, but as Abraham Lincoln liked to say, "[Y]ou can't please all of the people all of the time."

Never were truer words spoken.

Opinions are like noses. Everyone has them. And there's lots of people that like putting their noses in everyone else's business. They have their reasons. Most believe "they're just trying to help." Sometimes, they sincerely are. Sometimes, they actually do. And sometimes, we've asked them for their help and welcome their noses in our business because we value their opinions. We recognize their constructive comments can do us a lot of good.

But there are those personality types that deceive themselves into thinking their criticism is for our good, when it's really meant to put us in our place—meaning below *their* presumed place so they can feel better about themselves and their accomplishments ... or lack thereof. There's also those sour pickles that can't stand it that you've done something well, or are working hard to do something well. Again, it exposes their insecurities and feelings of inadequacy about what they've accomplished in life or career, maybe even their lack of trying. Throwing a wet blanket over your sunshine makes their gloom look a little bit brighter.

But there's another type of critic that really does have bad intent and gets sadistic pleasure out of undermining others and the good work they do. There are even destroyer personalities, abusive trolls that thrive on crushing people's good works and noble dreams. There are all types of people in this world. We face them every time we walk out our doors (and sometimes, even in our doors). When our stories, novels, and screenplays go out our doors, they're going to have to face the public, too. The good, the bad, and the ugly. *Wah-wah-wah.*

If we're hobby writing, we're pretty safe. We can write to our heart's content, stuff our story in a drawer or save it in a file on our computer, and we don't have to deal with our work being weighed and measured by the public. Nobody can touch us because nobody knows what we did. We locked it up and threw away the key.

But isolation is not communication—no exchange of ideas is taking place. Communication needs both a transmitter and a receiver. To transmit our stories into the minds and hearts of readers, we're going to have to expose ourselves. No, not like some person in a trench coat flashing passersby on the street. Sharing our creations with the public is far more revealing than baring a little skin. We're actually exposing our hearts and minds and creative abilities to outsiders when we seek publication, and that's a mighty big flash. And since there are all kinds of people in this world with their own tastes and opinions and even objectives, we've got to be prepared for that universal truth.

You can't please everyone.

Those that try end up pleasing no one.

Let's take a look at criticism, both the kind and the unkind, the helpful and the unhelpful, the constructive and the destructive. Learning how to deal with criticism will determine whether we will be happy or miserable as writers. In fact, it's so important, I believe it will determine whether we succeed or fail.

CONSTRUCTIVE CRITICISM

The word "criticism" carries negative connotations for most of us, but in truth, criticism is not in itself an evil term. Wikipedia defines criticism as "the construction of a judgment about the negative or positive qualities of someone or something."

See? Criticism doesn't have to focus on negative qualities, it can just as easily focus on the positive. We all love it when someone evaluates our work and says, "Good night, Westley. Good work. Sleep well. I'll most likely kill you in the morning." Okay, not that last bit, although it was a pretty funny commendation in William Goldman's *The Princess Bride*.

We might even ask a friend or mate to look us over and offer their opinion. "Does this dress make me look fat?" "Do I have anything in my teeth?" "Should I get involved in a land war in Asia?" Constructive comments meant to help can save us pain, embarrassment, even brutal conflict.

But here's a tricky one. When someone says to a writer, "Don't quit your day job," they're putting their nose in your business. Is that advice the good, the bad, or the ugly? Truth is, the apprentice period for a writer doesn't pay well, and even established bestselling writers often struggle to make ends meet. So the person with the nose could well be offering constructive criticism out of sincere concern for our welfare, and we would do well to weigh the cost of giving up a bird in hand for one or two in the bush.

But another person—even a sibling, mate, or parent—might have a different motive in making such comments. Perhaps they never pursued a dream they had, and it makes them jealous to see you doing so. They'd feel a lot better if you gave up your dream of getting published or becoming a full-time writer. Such criticism has nothing to do with helping you—it's selfish, meant to defeat or hinder you from reaching your heart's desire so they can feel better about their lack. If they persist in such talk, you'll need thicker armor, or you'll need to have a frank discussion to tell them to stop. If that doesn't work? You'll have to find a way to avoid the conversation or even the person to keep that toxicity out of your life. Writing is hard enough without someone trying to snuff your flame.

Back to constructive criticism. The newer we are at writing, the less experienced we will be, the more mistakes we will make. A humble writer recognizes this. He doesn't believe, "I writes, therefore I's brilliant." New writers that hope to progress recognize there are many things they will need to work on to finally create working stories that will sell. Even old dogs must learn new tricks to stay in the game.

One way to learn new tricks and avoid mistakes? It can be quite helpful to ask trusted readers to give us feedback on our stories. Sharing in critique sessions with good writing groups has helped many a writer advance—especially if there are some professional writers in that group with the pay-it-forward ethos. We all have our blind spots. The newer we are, the more we have. Helpful writing companions can kindly point them out, and if we listen carefully and don't take offense, we can improve our work.

And if an experienced mentor takes a shine to us? We've hit the jackpot, because a mentor's desire is to use their hard-earned knowledge to make the progress toward success easier for their mentee. This can happen at writing seminars and even in workshops. Good instructors work hard to uplift everyone in their classes, but speaking from experience, they have a special spot in their hearts for those doing the work that show promise. They can sense who is about to make a breakthrough, and will often give extra help and counsel outside of workshops to boost the process for advancing writers. Such guidance can be pure gold. As Napoleon Dynamite would say: *"Luck-ky!"*

But if none of these opportunities are open to you, don't despair. You can read an instructor's books on writing. You can listen to writing podcasts. Do constructive criticism on your work based on the knowledge you gain. There is an abundance of free material to help writers on the Internet. I know. I've created plenty of it for this purpose.

You can also pay to have your work analyzed by a professional. Some, like me, are writing coaches and professional editors with proven track records both in their own work, and in the writers' careers they have guided. Even one edit by a professional freelance editor can be revealing, giving you personalized guidance that can shave years off your learning curve. It's like hiring a personal trainer. You're going to get a customized program by a professional to beef up your writing muscles. *We're going to pump you up!* But please, make sure they are legitimate editors.

As in life, so in writing, we all have to learn how to take constructive criticism. Nobody is perfect. Getting good advice from good people trying to help us is how we grow. Iron sharpens iron.

I loved what writer Nnedi Okorafor (*Binti* Series) said about this in the Writers of the Future Podcast #233: "One bit of advice that I would give is if you are working with more experienced writers, be humble and listen …. Don't let criticism crush you. Be able to listen, be able to take the criticism and if it does crush you a bit, go cry in a different room. But always be able to take in the advice because those lessons are there where you can learn them and you'll be better off after you learn them, even if it's a painful thing."

Alas, there is another kind of criticism. It's not iron sharpening iron. It's hurtful words intended to stab us like a knife. That kind of criticism, we do not have to take.

But we must learn how to deal with it.

CLINICAL DESTRUCTIVE CRITICISM

My father had his good qualities, but he had very bad ones, too. My mother? She left us to go live with a boyfriend in Germany. In high school, I won many prestigious awards in creative writing, journalism, forensics, and debate. Each time I brought trophies home, Dad would only say, "You'll never make a living at this. You should come work for me as a Realtor. My name would carry you in town." He had won Realtor of the Year for our state many times and my goals didn't fit into his plans for me.

The comments increased in toxicity, becoming verbal abuse, and then physical. If you've suffered from such abuse, I'm not going to go deep, but I'll put a trigger warning here if it's hard for you. I do understand. Skip this section and move to the next. I have no desire to trigger bad memories; this is meant to be an upbuilding book. But we all know stuff happens. Or something like that.

Okay, here was my teenage home life. If my dad caught me reading a book, he'd beat me in the face with it. I had to hide to read, hide to write, and if he caught me doing homework instead of his endless chore lists on our hobby farm, I'd also get beaten. My stepmom had orders to put us to work on the farm as soon as we came home from school and the chores didn't end until it was too dark to see. I felt I was in a concentration camp, and longed for the day I could leave home after finishing high school.

Normal parents love having a child that excels scholastically. My father never commended me no matter how many trophies I brought home. That's tough for a kid. You base much of your worth on commendation and expressions of love from your parents. I'm certain underneath it all I worked harder than most students because I desperately sought acknowledgment that I had worth. But no matter how much I achieved, I'd be met by my father's cold grunt and a statement that I'd never amount to anything pursuing a career in writing.

The violence escalated. To make a long and painful story short, I finally ran away and got placed in a foster home. I finished high school with honors—my class even voted me Most Likely to Succeed, and a good college created a full scholarship including room and board to recruit me. My dad even showed up for my high school graduation and threw a party for me.

It was the most awkward party I've attended in my life.

Dad never said he was sorry, but I took it as a sign that he wanted to have a relationship. You only have one biological father. I forgave him in the form of letting go and I left the past in the past. And I *never* talked to him again about my writing.

Until a few decades later when he forced it out of me. I was now married and living in Eugene, Oregon. Dad took a flight from Minneapolis to Portland, and we drove up to pick him up. On the drive back, what's the first thing he asked about? You got it. My writing.

"You're not still doing that writing thing, are you?"

He knew we had our own company, had just built a home he had come out to see, and *this* is what he wanted to talk about? Passive-aggressive stuff, just like the days of old.

"Yes, Dad, I still write as I have the time."

"You're not getting published, though. Not making any money at it."

Here we go. "You know I've made money at it, Dad. I had that sale to Scholastic Corporation in high school."

"But not anything lately."

Dad knew how to push my buttons. My temperature had risen to boiling point. His first trip out to see me and we're back to this old saw from when I was a kid? I had started writing again and had won thousands of dollars in prizes, had written the winning ending to a romance novella contest by Nora Roberts, and had signed a nice publishing contract with Paramount and Pocket Books of Simon and Schuster. I never told him so he couldn't play head games with me. But it was a direct question, and I don't lie.

"Yes, Dad, lately."

"But not anything big. Not like you're making any *real* money at it."

That's when I lost it. "How does *Star Trek* sound, Dad? Is that big enough for you? I'm in every bookstore in America right now. They paid me $750 for my story, plus royalties. Does that sound like real money to you?"

He sat silently for a few moments, then played the victim card. "Why didn't you tell me?"

"Because I knew you would do this, Dad."

"Do what?"

It was not an enjoyable two-hour drive back to Eugene. The black ice on the road had nothing to do with it, either. There was plenty of it in the car.

Some people have made such a habit of gaslighting, they don't even know they're doing it. You just have to feel sorry for them and how insecure they must be within, and if you're fortunate, not give them the opportunity to do it to you. When they're family, this can be extremely hard to avoid. They know you well, they know your weak spots, hell, they've created those weak spots so they can watch you crumble when they push on them. It's a mental sickness on their part, but it can be damaging and even dangerous to your own mental health and life if it's allowed to persist.

I am not a mental health professional. But I do know it is nearly impossible for a leopard to change its spots without professional help with things like this. To change, the passive-aggressive and outright abusive person must recognize they are hurting people with their words and actions and recognize the need to get help.

From experience I can say the longer you're around people with mental health disorders of an abusive nature, the more they will undermine your belief in yourself. If it's family, you can lay it on the line and tell them what the cost will be if they keep it up. Make sure they know you mean business. If they refuse and persist in denigrating you, distance yourself as much as you can. In our case, we moved across the country. You can't choose your family. But you can limit your exposure to them when they're toxic.

If it's friends or associates that are denigrating you and your writing, that's a little easier. You can have a serious talk with them and let them know how much writing means to you. If they're a true friend and really care about you, even if they can't understand why you write, they should understand your need to feel fulfilled, your desire to excel, and the time you need to dedicate to your craft to do so. True friends want what's best for you, not for them.

But if they persist in trying to kill your dream after you've asked them to stop, it's not you. It's them. Cut them out of your life. Period. And if they have a personality disorder like I've described, they're not going to change by having a talk with them. In fact, they'll often double down on you. Don't keep exposing yourself to destructive speech and the individuals that spew it. It will erode away your confidence and your faith in your abilities.

And that's exactly what they want to see happen.

35

DEALING WITH CRITICISM, PART TWO:

And The Ugly

Y ou don't have to worry about this one. Everyone in the writing community is kind and friendly, ready to extend heartfelt advice and lend a helping hand to assist you to succeed. *Kumbaya. All we are saying is give peace a chance.*

Um, what brand of flavor-aid drink have you been imbibing?

In truth, most writers are quite nice, even the extremely successful ones. They remember their roots, they remember what it took to get where they are, and they do good things to help writers get a leg up as they're able. But they are busy people with lots of deadlines to meet and many demands on their time. If they can't help when you ask or sound curt in an email or at a convention, remember that professionals get buried in emails and requests for help each day. If they don't protect themselves and their writing time, they could spend all of their time helping everyone else and have no time left to advance their own career. Don't ask me how I know.

And yes, there are a few downright cranky and crotchety writers. And pompous ones, too, that make a point of letting everyone know that they are the smartest and most successful writer in the room. God help you if you get on a panel with them at a convention. If they give you the opportunity to speak at all, they will quickly interrupt to tell you how deluded your viewpoint is and how right they are.

But isn't this how it is in any profession? In any cut of society? Lots of friendly outgoing people, lots of kind but reserved people, and then some less than kind people that believe they're above the rest of us, or don't believe they're above the rest of us but do feel better if they can trample us under their boots.

People are people no matter what profession we choose.

That said, I do have a fond spot for creatives. They have powerful emotions that drive them to create art in all of its forms, and unlike many other professions, the years creatives spend in their apprentice-ship learning their craft does not pay well, if at all. I do believe creatives that suffer for their art but persevere into careers remember their pain, and are more sensitive to the struggles of those behind them. It's why we look for ways to help, like moderating on writing forums or offering to read manuscripts or forming writing groups or going on podcasts to share knowledge. There is a "pay it forward" ethos in creative communities, and you respect those that are generous with their knowledge and time.

This is the way.

Where it might not be the way, is among your peers. Oh, everyone is happy in your circle of friends when you appear to be swimming at the same level and speed that they are. Often, this is why you became friends, forging bonds with those with similar aspirations, working to reach your goals and dreams together. Writing partners, writing circles, and writing groups generally form around commonalities, like genre, locale, and experience. Locale has become less relevant in our digital age, but experience has not. Either you have sales to respected markets, or you do not. And if one peer starts breaking out in their sales and career and the others in their circle do not, status quo is put to the test. Everyone in the group wants those same sales and publishing credits for themselves, and it can be hard to watch someone else get them while we may feel left behind.

It's only natural to want good things to happen for us if we've been working hard to achieve them. We are happy for our friends, but darn it, we've been doing the same work, and maybe we've been at it longer, too. Why are they suddenly getting their stories published, and we are not?

DANGER, WILL ROBINSON. DANGER! DANGER!

If we don't keep such feelings in check, we might be smiling and congratulating our friend on the outside, but inside we could be secretly seething with jealousy. Worse, if they have a string of good results, we could steep in bad feelings and become envious. Suddenly, we're the ones making snide comments meant to trip our peers up or even to knock them down a peg. And if that doesn't work, we could even grow to hate our friend that hasn't done anything but succeed at a task we've all been trying to help one another succeed in. Instead of being happy for them and doubling down on our own work to help us succeed, we might try to undermine their success. And if that doesn't stop them from advancing, we might even impute bad motives and speak malicious gossip and slander designed to damage their good reputation.

It happens. Fish like to swim in schools where the rest of the fish are about the same size. There's security in that. But if one fish appears to be growing larger than the rest, the littler fish can become insecure and gang up on the bigger fish to push him out.

Over the decades, I've seen this happen in writing groups. It's not pretty, but it is imperfect human nature. And it doesn't have to happen. We should be happy for that writer—we've watched them do the work to get where they're at. It should encourage us that if we keep slugging away, it will happen for us, too. And we have a bonus —our friend figured something out, and as our friend, they'll be happy to share with us what helped them level up.

Unless we're jealous. Unless we start making snide comments about how that story wasn't really all that great, or that writer only got published because they're friends with the editor, or that their popularity isn't based on meritorious work but only because they have a cult following. (Yes, I've had this said to me more than once!) What happens then? That friend that would have given the shirt off his back to help us succeed now has to draw away to protect himself. Because the relationship or even the group he or she was once a welcome member of has now become toxic.

And that would be a shame. But it does happen. So much so that bestselling writers Kevin J. Anderson and Rebecca Moesta do a presentation every year at the Writers of the Future Workshop in Hollywood on career advice. I've heard them give this presentation several times now. One of the things they warn emerging writers about? That when others see your career taking off and theirs is not, they can get jealous. In fact, Kevin and Rebecca come right out and say, "It's going to happen." Their solution? "You're going to need to get new friends."

I remember hearing this for the first time at the workshop and feeling a little shiver go down my spine. We're writers! Comrades in the trenches together, fighting for the same cause, brothers in arms, trying to get our stories out to the public so we can change the world! Why would we ever turn on one in our brotherhood after working so hard to get here? I must confess Kevin and Rebecca's warnings baffled me, but I knew they were sharing from their own years of experience. I took the warning to heart.

Boy, were they right.

People are people. Hang on to the good ones in your life. Cherish those friendships. Give more than you get to them. They will always stand behind you and be happy you are succeeding at what you do. Especially if you are giving back to others along the way.

And if you feel that weed of jealousy creeping up in the garden of your heart? Nip it in the bud. Our relationship doesn't have to shift. We can be happy we've got a bigger fish in our school. That big fish is our friend. It's good to have some big fish in our lives.

They keep predators at bay.

∼

PUBLIC COMMENTS AND REVIEWS

"An action-packed thrill ride!"
"A rollercoaster thrill ride!"
"A thrilling thrill ride!"

"This story is amaze-balls, and not just because my brother wrote it, either! Totally tubular thrill ride! FIVE STARS!!!"

We all love sincere commendation, especially on something we worked hard on, like our stories. Although I'm guessing movie critics must all write at amusement parks because boy do they love writing *rollercoaster thrill rides* in their reviews!

Whether we're an indie writer or traditionally published, when our work goes up on an online retail platform, there will be a place for readers to leave reviews. As mentioned, there are all kinds of people in this world, just like there are all kinds of noses. Everybody has a right to their opinion, and these platforms give the general public (hopefully verifying whether they actually bought the book) the opportunity to tell others what they thought about it.

Some of those opinions will be glowing. Some of them will be blah. And some can be negative, even derisive. Having tracked a few of those making derisive ones, it does appear to be their modus operandi. That can actually help in dealing with their negative criticism—they do this to everyone, as if nothing written in this world is good enough for them, and they take pleasure in letting everyone know it. Doesn't sound like a happy way to live your life or to make friends, but you did choose to put your work before the public eye so it would be read. Some of these types will be more than happy to pounce on it.

How do you deal with this? Some choose to never read their reviews and even advocate ignoring them. If we tend to take it personally or even get angry about it, that might be a good idea. But what about those good reviews? They can really lift us up and put wind in our sails. What's more, they make wonderful grist for our social media mill. In public relations, it's always better if someone else praises your work. We do need content, and a nice review can provide it. Learning how to take the bad with the good will be a helpful skill to develop.

An easy way to write those bad ones off is to remind ourselves we never intended to please everyone. That's impossible. Why should we care what a total stranger thinks? They're obviously not our people. Focus on the ones that are. Those are the ones we build our fanbase from. Those are the followers that will give us the privilege of having a career.

Sometimes, the troubled author will try to reach out to the person that wrote a nasty review or posted a negative comment on social media. The author might even post a counter to their review in defense. Don't. It's a waste of your time and energy. And some of these people are purposely baiting you so they can start a flame war to get attention. Don't feed their negative fire. It will die out.

Normally. I offer one caveat. There are times where an instigator, not getting the results they want on their own power, will stir up a group with false statements and outright slander to make it appear through volume of comments that their slander is truth. If they can't control you, they'll seek to control the narrative about you to harm your reputation. If you believe the slander is significant and actually does have the power to hinder your career, you may find it necessary to weigh in publicly to get the truth out there. But after doing so, it's usually wise to let it go and let the public decide instead of getting embroiled in an ugly public debate with the instigator.

As Shakespeare said, "Truth will out." It can be trying waiting for that day to come, but keep shining on your part. It's how we overcome the darkness.

$\sim$

PROFESSIONAL COMMENTARIES

There are professional critics, hired to write reviews for magazines and online review sites. They do have a job to filter through the overwhelming amount of published material out there and shine a light on those stories and books they feel should get more attention. Some are very generous to the authors they review, and some are quite stingy with praise. Remember my comment that there are all kinds of people? There are all types of critics as well.

What if you get one like the food critic in the animated movie *Ratatouille*? What if that critic has written your establishment off and pronounced it dead, and here you are, open and serving the public in spite of their official decree? It happens. Your writing won't appeal to everyone. People are people, and critics are people—they all have their own noses and tastes. One critic's treasure is another critic's garbage. Their job is to write their honest opinion, whether you like their opinion or not.

There's not much you can do about a negative review. Except become the duck that lets the bad reviews roll like water off their back. Remembering it's just one person's opinion can help. Perhaps they're not even a writer and have little in the way of credentials. They often write under pseudonyms so there's no way to know. Some could even be doing their article on a writer as a hit piece meant to gain media attention or to grind a jealous ax they're carrying. You might even know of some cases like this. It happens. If it can happen to the big names, why couldn't it happen on a smaller scale? People are people, some with good motives, some with bad.

I'll share some tricks I've found that help me when I get professional reviews—and if you're published in a professional publication, you're likely to get one. The positive reviews go up on a corkboard on my office door so I can read them often. I also share excerpts from them on my social media and websites. Good news drowns out the bad. Other professionals have said wonderful things about my work. I choose to give those reviews my focus. They're obviously the wise and intelligent critics that know quality when they see it. Hey, it helps!

The other trick is really no trick at all, it's a cold hard fact. An editor that knows their business paid you money for your story and published it. Just appearing in their publication is a sign you wrote a good story. That really is the only opinion that matters. The editor thought your story was so good, they paid you money and published it. Often out of hundreds or even thousands of other stories they could have published. Remind yourself of that, shake off the negative review, and move on to writing your next. Besides, even in negative reviews the critic often says something positive, just to hedge their bets. They too know the editor saw merit in your story or they wouldn't have published it.

Finally, as your writing skills improve, thoughtful editors at the publications you submit your work to will often take time to jot you a helpful note, known as a personal rejection. Editors are busy people, often working a day job to support their project of love, so when you get your first personal, jump for joy and post it on your corkboard. They only write personals when they feel your work shows promise. They're trying to help.

Whether it *will* help is often determined by their level of experience and reputation. It doesn't hurt to analyze the validity of what they said to see if it will improve your work—especially if you are new at your craft. And if they asked you to send more stories, they mean it! Be sure to send them your next if it fits with what they publish. Some editors keep lists to remember those they want to keep an eye on. Editors love being the first to discover and publish new writers.

Here again, everyone has their personal tastes, even editors. And even experienced editors, agents, producers, and publishers can let a precious gem slip through their fingers. Often, they reject stories they'd love to publish, but it doesn't fit with their theme. But they do have bad days and make bad calls just like the rest of us. Nobody is purr-fect.

I once submitted a story to a professional publication where I was on friendly terms with the editor. He wrote back with comments and said he felt the potential was there, but the story was like taking a few perfectly good ingredients and cooking a tuna-and-marshmallow casserole. *Ouch.* But that was his opinion, and because I'm experienced, he felt I could handle it.

Because we're friends (don't you do this!), I wrote back and said, "Thanks again for taking the time. Now to find an editor that likes tuna-and-marshmallow casserole. There's got to be at least one in this world."

He replied, "You're absolutely right that it only takes one editor who will love the story. Sorry that wasn't me! …. I hope you prove me wrong and land this at a good home." He acknowledged another editor might have an entirely different opinion, and hoped I would sell it. That's a good editor.

The next professional market I sent it to? *Deep Magic* magazine. The editor there was also an experienced professional, actually a *Wall Street Journal* bestselling author. He loved the story and published

"Muzik Man" in *Deep Magic*, Fall 2020. He even posted on Goodreads that he thought it would win awards. *Tangent Online*, a premiere reviewer of speculative short fiction, reviewed the issue. The critic likened the power of my story's plot arc to *Star Wars* and concluded: "… Moon shows he can masterfully construct a triumphant feel-good finish. Recommended."

Sure enough, "Muzik Man" won Best Science Fiction and Fantasy Short Story of 2020 in the Critters Readers' Choice Awards, a stellar honor. This is one of their largest categories and thousands of readers from around the world vote in that contest. "Muzik Man" also received a star on the 2020 *Tangent Online* Recommended Reading List, an end-of-the-publishing-year list every speculative fiction writer hopes to be on—those stars to our writers are like Michelin stars to restaurateurs. And finally, when *Deep Magic* had their editorial staff choose their best stories from multiple years of publication, "Muzik Man" was chosen for *The Best of Deep Magic Anthology 2*.

Was that first editor's opinion wrong? Not at all. The story obviously wasn't right for him, but he recognized it might be right for someone else. And it was! One editor's tuna-and-marshmallow casserole is another editor's Chateaubriand with *maître d'hôtel* butter. Editors' varied tastes are what make the flavor of stories in each publication unique, and we should respect that. Our job is to finish our stories, have faith in them no matter what comments might come back, and keep sending them out to respected markets until we find the editor that loves what we're serving. *Bon appétit!*

In conclusion, if you want to be read, you have to expose yourself to the public. The good, the bad, and the ugly. They're all out there. If you try to please them all, you'll please no one. Instead, hunt for your people. Gather your people to your social media platform, website, and newsletter. The critics will still be around because everyone has the right to their opinions, and some are quite loud about theirs. But they'll be easy to ignore if you're surrounded by fans that love your work.

Don't hide your writing from the world to be safe from the critics. There is only one way to enjoy success: *Do something, say something …and be something.*

36

THE SECRET INGREDIENT

I love to cook. Cooking is an immensely creative and fulfilling process when your goal is hitting that perfect blend of flavor profiles with the ingredients you have to work with, highlighting the star component of the dish. I rarely follow a recipe unless I'm recreating one of my own dishes. For me, it's all about the challenge. I get a thrill out of pitting my mind and knowledge to unite a medley of harmonizing flavors to make a perfect melody on the plate and the palate.

When I serve one of my creations to visiting friends, my artist's eye turns to the plating. We eat first with our eyes—visual impression is the true appetizer—so I collect serving sets because I know the plate makes the colorful stage for my creation to dance upon. When I plate the meal and guests take that first bite and say, "*Oh, my,*" I know the magic I've planned has happened on their tongue.

But it's not just flavor magic. I've transferred *love* to them. My care for their happiness and well-being is reflected in the details I've tracked through the prep and cooking and serving process to ensure they know I care. Our meal is enriched, my guests feel warmth and joy, and our dinner and conversations are uplifted to a higher plane. And as we hug our friends at the end of the evening and send them on their way, I'll shut the door and my wife will often say, "Did you write that recipe down? Well you better. It was perfect and I'd like to have it again."

I appreciate the compliment—creating a great-tasting dish takes hard work and tremendous focus to make it come out right. However, it's never perfect. I know better. But I did hit a mark of balance where all the ingredients came together and worked like a well-rehearsed dance troupe on a stage. That part does not happen by chance. I've been cooking for a long time: first, at home as the oldest of seven siblings where I often cooked for everyone in the household, and then, in a restaurant where I was trained by a skilled chef. There is art in cooking, talent in improvisation. But it takes knowledge of the fundamentals and fine-tuned skills—the result of years of dedicated practice —to make the deep magic happen.

How does this relate to writing? Let me show you.

~

COOK VS. CHEF

There are cooks. And there are chefs. One cooks to live; the other lives to cook. When you are served in a restaurant, you don't have to go to culinary school to know the difference. Without ever meeting the person that prepared your meal, you can tell whether that person in the kitchen is a cook or whether they are a chef. It's obvious by their attention to detail and if they gave your dish some love.

It's even more stunning when the person has the gift and hones that gift through skilled education and training. When those people start experimenting, all of that knowledge and skill they've mastered flows into the experimentation. That's the deep magic. That's when the dish becomes a miracle, and you were there to experience the joy of that miracle working on the plate. Such a meal becomes a full sensory experience, enveloping you through the ears (hear those fajitas sizzle?), the eyes (just look at the riot of color from those peppers!), your nostrils (smell that smoky char?), and on your tongue (it's a party in my mouth!). It even gives you a sense of well-being. Your hunger has been pleasingly sated. Life can go on.

Writing is like cooking. There are many similarities. Guess what? I already know you have the gift, that cheffy fire burning within you, yearning to create, or you would not have read this far. Good on you, mate! I designed this book to advance writers from prep cook to line cook to chef. Okay, maybe some of you are like me when I got my start, working my way up from dishwasher. There's no shame in it. Half the famous chefs you know got their start as humble dishwashers. They knew they wanted to be chefs, and dishwashing was their chance to enter the kitchen. The point is, you don't start as a chef, *you work your way up to being a chef.*

The Super Secrets are for writers that are serious about working their way up the line. To do that, one must learn the craft of writing, creating written works that are viable, and serving up those works to be read/heard/felt/seen by an audience. I've been straightforward in detailing to you what this requires, right? I'm known for being nice but not mincing words. It's the only way my words will help. So here's the kicker: I know you would have quit reading long ago if you weren't a true writer, a doer instead of a wisher.

You are a writer. You may not be a published writer yet, but you are writing and investing your time and money to improve your craft. Instead of simply working the line in the kitchen with what's provided, you've bought your own knives (ooh, are those the Shun Premiers with thirty-four layers of high carbon Damascus steel cladding? *Noice!*). You're taking this seriously, working with quality tools instead of a $9.95 Ginsu knife. That's going to show up in your craft.

And if you're already published? Studying the craft and taking workshops is like a cook going to culinary school. Master chefs are there teaching the fundamentals, passing on their knowledge from one generation to another. Many cooks also seek to work in the kitchens of award-winning chefs. There, they hope to find a mentor that knows the alchemy of combining ingredients to their maximum effect to make miracles occur on the plate. Many famous chefs are willing to share their secrets with a mentee.

With knowledge, training, smart practice, and intelligent experimentation, a chef's work can rise above that of others, creating a culinary experience only that unique chef can satisfy. These are the cooks that become award-winning chefs, creating their own establishments with loyal fans that will follow them anywhere they go.

Some even become celebrities, but my favorite chefs aren't the ones that crave the limelight. They're the ones in the kitchen making miracles happen out of pure love for their art. Oh, there's plenty of experimentation, but the foundation of every experiment is built from cooking fundamentals they fought hard to learn and master. It's what makes that dish on the plate look and taste like real magic.

But creation of the dish is only part of the equation for great chefs. It's the *sharing* of the dish that gives them fulfillment. You'll see them at times, slipping out of the kitchen for that front-of-house moment to watch a customer take their first bite. When they see the smile of delight as the flavors burst upon the diner's tongue, the chef's heart is warmed. Someone appreciates all the care they took to make that magic happen. Their love has been transferred into the food, sustaining the partaker of that love.

The chef slips back into the kitchen, the circle complete. They're ready to make the magic happen again, one plate at a time.

Would you like to know the mindset of cooks that became chefs? The ones that achieved the devoted followers and critical acclaim that helped them create their own establishments that sustained them while pursuing their art? There are lessons to be learned for writers here. And I have one last secret ingredient yet to share with you that I guarantee will make all the difference in your cooking.

Fire up the grill.

~

THE MASTER CHEF MINDSET

Earning Michelin stars is a crowning achievement for chefs. It's nice to get recognition for all the hours one devotes to their craft to become a master. Kitchens are hot, tempers flare from stress, and the hours are grueling. Watch a *Hell's Kitchen* show, and the charbroilers aren't the only things flaring!

But note what keeps chefs in the game in spite of the pain. Here's a quote from Chef Jarrod Wentworth from the Chicago restaurant Moody Tongue. With ten Michelin stars to his credit at the time of this 2021 CBS interview, Chef Wentworth certainly would know what motivates him to be a chef. Take a look. His answer may surprise you.

"I've been blessed, and part of that's through a lot of hard work, a lot of suffering for your art, essentially. I've kept Michelin stars pretty much throughout my whole tenure in Chicago, I never take it for granted. Do we want stars? Of course we do, but we work our asses off to get that. For me, it's the satisfaction of seeing a smile on a diner's face. And I think it's the biggest thing, it's that instant gratification of making somebody happy. Cheers!"[1]

Successful writers feel the same way. Awards and accolades from peers are nice, but the real joy is in writing your truth and seeing how it touches the hearts and minds of readers. Hearing that your story put a smile on someone's face? That your dear character's triumph or tragedy brought tears to their eyes? Priceless. This is why we write.

Here's a comment from a pizza chef on how to create an amazing product consistently. His name is Dan Richer, owner of Razza Pizza Artigianale, continually ranked as creating some of the best pizza on the planet (if you live near Jersey City, New Jersey … *Luck-key!*). Does Richer just wing it to make his knock-out pizzas? Notice his secret ingredient to his success: "So we have to understand the science in order to create a really amazing pizza … on a consistent basis."

Science behind pizza? Whodathunk? Well, Dan Richer, obviously. It's how he makes his amazing crusts and how he became one of the top pizza creators in the world. Yes, he experiments, but like I've said, those experiments work because he understands the fundamental principles necessary to make them work … the science! That knowledge allows him to turn out quality product on a consistent basis. That's also how you build a following. Sound like what I've taught here in these Super Secrets? You bet! Knowledge, *accurate knowledge*, is power. When you understand a process, you can control that process and make it work for you.

Here's a quote from a chef that never gave up on that fire burning within her. This is chef Nasim Alikhani, executive chef and co-owner of Sofreh, a restaurant that features her Persian cooking in Brooklyn, New York. She's cooked for the White House, she's been a finalist for the James Beard Award for Best Chef, but what's so incredible about her story is that although she had been cooking for family all her life, she didn't become a chef until she was fifty-nine years old. It's never too late to chart a path to our heart's desire! Here's her story, as she told it, and may it inspire you:

I announced to my husband I am opening a restaurant.

"May I ask why?"

"Because I have one dream that I have kept all these years. I have to be able to look at this person in the mirror, which is me. I say, 'What was your reason for not reaching your dream?' I can't, I don't have an answer for that person five years from now, ten years from now? I'm going to do it. And if it fails, I tell that person, 'You tried. Didn't work. Tough luck.'"[2]

Instead of tough luck, by making the leap of faith, Nasim's belief became reality. Because she never gave up on her dream and was proactive about doing something about it. All of those years she spent cooking for family? That was her apprenticeship. She learned her craft and featured unique flavors of Persian cooking that made her dishes stand out. Her restaurant and late-life career has been an amazing success.

When you look at yourself in the mirror, what's your dream? What goals do you need to set in order to chart a course to reach your dreams? We write about proactive characters with dreams, and we make them fight in our tales to achieve them. Like Nasim, will we be able to tell ourselves one day that we tried? That we gave it our best?

It's the only way to make dreams become reality.

$\sim$

THE SECRET INGREDIENT

Chef Nasim Alikhani made another insightful comment in that interview. "What you bring to your food is not your culinary experience, it's your life experience. And if you can bring them together, you have a successful recipe."

This is why many chefs travel. They are increasing their life experience, absorbing the food and flavor of other cultures in order to enrich their own. Enhancing one's life experiences makes us richer people with more to draw from in our creations, whether we're chefs, painters, songwriters, poets, or yes, writers in all the various forms. Drawing from a deep well can make our writing deep, authentic, powerful. It's how we speak our truth, even as we're entertaining others through our stories.

Have you watched the first *Kung Fu Panda* movie? Spoiler alert if you haven't. Go watch it and come back, it's super cute. Done? Okay, good. Thanks for not saving me any popcorn! Where were we? Oh. The story of Po, an overweight panda that by an apparently monumental accident gets chosen to become the next Dragon Warrior. As the plot progresses, there's a big deal made about the Dragon Scroll, a sacred Kung Fu scroll in the Jade Palace that can unlock unlimited power for the one deemed worthy to read it.

When the village in the Valley of Peace is about to be attacked by Tai Lung—an evil snow leopard with supernatural strength—our reluctant hero is given the scroll by his sensei. Po opens it, ready to become the Dragon Warrior by unlocking all the secrets that lie within. Finally, ultimate power shall be his! The village is saved!

He opens the scroll.

It's blank.

He opens it again.

Nothing there.

His sensei takes it from him and is shocked to find it's true; the shiny Dragon Scroll has absolutely nothing written on it. Hope is lost. Unleashing the power held within the scroll was the only chance both Po and his sensei believed they had to save the village.

As the town evacuates, Po leaves the Jade Palace and goes to help his adoptive father, Mr. Ping, a goose that owns a noodle shop. His father has kept the secret ingredient for his famous soup secret all his life, even from his son, but Mr. Ping believes the time has come to reveal it.

He tells Po the secret ingredient is … nothing. There is no secret ingredient!

Po: "Wait, wait … It's just plain old noodle soup? You don't add some kind of special sauce or something?"

Mr. Ping: "Don't have to. To make something special you just have to believe it's special."

Po looks at the scroll again and sees his reflection in it.

Po: "There is no secret ingredient."

Po has an epiphany at that moment. He recognizes a monumental truth. True power to transform us does not come from outside, it comes from within. All that we need. The secret ingredient is *you*. We simply need to recognize that fact, believe in ourselves, and unlock the power. Until we recognize that all that we need to succeed is within us, we cannot become the Dragon Warrior.

But when we do, when we truly believe, anything is possible.

Have a dumpling.

AFTERWORD

"Life finds a way."
—Ian Malcolm, *Jurassic Park*

"Writing finds a way."
—Wulf Moon, Olympic Park

We have come to the end. And so, we go back to the beginning, for all great stories come full circle. In the opening chapter, I made the point that you can't ski what you can't see. But if you have a guide that knows the trail, they can help you see what you might not. They can make that run down the mountain so much easier, preventing a wipe-out, or worse, a game over if we strike a tree. We don't have to take *Widowmaker*.

What we have to do is learn the course and build our skills. I've done my best here to show you what that course looks like. I've marked it as clear as I know how, and hopefully you smiled and laughed as you skied along with me. It's not a perfect trail—no trail is.

But it will get you where you need to go if you follow it at a pace that's right for you. Use what you need to help you stay the course.

That's really what success is all about. Staying the course. Getting up one more time than we have fallen. The ones that steadfastly get back up and put one foot in front of the other eventually get to where they are going. The ones that stay down don't. You simply have to decide which of those two you want to be. And then do everything in your power to head toward your goal, whatever that goal may be. If you're new to writing, it's completing a story. If you've been writing for awhile, it's likely getting published. And if you've been published, many a published writer would like to make a career of writing, which is making their living doing what they love.

After all, a writer's heart's desire is to write. And to be read.

I gave you three life lessons I learned that day on the mountain that I am confident will be helpful to you:

1. Belief determines reality.
2. What we think is the absolute limit of our ability is not even close.
3. Everything worth achieving is on the other side of fear.

Guess what? All of that rests with you now. You must be the proactive character in your own story and make your heart's desire a reality. A mentor can show you what you must do based on their own experience, but you're the one that must do the work. You'll stumble a lot in the beginning. It takes time to build up our muscles. But if you stay the course, you'll get your footing. And you've got a decent map with you in case you stray. That's why I wrote this book. It's a map. Refer back to the principles often. Highlight the ones you need to work on. They'll keep you on track. As they have done for so many others.

If you'd like extra help, I have workshops, both live and recorded. There's the *Illustrated Super Secrets of Writing* workbook as well with bonus chapters, questions, and places to record your goals. You'll find all these and more on my website. There's a second book coming, too, and a second workbook. I've also built up a Wulf Pack you can run with, my Wulf Pack Writers group. It really helps to have allies that understand the process and work together as a team to aid one another in accomplishing goals. As Rudyard Kipling said: "For the strength of the Pack is the Wolf, and the strength of the Wolf is the Pack."

I know the power of belief. I know the power of those that will try to steal that belief from you. They have no desire to see you succeed in your quest. But if you know in your heart that you're a writer, then you must not allow anything or anyone get in your way. Writing is the only way you will be able to feel truly fulfilled. We must be true to who we are. We cannot be truly happy without being true to ourselves.

I hope I've made that truth a little easier for you to see. I know I've done that for others. I've asked some to tape my saying, "Belief determines reality," to their monitor or workstation so they can be reminded of it daily. You might benefit from doing that as well. For when we truly believe that we have the power and do the work to unleash it, *nothing* can hold us back from our destiny.

What could these writing principles do for you? Nothing, if you don't apply them. Nothing, if you don't try.

But everything can happen … if you do.

Writing finds a way.

Go and write some howling good stories. I look forward to hearing of your success!

All the beast!

Wulf Moon

GLOSSARY

alliteration: the repetition of the initial consonant sound in words that are in close proximity to each other. *SEE EDITOR*

alpha reader: also known as *first reader* or *wise reader*, they're a trusted reader you share your story with first for feedback. Writing knowledge is not necessary; wide reading experience is a huge plus.

antagonist: the person or organization that stands in the way of your protagonist's ability to obtain their Heart's Desire. Also known as the villain, but today's villain usually isn't the moustache twirling tie-the-damsel-to-the-train-tracks type of person. *Muahahahaha!*

authorial intrusion: when a writer breaks the story's narrative and addresses the reader directly, like when you're reading stale glossary terms and the author breaks in and says, "How's it goin', bud? You wanna keep reading these or should we head to bar con for a drink?"

bar con: when writers, editors, publishers, and agents gather in a bar after sessions at a seminar or convention to visit and network, and yes, to wet their whistle. Didn't I just see you over at authorial intrusion?

beta reader: a Siamese fighting fish that loves to read. Oh wait, that's *betta* reader. A *beta* reader is a person who reads an unpublished work for a writer to mark errors in the manuscript and to suggest improvements. Typically a service provided by a writer to help a fellow writer, the rate of exchange being, "I'll read yours if you read mine."

blind submissions: when a market or contest requests that any information that might indicate who the author is be removed from the manuscript, file name, and metadata.

comedy: (1) a humorous story, or (2) stories that end with a positive outcome for the protagonist. *SEE POSITIVE ENDING STORIES*

cover letter/submission letter: for *short stories*, a brief letter or email stating the title of the story, word count, genre, and a few noteworthy writing credits, if the writer has them. You *do not* describe or pitch the short story. For *novels*, a cover letter is a short letter which introduces you and your novel to an agent or publisher, giving them the title, word count, and genre. But the main purpose is to entice them to read your manuscript through a brief pitch, market comps, and a little about you and your noteworthy writing credits.

crossing the threshold: when the protagonist commits to the quest to obtain their Heart's Desire, moving from their ordinary world into the unknown world of their quest. It is also the term for the custom of a groom carrying his bride into their home after the wedding, causing many a slipped disc on an important night for the groom to be functional.

dark night of the soul: "Woe is me; all is lost! I shall retreat to my refrigerator and OD on Ben and Jerry's Chunky Monkey!" The pit of despair the protagonist sinks into after failing to achieve their objective and experiencing a soul-crushing defeat.

Denouement: (pronounced Dey-Knew-Ma) after the climax, a scene in short stories (can be chapters in novels) where the protagonist receives validation for a job well done in a positive ending story, or lots of *tsk, tsking* by onlookers in a negative ending story. This is where loose ends are tied up and proof is provided that the protagonist achieved their stated Heart's Desire at the start of the story, or failed to achieve it in a negative ending story. Also commonly referred to as the Resolution or Validation scene.

echo words: *hello, hello, hello.* When a word or phrase gets repeated in the same sentence, paragraph, or even on the same page.

editor: a possibly underpaid and perpetually overworked productive person you should be patiently polite to particularly because not only are they a fellow participant in project humanity, they work for the publisher, possibly *are* the paramount publisher, and they have the plenary power to pay for your production and publish it in the peerless publication they prudently produce. *SEE ALLITERATION*

elevator pitch: similar to a logline, but the term came from trapping an editor or literary agent in an elevator, sweeping the buttons from Parking to Penthouse, and pitching the plot of your novel to them from Aardvark to Zebra. *SEE LOGLINE.*

Escalating Tension: the ever-increasing risk to the hero's obtaining their Heart's Desire as they strive to achieve it. Stakes must ratchet up. THINGS GET WORSE.

first reader: *SEE ALPHA READER*

Flow state: "In the Zone." A concept of positive psychology studies, defined as a heightened state of productivity the mind enters by being completely immersed in a challenging but achievable task.

full-circle ending: repeating or echoing an important phrase or idea presented at the beginning of the story at the ending. Full-circle endings provide closure for the reader because the story began with a promise of what the story would be about, and the ending concludes with reminding the reader of whether or not that promise was fulfilled, but perhaps not in the way they expected.

Heart's Desire: Heart's Desire is a person, thing, or state of being that the protagonist values and desires. It can be something precious to them that they hope to gain, or something precious that they have and don't want to lose.

hero: *SEE PROTAGONIST*

Hero's Journey: a universal narrative structure postulated by Joseph Campbell where a hero accepts a call to adventure, leaves their normal world and enters the unknown, gains mentors and allies, confronts challenges and temptations, comes off victorious, and returns home with a boon. Also known as the Monomyth.

hybrid author: an author with works published both independently and through a traditional publishing house.

in medias res: when the narrative starts "in the middle of things." Have you seen teaser openings of Hollywood movies that begin with wild car chases or crazy gunfights and you have no idea who the story is about and why this scene is happening? That.

inciting incident: the size-sixteen combat boot that drops down on your protagonist's normal world and what they hold most dear (or hope to hold) and shatters it. It's the initial event that incites the protagonist to take action against the problem (opposing force) behind the incident.

indie, independent author: a writer that self-publishes and markets their own work, retaining control of their publishing rights.

internal character arc: an internal hang-up within the protagonist that holds them back from reaching their full potential. The external plot arc is designed to expose this weakness at the start of the story, make the protagonist pass through trials by fire that force their weakness to come to the surface. The protagonist gains a level of mastery over their issue through the course of the journey, and they come off refined and improved in dealing with their weakness, perhaps even healed of it, by the end of the tale.

literary genre: the classification and organization of works based on specified characteristics of each grouping. In broad strokes, the fantasy genre has magic as a characteristic, the science fiction genre includes science principles, the romance genre centers on love interests, the horror genre explores fears, and the Canadiana genre explores a fantasy land where everyone is polite, drenches maple syrup on everything, feasts on poutine, and greets you with, "Beauty day, eh?"

logline: a one or two sentence summary of a short story, novel, or screenplay. Includes the protagonist's name, some idea of who they are, where the story is set, what's their Heart's Desire, and who or what is trying to keep their Heart's Desire from them.

MacGuffin: a *fake* Magic Sword. A plot device that appears to have the power to help the protagonist achieve their Heart's Desire, so characters in the story assign it value and desperately seek it. In the end, it turns out to be much ado about nothing.

Magic Sword: unlike a MacGuffin, an archetype (think Excalibur) that represents a thing of real power wielded by the protagonist to defeat their adversary. The Magic Sword can be internal (power latent within the hero) or external (an item of power or knowledge outside the hero). *SEE MACGUFFIN*

Mary Sue story: a story about a protagonist that is charming, powerful, intelligent, and comes up with an instant solution to any trial faced. While the origin of the term came from the female character in a *Star Trek* fanfiction story "A Trekkie's Tale" written in 1973 by Paula Smith, this type of story with an idealized protagonist is not gender specific.

pantsers: explorative writers that eschew outlines and detailed planning and view the writing process as organic discovery. The term comes from referring to this group as those that "write by the seat of their pants." *SEE PLOTTERS, PLANTSERS*

past tense: stories or scenes describing events that have already happened.

plantsers: the no man's land between pantsers and plotters. They utilize a bit of both systems, and try not to get shot when pantsers and plotters face off.

plot: the series of events in a story from start to finish.

plot arc: a graph of events in a story beginning with the status quo, the rise through events of escalating tension, the peak event occurring at the climax, and the falling action down to the denouement and last line. Also known as narrative arc or story arc.

plot points: the critical events in a story that impel the protagonist to advance on the plot arc.

plotters: planning writers who meticulously plan and outline their stories before they begin writing. The term comes from this group's system of plotting out or mapping out the events and details that will occur in their story. *SEE PANTSERS, PLANTSERS*

positive ending stories: a story that ends with a positive outcome for the protagonist—they get their Heart's Desire, or they get an upgrade for no extra charge! Who am I kidding? Anything of greater value requires a greater price. *SEE COMEDY*

POV: the point of view the narrative is told through. There are three types of POV:
    1. first person: we see the events of the story and read exposition

exclusively through the viewpoint of the person telling the story. "I picked up the gun." Uses I, me, mine, my.

2. second person: the narrator is speaking to you, telling you what you see, where you will go, how you will act. "You picked up the gun." Uses you, your.

3. third person: an authorial narrative from a viewpoint outside the story, not a character within it. "He picked up the gun." Uses he, she, they, their.

present tense: stories or scenes told in the present that are currently happening.

protagonist: the principal character of a story, also known as the hero.

publisher: an organization that publishes newspapers, magazines, or books. Publisher is also the title of a person in the organization who is responsible for publishing their product.

red herring: a wild goose chase plot ploy designed to take the reader down a false path.

resolution: a scene or a series of scenes (or chapters in a novel) that tie up the loose ends at the end of a story after the climax. *SEE DENOUEMENT*

single sensory weaving: writing that lacks an immersive sensory experience that utilizes all five senses; instead, the story is told almost exclusively through visual descriptions.

slush pile: oh man, do I know slush! I lived for many years in Wisconsin and Minnesota. Those roads and sidewalks are slopped in melting piles of snow in the spring. Much like the mess editors used to have in the paper submissions on their desks. Hundreds of globs of manuscripts all chaotically stacked or slushing around in bins waiting to be read. Today it's the mass of electronic submissions sent to a digital mailbox that an editor, literary agency, or publisher receives manuscripts from hopeful writers.

story: a narrative about someone that wants something, and someone or something is standing in their way of getting it.

Super Secrets of Writing: my writing principles and tips to help writers identify the elements of solid stories and what makes them tick, allowing them to duplicate these elements in their own work to experience greater success.

trad/traditional author: a writer that allows a publishing company to publish and market their written work, normally giving up rights to their intellectual property for a specified period in order to receive payment and/or royalties.

Tragedy: stories that end with the hero failing to achieve their Heart's Desire, or they achieve it and it does not give them the boon they hoped for.

try/fail cycles: *SEE ESCALATING TENSION*

try/succeed cycles: with each attempt by the protagonist to achieve their goal of obtaining their Heart's Desire, it appears to the protagonist that they are succeeding. However, the reader knows the truth— each apparent success is actually bringing greater troubles upon the protagonist, and they will have to deal with it by the end. *Bring on the heat! SEE ESCALATING TENSION*

validation: when you visit a posh restaurant downtown and they validate your parking so you'll linger and buy dessert. (May I recommend the crème brûlée served with decaf espresso? Excellent choice!) It's also the proof at the end of the story that your protagonist got what you promised in the opening, or that your protagonist got upgraded to something better. Validation is often referred to as another term for denouement, but it's actually just one the elements in a properly executed denouement. *SEE DENOUEMENT*

writer circles: a small group of writers with similar goals that work together to achieve them.

writing group: as I like to call it, your wolf pack. A group of writers that have your back and meet in person or online to discuss writing, markets, one another's work, and to provide encouragement and accountability to meet writing goals. Many offer a venue for group critiques. They provide a shoulder to cry on when rejections get you down, and peers to howl with you in joy when you receive an acceptance. "For the strength of the Pack is the Wolf, and the strength of the Wolf is the Pack."—Rudyard Kipling

100 HOWLING GOOD WRITING PROMPTS

In my workshops, I use writing prompts to spark ideas. Writers that practice with them on a regular basis discover in short order that they can write stories on any subject, in any genre. I've watched many turn my prompts into works that became their first published stories, or even their winners in international writing contests.

This is Super Secret Prompt Generator #2. The first is in *The Illustrated Super Secrets of Writing, Vol. 1* workbook. Here's how it works. If you're a D&D campaigner (true claim to geekdom here, I used to compete in tournaments at TSR headquarters in Lake Geneva where Gary Gygax presided), you've got a d100 die at the ready. And if you don't, use the Internet's random number generators. I've given you one hundred prompts to light your forge. Roll and work with whatever the random gives you, tricky though it may be. The point? Get words flowing on the page in a stream-of-consciousness timed writing session that you establish without judgment. Sort it out later. Ready? *Roll the bones!*

1. Fire sale
2. Creature comforts
3. Portal of peril

4. Delusional truth
5. Caught in a loop
6. Border crossing
7. Cosmic cowgirl/cowboy
8. Note to self
9. Living the dream
10. Corrupt judge
11. Letter of the law
12. Star path
13. Dragon's eye
14. Nosy neighbor
15. Tiny visitor
16. Ignored prophet
17. Road rage
18. Coffee shop mystery
19. As the mercury climbs
20. Side hustle
21. Phantom lake
22. Sending out an S.O.S.
23. Soul food
24. Bird of prey
25. Plan B
26. Bon voyage
27. Forbidden love
28. Not without my kangaroo
29. Deadly surf
30. Along the watchtower
31. The shipping channel
32. One chance in hell
33. You take my breath away
34. Solar flares
35. Mausoleum of madness
36. Snake eyes
37. Zero tolerance
38. Claim jumper
39. Sensory hallucinations

40. Spontaneous combustion
41. Drone activity
42. Cat's pajamas
43. Cryptic cove
44. A.I. anxiety
45. Mangled multiverse
46. Screaming chasm
47. Cosmic dust
48. Timeline's curse
49. Hellscape
50. Destiny broken
51. Rising from the ashes
52. Into the mystic
53. Scarred perfection
54. To hell and back
55. The shield wall
56. Shimmering mirage
57. Optical oasis
58. Hunger pangs
59. Toxic treasures
60. Shards of time
61. Scarce commodities
62. Hidden refuge
63. Love betrayed
64. Hidden hatred
65. A plot to kill
66. Mistaken identity
67. Chasm of chaos
68. Alone though surrounded
69. The opulent realm
70. The summoning
71. Salvaging starships
72. The parting glass
73. The Four Horsemen
74. Secret strike
75. The butcher

76. Bounty hunter
77. The green woman
78. Poisoned chalice
79. From hero to zero
80. Happy campers
81. Secret embryo
82. Belly of the beast
83. Possessed fire alarm
84. Shattered heart
85. Fantastic felines
86. Watcher in the closet
87. Fox in the henhouse
88. Death squad
89. Jackal's smile
90. Special order
91. Veil of fear
92. Witch hunt
93. Mood ring
94. Pirate's parrot
95. Bumbling boneheads
96. Blinding pain
97. *Kintsugi* gold
98. Spellcasting spies
99. Ghost dance
100. Alien shore

ACKNOWLEDGMENTS

"Sweet is the breath of vernal shower,
The bee's collected treasures sweet,
Sweet music's melting fall, but sweeter yet
The still small voice of gratitude."
—Thomas Gray, *Ode for Music*

My gratitude to my wife Jules, who has stood loyally by my side in every venture, ready to lend her ears and eyes whenever I step out of my office and interrupt what she's working on to say, "How does this sound?"

My gratitude to my friend, mentor, and publisher, Mark Leslie Lefebvre, who believed in my project from its inception and taught me that you can do more with a hundred dedicated fans than you can with a thousand random ones.

My gratitude to Ruth Nickle for the gorgeous cover of this book, and to Catherine Weaver for her thoughtful copy editing and speedy service.

My gratitude to Scot and Jane Noel—Scot for inviting me to create a featured series on writing for *DreamForge Magazine* we called Wulf Moon's SUPER SECRETS, and Jane for beautifying every article with her masterful illustrations.

My gratitude to the members of my Wulf Pack Writers group that were there the moment the Kickstarter campaign for *How to Write a Howling Good Story* launched. This project fully funded in an unbelievable seven minutes, and went on to achieve 1124% over its funding goal. Special thanks to Jenny Perry Carr that backed as Supreme Wulf, boosting the campaign with its initial thrust that sent the project skyrocketing into the stratosphere.

My gratitude to the 330 backers in the Kickstarter campaign for this book, and their patience as the project became delayed by several months due to my dealing with recovery from long-COVID. I am truly grateful for the support from every backer, but to make it easier to compose the following list, I limited acknowledgment in the backer rewards to those backing at the trade paperback level and higher. These are:

Dawn Hebein, Ed Ryder, Tyson Dutton, Joshua Dyer, Kelly Morgan, Rebekah Wells, Amey Zeigler, Wendy Sornberger, Irene Stanhope, Samantha Rutenber, Mike Jack Stoumbos, Jackie Payson, Cynthia Waldron, Yelena, Kate MacEachern, Alexander Barrett, Stephen Sottong, Kari Wolfe, Tarry, Louis Schlesinger, Devin Miller, Bethany White, Chuck Lang, Rob Vagle, Tony Dutson, Granibug65@gmail.com, Matthea W. Ross, Spencer Erdman, Katie Dresel, Greg Tausch, Heather Lee Dyer, Brittany Perry Rainsdon, Elaine, Zeet, Kate Mergener, Jeffrey Frisone, Sarah Tullipan, Melissa Bianco, Meredith Carstens, Ari Officer, Phil Hall, Vickie Smith, K. Z. Richards, Jennifer Probst, mgvaughAn.com, Debbie Day, Peter Medeiros, John M. Campbell, nicole.tate23@yahoo.com, sparkerc@gmail.com, Denise Gaskins, Steven Mosbrucker, Angyne Smith, aisleyclaireextraordinaire@gmail.com, John K. Patterson, Zachary Helmick, Wmeese, Candida Norwood, Emily Walter, Ashley M. Orndorff, Luke Italiano, RJK Lee, Winston Malone, BK Leona, Natalie Keller Reinert, Lauren C. Teffeau, Charlotte, Matt Frankie, Evan S., Isaac Semko, H. Dietz, Stace Johnson, Benn Liska, Crystal Crawford, Samara Lipman, Kelvin Neely, Jessica Guernsey, Joe Monson, Tyler Hulsey, Davina Tang (davinadiva), dewilliams0327@gmail.com, Sandra Skalski, Lawrence Dunmore III, Charlotte Henley Babb, Martin L. Shoemaker, Teague Summerlin, Viannah E. Duncan, Christopher Rightmyer, Wendy Landes, Tai Estopy, Brandon Harris, Beth Caudill, John Eric Schleicher, Christoffer Miller Dahl, Richard Novak, Paul and Courtney Martin, Anna, Jb11rx@gmail.com, Debra L. Foust, Ozymandias Aurelius, Estey Nesmith, Christine Pointeau, James T. Lambert, Shannon M., StraySpectre, Jamie Dill, Cherise Papa, Allison Mann,

Corbin Rogers, Catherine Barrett, Richard Sayer, Anita Buckowing, Mark Leslie Lefebvre, Jan MG Nerenberg, Shannon L Miller, Jacob Perez, Steve Pantazis, Patric Ryan, Debbie Culver, Kallan Aventyr, Danuta Raine, Glenn Witt, Tracy Hughes, P Mickevicius, Tammy Burke, William F Sattelmeyer, Dennis Donlan, Kenton Erb, Robert Martirosyan, Tyberious Barnett, Tim Geoghegan, Todd S. Jones, Duchele Long, Alexander Baban, Charlene Harmon, Mark S R Peterson, Dennys Antunish, Charles Thompson, Josef B. Wilke, Hermione Lee, William Pelecanos, Anna X, Ryan Connor Cadigan, Brenda Carre, Ruth Nickle, Shannon Fox, Adelaide Winters, A. G. Nurse, Alex Harford, Marla Green, Cathy Peper, Jarrod K Williams. Nicole Van Den Eng, Doug Triplett, Martha E Pedersen, Candice R. Lisle, Danny Hankner, Brandi Kalena, KT Magrowski, Scot Noel, Martha E Pedersen, Angelique Fawns, Catherine Weaver, Huw Nicholas, Daniel M. Cojocaru, Terri Burton, DD Haeg, Rick Johnston, Lauren Diana Scalf, Martin Greening, Terry Ebaugh, Khadija Hussain, Kristin J Haggard, Catherine Weaver, Jade C Wildy, Eric Stallsworth, David Hankins, Amy R. Wethington, Jared Nelson, Carol Hendrickson, Ben Kesler, Desmond Astaire, Jennifer Lesh Fleck, Fred Wehling, Robert Stahl, Rachel Unger, Jami Fairleigh, Tarry Perry, A. X. Ander, Nancy D Greene, Darren Lipman, Celestine de la Tour, Gregory Miranda, Winter Navi, Maythaporn Narthanon, Shean Pao, and Mark Fetherman.

Finally, I am grateful to you, dear reader, that supported my labors by purchasing this book. Cheers!

ON-DEMAND WORKSHOP RECORDINGS

WULF MOON'S
SUPER SECRETS

"Not only is Moon a charismatic and engaging educator, I am continuously awed by his authenticity and generosity. Going to a Wulf Moon workshop means coming away with so much more than you could have possibly imagined."—Ana Sun, UK author

Webinar Recordings

- *"Title is Your First Hook: A Rose by Any Other Name is Not Just as Sweet"*
- *"Magic Sword: The Powerful Story Element Everyone Forgets"*
- *"Modern Marketing: Let Your Light Shine"*
- *"Denouement: Stick Your Landings"*

Masterclass Recordings

- *"The Illustrated Super Secrets of Writing"*
- *"Heart's Desire and the Reader/Hero Bond"*
- *"KYD: The Kill Your Darlings Exercise"*
- *"Flow State: Release the Kraken Within You!"*

"Moon's teaching style is engaging, authoritative, and friendly. Not only does he know his subject matter inside-out, he clearly enjoys it and cares for other writers who want to do what he does. The man is a treasure of writing wisdom and encouragement, and I heartily recommend Wulf Moon's classes to anyone who wishes to improve their artistic work and their enjoyment of the writing life."—Nathaniel M. Barret, writer

Order Today and View Immediately at:

www.TheSuperSecrets.com

Would you like more?

Get the workbook companion to this book!

Proven results

The Illustrated Super Secrets of Writing

BONUS Chapters. REVIEW Questions. GOAL Affirmation.
Full color, 8.5" x 11" Fully Illustrated.

ABOUT THE AUTHOR

Wulf Moon was fifteen years old when his story won the national Scholastic Art & Writing Awards, the same contest that first discovered Stephen King, Peter S. Beagle, Joyce Carol Oates, and a host of iconic names in the arts. He sold the story to *Science World* that same year, making it his first professional sale. His stories have received recognition numerous times in best-of-the-year lists and awards, and have appeared in professional magazines and bestselling anthologies that include *Writers of the Future Vol. 35, Best of Deep Magic Anthology Two, Galaxy's Edge*, and *Star Trek: Strange New Worlds 2*.

Wulf Moon has won over forty awards in writing, and thirty in public speaking. Moon's award-winning *Super Secrets of Writing* online resource has had 850,000 views, and his articles on writing are a regular series in *DreamForge Magazine*. Moon is a freelance editor and voice-over actor. He is the leader of the Wulf Pack Writers group, teaches the Super Secrets of Writing Workshops, and is the author of the award-winning *The Illustrated Super Secrets of Writing*, and *How To Write a Howling Good Story*. To invite Wulf Moon to conduct his workshops or to speak at your event, please query through the contact form on his website.

Learn Moon's secrets at www.thesupersecrets.com or on his Patreon at https://www.patreon.com/wulfmoon where you can *Join the Wulf Pack!*

NOTES

27. SHARING YOUR WORKS WITH THE WORLD

1. E! News, February 27, 2015

28. BABY STEPS

1. Thomasedison.org

30. BETA READERS, WRITING GROUPS, FREELANCE EDITORS

1. Quotestats.com

34. DEALING WITH CRITICISM, PART ONE:

1. 1909 November 7, Cleveland Plain Dealer, Hubbard Praises Mayor Johnson: The Fra, Here on Lecture Bent, Quote Page 10-D, Column 5, Cleveland, Ohio. (GenealogyBank)

36. THE SECRET INGREDIENT

1. *CBS Saturday,* December 4, 2021
2. *CBS Mornings*, August 21, 2023